Pronouncing American English

Sounds, Stress, and Intonation

Second Edition

Gertrude F. Orion

Professor Emeritus

Queensborough Community College

City University of New York

Heinle & Heinle Publishers

I(T)P **An International Thomson Publishing Company**

Pacific Grove • Albany • Bonn • Boston • Cincinnati • Detroit • London • Madrid • Melbourne
Mexico City • New York • Paris • San Francisco • Tokyo • Toronto • Washington

The publication of *Pronouncing American English, Second Edition,* was directed by the members of the Newbury House Publishing Team at Heinle & Heinle.

Editorial Director: Erik Gundersen
Market Development Director: Bruno R. Paul
Production Services Coordinator: Kristin Thalheimer
Associate Editor: Ken Pratt
Vice President and Publisher: Stanley J. Galek

Also participating in the publication of this program were:

Project Manager: Angela Malovich Castro, English Language Trainers
Production Editor: Maryellen Eschmann Killeen
Associate Market Development Director: Mary Sutton
Manufacturing Coordinator: Mary Beth Hennebury
Compositor: Christine E. Wilson, IBC
Interior Designer: Carol H. Rose
Illustrators: Bob Holmes, Charles Martin
Cover Designer: Gina Petti, Rotunda Design

Library of Congress Cataloging-in-Publication Data

Orion, Gertrude F.
    Pronouncing American English : sounds, stress, and intonation / Gertrude F. Orion.
       p.   cm.
    ISBN 0-8384-6332-0
     1. English language—United States—Pronunciaton.   2. English language—Pronunciation by foreign speakers.   3. English language—Textbooks for foreign speakers.   I. Title
PE2815.O7   1997
421'.54—dc21   96-51549
                                                 CIP

Heinle & Heinle Publishers is a division of International Thomson Publishing, Inc.

Manufactured in the United States of America

ISBN 0-8384-6332-0

10 9 8 7

Acknowledgments

I am indebted to a number of individuals who helped in various ways with the preparation of this edition: Ken Pratt, Associate Editor at Heinle & Heinle, and Angela M. Castro of English Language Trainers for their gentle prodding to finish the manuscript and to all the reviewers for their invaluable criticisms, comments, and suggestions. A very special thank-you goes to my students, who helped to develop and refine the material in this book and without whom it would not have been written.

The author and publisher would like to thank the following individuals who offered many helpful insights, ideas, and suggestions for change during the development of *Pronouncing American English, Second Edition.*

Susan Carnell, *University of Texas, Arlington*

Cindy Chang, *University of Washington*

William Crawford, *Georgetown University*

Roberta Hodges, *Sonoma State University*

Alison Stevens, *University of Washington*

To the Memory of My Parents

Contents

Guide to the Exercises

x

Introduction

The second edition of *Pronouncing American English: Sounds, Stress, and Intonation* enhances and expands upon the comprehensive array of activities offered in the first edition.

To make learning and teaching with *Pronouncing American English* more effective and satisfying, the second edition has been correlated with the following publication:

> *The Newbury House Dictionary of American English.* Containing more than 40,000 entries with clear and simple definitions, *The Newbury House Dictionary of American English* is the first learner's dictionary developed from an American English vocabulary base. *Pronouncing American English* and *The Newbury House Dictionary* have been designed as companion volumes; both employ the International Phonetic Alphabet (I.P.A.).

For those who are not familiar with the first edition, *Pronouncing American English* is a pronunciation text for students of English as a second or foreign language. It is suitable for high-beginning-level learners who are developing this skill, as well as for intermediate and advanced students who wish to perfect their pronunciation. Beginning students can learn "correct" pronunciation in the very early stages of speaking, and intermediate and advanced learners can improve their oral proficiency.

The materials in the second edition retain the comprehensive approach used in the first edition. The text is still as complete and appropriate for individual use as it is for class use. What makes this edition different from the first is the addition of subjects that had not been included or fully developed in the earlier edition. New sections, exercises, and activities, along with more pair work and pair-practice activities, have been added. The use of authentic language in these exercises and activities serves to encourage the student to independent self-monitoring.

More definitions of vocabulary that students may not be familiar with have been added, with more illustrations and footnoted words. The vocabulary used is accessible to students at a variety of levels. Boldface letters, instead of capital letters, are now used to indicate the stressed syllable in words of two or more syllables. Several of the illustrations of the mouth charts for the production of the vowels and consonants have been made clearer, as have the explanations for place and manner of articulation.

This text addresses the problems shared by speakers from various countries of the world who have large categories of speech difficulties in common. It can be used in a classroom with the teacher modeling the material for the students, with the tape cassettes in a language laboratory class, or with the tape cassettes by students working alone, in pairs, or in groups.

Text organization

Parts 1 and 2

Pronouncing American English is divided into four parts. **Part 1,** "An Overview: Sounds of American English," consists of Units 1 and 2. Unit 1, "English Spelling and English Sounds," includes the problems encountered with English spelling as opposed to sounds, and the use of a phonetic alphabet. Unit 2, "The Speech Mechanism," describes the articulators that help us produce sounds and the rules governing voiced and voiceless sounds.

Part 2, "Stress and Intonation," consists of Unit 3, "Syllable Stress," Unit 4, "Vowel and Consonant Length," Unit 5, "Content Words and Function Words," Unit 6, "Word Stress and Phrasing," Unit 7, "Intonation," and Unit 8, "Using a Dictionary for Pronunciation."

Unit 3, "Syllable Stress," concentrates mainly on the stressing of two-syllable and polysyllabic words. *Syllable stress* refers to the syllable that is given primary stress in a word, and *word stress* refers to the word that is given stress in an utterance. This terminology proves to be more logical and understandable to students than "word stress" and "sentence stress," since students are taught to think in terms of which syllable is prominent in a word and which word or words are prominent in a phrase or sentence.

Only primary and weak stresses are discussed. Contrasts are made between the primary and weak stresses of syllables in words and the stressing and unstressing of words in phrases or sentences. The rationale is that if students learn this from the very beginning, or if they succeed in changing old habits by concentrating on these two stresses, the other stress patterns will fall into place more easily and can be described and detailed extensively, if necessary, when the students are well advanced in their knowledge of the English language.

Syllabification indicating primary stress, in some instances, may not follow established practice. For example, in dictionaries, the words "annoy" and "suppose" are syllabized "an-noy" and "sup-pose," although the doubled letters "n" and "p" each indicate one sound. The basis for this appears to be that words are divided into syllables arbitrarily, based on historical precedent, and not on a phonetic one. In this text, for simplification purposes, doubled letters are syllabized phonetically and stress in such words is indicated by boldface letters, as in "a**nnoy**" and "su**ppose.**" Throughout the exercises, all words of more than one syllable have their primary stress indicated by letters in boldface.

Unit 4, "Vowel and Consonant Length," replaces Unit 3, "Long and Short Sounds," in the first edition. The terminology has also been changed so as not to be confused with the definitions of "long" and "short" vowels used in the teaching of phonics and those definitions customarily found in dictionaries. "Vowel and Consonant Length" is concerned with duration: the lengthening and shortening of vowel and consonant sounds in particular environments. In this unit, duration is treated in more depth and the unit contains more exercises and activities for students than in the first edition.

Unit 5, "Content Words and Function Words," has also been expanded, and the use of colloquial language has been added.

Unit 6 and Unit 7 tie it all together. Unit 6, "Word Stress and Phrasing," covers stress, rhythm, linking, and pausing. In addition, the use of different types of numerals has been included along with more exercises and activities.

Unit 7, "Intonation," covers rising and falling intonation. Although there are several intonation patterns in American English, only two basic ones are covered here: rising intonation and falling intonation. Once again, if the student learns how to use them from the very beginning or succeeds in changing old habits by concentrating on these two intonation patterns, the others will fall into place more easily and can also be detailed extensively at a later date.

Unit 8, "Using a Dictionary for Pronunciation," describes how to use the dictionary to find the "correct" pronunciation of a word.

Parts 3 and 4

Parts 3 and 4 contain the vowel and consonant units, respectively. These units need not be taken in order but may be assigned according to individual or group need. However, before studying them it is vital that the students cover the materials in Parts 1 and 2 because these sections are the bases for the study of the vowel and consonant sections.

Each unit in Parts 3 and 4 introduces either one or two sounds and their common and sometimes less common spellings in initial, medial, and final positions, wherever applicable. Letters representing the target sound in a given unit are underlined. A key word for a given sound is included in each unit. Students should be encouraged to memorize this key word, or find one of their own, as a way to self-monitor and self-correct when doing the exercises. In addition, there is an illustration and description of how to produce each target sound. These illustrations and descriptions are teaching aids and are not scientifically exact diagrams or descriptions. They should be referred to when the student cannot produce the sound in a satisfactory manner through auditory stimulation.

The "Contrast" section of each lesson includes auditory discrimination exercises. For a variety of reasons, it may be difficult for students to discriminate between particular sounds, especially in the context of a word. Even when they can, it does not necessarily follow that they will be able to produce them acceptably. In these exercises the student listens to the target sound in isolation and repeats it after the instructor or the tape voice, first "normally," then in an exaggerated manner, then "normally" once again. The sound is then practiced in words. It is important to impress upon the students that we do not normally make sounds in an exaggerated manner but that this is merely a training exercise. Exaggerating the sound allows the student to "hear" it and to "feel" both the place of articulation and the movements of the articulators. It is one way of practicing the target sound and another method of self-monitoring and self-correcting. Also, students should be encouraged to use mirrors to help them see, wherever possible, the movements of those articulators that are easily visible.

In the "Check Your Listening" exercises, if students are listening to the classroom teacher or to the tapes, a good technique is for the students not to look at the instructor or the printed words as they are said. In this way they receive no visual clues and must rely solely on their auditory perception.

Some students will probably need more practice in auditory discrimination than others. When more is needed, the instructor can review the "Contrast" exercises and, for variety, use additional words from the lesson. It is important that students be successful in this aspect of the instruction before proceeding with the rest of the lesson.

Minimal paired words and sentences, under the heading "Practice the Contrast," are also part of each unit. The purpose of this exercise is to help the students further sharpen their auditory discrimination, to heighten their awareness of the differences between sounds, and to impress upon them that even small differences in pronunciation can indicate changes in meaning.

Exercises are provided for students in a classroom situation to pair off and practice with each other. This offers students an opportunity to engage in a communicative activity among themselves and, in addition, affords them another form of repetition and practice.

At least one exercise in each unit of Parts 3 and 4 is devoted specifically to stress and intonation to aid in carrying over content from Parts 1 and 2. Sentences and dialogs emphasize affective meanings such as happiness, curiosity, surprise, annoyance, anger, humor, and disappointment.

The student is always directed to practice aloud, wherever the assignment is being done. There are exercises that can be done in class as well as assigned as work to be done at home; these can be graded.

Theoretical explanations have been kept to a minimum throughout the text. The emphasis instead is on considerable oral practice. Listening and speaking are coordinated in each unit, and students are encouraged to listen carefully as well as to speak. A great deal of practice and repetition is included and it is desirable for students to get a feel for the rhythm and flow of American English.

The pronunciation described in this book is standard American English, heard with some variations, and is spoken by the majority of educated people in the United States and Canada. It is the speech that is most often heard on radio and television.

There will always be some words the students do not know. They should be encouraged to look them up in a dictionary, wherever possible, to expand their vocabulary.

Many of the definitions of words in this text were taken from *The Newbury House Dictionary of American English*, Heinle and Heinle Publishers.

The symbols of the International Phonetic Alphabet are used, with modifications. These were made for purposes of simplification, especially for the vowel sounds; both vowels and diphthongs are classified as vowels.

An appendix has been added to this edition. It includes a list of one hundred homophones, their pronunciation and their use in sentences.

The symbol indicates the exercises that have been recorded on cassettes.

The first edition of *Pronouncing American English* came with an answer key to the exercises in the text. This second edition is accompanied by a manual that not only includes the answer key but also serves as a quick reference to the phonetic and linguistic areas that apply to each unit. It covers a variety of techniques that can be used by the less-experienced teacher in the identification and correction of specific common segmental and suprasegmental problems. It may also be of use as a refresher/reminder for more experienced instructors. Also, the manual includes contrastive analyses of the phonology and prosody of selected languages commonly spoken by foreign students.

To the Student

Acquiring good pronunciation is the most difficult part of learning a new language. As you improve your pronunciation, you have to learn to listen and imitate all over again. Not only do you have to learn to use your voice in a different way; you also have to learn to make new movements with your tongue, lips, jaw, and other organs of articulation in order to make the new sounds and even old ones in a new way. You are developing a new skill.

We know there are certain movements that are important to the production of any given sound. For example, everyone's handwriting is different. The letter "f" can be written in various ways: f, f, f, f. However, we know that this letter has to have a certain form; otherwise, we will not be able to recognize it and will have difficulty understanding the written word. So it is with pronunciation. If you don't shape the sound with the necessary movements, if you don't stress the proper syllable in a word, if you don't learn the flow, the rhythm, and melody of American English, your listener may have difficulty understanding you.

You may be able to produce some of the sounds by listening and imitating; for other sounds, you may need to refer to the illustrations and descriptions given at the beginning of each vowel and consonant unit. In the beginning, it is usually difficult to "hear" yourself. When this happens, you might find it beneficial to place the palms of your hands over your ears and then listen to yourself.

One can also compare speaking to playing the piano or singing a song. We can recognize the same piece of music played by two different pianists as well as the same song sung by two different singers. Even though each may play or sing in his or her own style, there are still certain notes that must be played or sung for us to recognize the tune as being the same. So it is with pronunciation. There are those necessary movements the speaker has to make for the production of any given sound, and there are also certain "notes" the speaker must combine in order to give meaning to his or her words.

Some of you may be reluctant to speak because of your "foreign accent." Foreign accents can be very charming as long as the person speaking is able to communicate. So losing your foreign accent or trying to sound like a native American English speaker is not necessarily the goal you should try to reach. Everyone's handwriting is not exactly the same; neither is everyone's pronunciation. What we are aiming for is easily understandable conversational speech.

How do we achieve this? A concert pianist may practice a piece of music for two years, eight hours a day, and an opera singer may work just as long on an operatic role. The same holds true for a person learning to speak a new language. As with any activity you wish to do well, you have to practice, practice, practice, and then practice some more.

But, before you begin to practice, how do you know you are hitting the correct notes?

When you begin to learn to play the piano, you first learn the names of the notes and which ones correspond to which keys. You are also learning to listen to the melody. As you begin to play, you look at the music and then at the keyboard to make sure your fingers are "hitting" the correct keys. You are now attempting to get the rhythm and the melody of the music. You judge whether or not you're on target. If not, you compare the notes to the keys and make the correction. Once you have the rhythm and melody, you go back and practice the individual notes to make sure you are doing the piece correctly.

The same can be compared to speaking a new language. You first must learn the "correct" rhythm and intonation (melody). You do this by learning to "listen" all over again. Are you "hitting" the correct syllable stress in words? Are you "getting" the rhythm and melody? You compare what you are saying to a model (your instructor or tape voice). You judge whether or not you're on target. If not, you adjust and try again. You are correcting.

So first you become familiar with your target. You learn to recognize it. You do this through ear training (recognizing your target and being able to tell the difference between it and what is substituting for it). You compare what you are saying to a model. If you are not on target, then you do some adjusting until it is correct.

In this text, stress and intonation are presented first for a reason. The reason is if you do not learn the stress and intonation patterns of American English, no matter how well you articulate the individual sounds of the language, you will still not be easily understood. Neither will you easily understand what is said. Research has shown that while communication is taking place, the native English speaker relies more on stress and intonation to understand what one is saying than on the individual sounds of the language.

You may be reluctant for a variety of reasons to really "get into" the language. Some of my students have said that "it feels funny." Well, if "it feels funny," you are probably doing it correctly.

Remember that you cannot accomplish good pronunciation overnight. Improvement takes time. Some students may find it more difficult than others and will need more time than others to improve. However, with practice, you can reach your goal.

Part 1

An Overview: Sounds of American English

When it's English that we speak

Why is *break* not rhymed with *weak*?

(Because they rhyme with *steak* and *seek*.)

Will you tell me why it's true

That *sew* does not rhyme with *few*?

(Because they rhyme with *oh* and *you*.)

We say *cow,* and that rhymes with *how.*

But *low* doesn't rhyme with *now,*

(Because they rhyme with *owe* and *bough.*[1])

And since *pay* is rhymed with *may,*

Why not *said* with *paid*?

(Because they rhyme with *bed* and *made*.)

---

[1] *bough:* a branch of a tree

Now here's another one for you:

Beard does not sound the same as *heard*

(Because they rhyme with *weird*[2] and *bird*.)

We have *blood* that rhymes with *mud,*

Food that rhymes with *rude.*

And *good* that rhymes with *could.*

Shoes is never rhymed with *toes,*

But is with *whose* and *blues;*

And I can also think of *zoos* and *chews.*

Are you surprised to know

That *toes* rhymes with *hose*

And *beaus,*[3] and *foes,* and *loaves*?

And what's more,

Horse sounds like *course*

And *worse* sounds like *curse*?

I've hardly made a start, gee,

I'm sure you will agree

In the way that sounds and letters disagree.

---

[2] *weird:* someone or something that is strange or unusual

[3] *beau:* the sweetheart of a woman or girl

As you can see from the above poem, in the English language there is a difference between sounds and spelling. The influence of English spelling is so strong, however, that many speakers find it difficult to think in terms of sounds. Therefore, it is very important to get into the habit of listening to and thinking of the sounds in words.

There are some letters that represent more than one sound and some sounds that represent more than one letter. Some letters represent no sound at all; they are sometimes called "silent letters." Since there is no simple relationship between sound and spelling and since the English language has twenty-six letters and more than forty sounds, a special *phonetic alphabet* is used. In this alphabet one phonetic symbol represents one distinctive sound. It includes some of the letters you already know and adds some new ones to represent additional sounds.

The organs of speech that help us form these sounds are called *articulators*. They include the lips, teeth, tongue, roof of the mouth, nose, jaw, and vocal cords.

The sounds of the language are divided into vowels and consonants. When the vocal cords vibrate, the sound is *voiced*. When the vocal cords do not vibrate, the sound is *voiceless*. All vowels are voiced, but consonants may be either voiced or voiceless. In addition, all vowels and some consonants can be held for a shorter or longer period of time, depending on which sound precedes or follows the sound.

The phonetic alphabet of American English consonant sounds is on page 7, vowel sounds, on page 8.

Unit 1

English Spelling and English Sounds

1. The Spelling System

The English spelling system is not easy to learn. It is confusing for both non-native speakers and native speakers.

The following exercises will help you understand some of the differences between English spelling and English sounds. Boldfaced letters indicate syllable stress.

> Reminder:
> - The English alphabet has 26 *letters* but has more than 40 *sounds*.
> - The sounds of English consist of vowels and consonants.

A. Same Letter, Different Sounds

Each of these seven words has a different sound for the underlined letter "a." Listen and repeat.

A = 7.

1. h<u>a</u>t	3. <u>a</u>ll	5. <u>a</u>rt	7. **or**<u>a</u>nge
2. <u>ai</u>m	4. **an**y	6. <u>a</u>**bove**	

Listen to and repeat these four different sounds for the underlined letter "s."

5 = 4

8. <u>s</u>ee	9. <u>s</u>ure	10. **bu**<u>s</u>y	11. **A**<u>s</u>ia

B. Same Sound, Different Letters

These words all have the same vowel sound, but each vowel sound, which is underlined, has a different spelling in each word. Listen and repeat.

1. **ba**by	3. st<u>ea</u>k	5. r<u>ai</u>n
2. th<u>ey</u>	4. v<u>ei</u>l	6. m<u>ay</u>

Listen to and repeat these four different spellings for the underlined consonant sound /f/.

    7. <u>f</u>ell   8. stu<u>ff</u>   9. **pho**to   10. tou<u>gh</u>

 C. Letters Representing No Sound

These words have "silent letters," which are indicated by a slash mark. Listen and repeat.

    1. rig̸ht   3. **i**s̸land   5. bomb̸

    2. de**sig**n   4. h̸our   6. w̸rong

2. Check Your Listening

Sometimes a word has more letters than it has sounds. Other times, a word has more sounds than it has letters.

A. More Letters Than Sounds (Silent Letters)

Count the number of letters in each of these words and write the number down. Then say each word aloud. Write down the number of sounds you hear. (*Hint:* "th," "kn," "bt," and "ou" represent one sound each and "gh" is not pronounced.)

1.	knee	_4_ letters	_1_ sounds
2.	debt	_4_ letters	_1_ sounds
3.	night	_5_ letters	_1_ sounds
4.	**off**ice	_6_ letters	_2_ sounds
5.	though	_6_ letters	_2_ sounds
6.	**Wednes**day	_9_ letters	_3_ sounds

B. More Sounds Than Letters

Write down the number of letters in each word. Then say each word aloud and write down the number of sounds. (*Hint:* "x" represents two sounds—/k/ and /s/).

1.	fix	_3_ letters	_3_ sounds
2.	**ex**tra	_5_ letters	_2_ sounds
3.	**tax**i	_4_ letters	_2_ sounds

4. **ex**it	_4_ letters	_3_ sounds
5. **ax**is	_4_ letters	_2_ sounds
6. ex**pel**	_5_ letters	_2_ sounds

C. Work with a partner. Discuss your answers. Check your answers
with a dictionary.

> Reminder: The influence of spelling on speaking is very strong. Many students remember
> the spelling of a word and then have trouble hearing and saying the correct sounds. Get
> into the habit of listening to the sounds of words.

3. The Phonetic Alphabet

In English there is no simple relationship between spelling and sounds. As a
result, people have invented different systems to represent English sounds. These
systems use one letter or symbol for each sound. An alphabetic system with one
symbol representing one sound is a *phonetic alphabet.*

The phonetic alphabet in this book includes most of the twenty-six letters of
the alphabet, along with some new symbols. We write these phonetic letters and
symbols between slash marks. For example, the symbols /k/, /ɪ/, and /æ/ represent
sounds, not letters. The sound /k/ is the first sound in the words "kiss" and "cat."
The sound /ɪ/ is the second sound in "kiss," and the sound /æ/ is the second sound
in the word "cat." Phonetically, the word "kiss" is written /kɪs/, and the word
"cat," /kæt/.

For those students who are familiar with the International Phonetic Alphabet
(I.P.A.), as an aid in transition to the system used in this book, the I.P.A. symbol is
noted next to its equivalent sound on the consonant and vowel charts, when the
I.P.A. symbol is different. The phonetic alphabet used in this book is on pages 7
and 8.

> Reminder: One phonetic symbol represents only one sound.

The following charts list the phonetic symbols for all the consonant and vowel
sounds of American English. Most of these sounds occur in initial (beginning), medial (middle), and final (end) positions. There are examples for each sound. *Memorize
one key word.* It will help you remember the sound for each phonetic symbol.

A. Consonant Sounds

The symbols in this chart look like letters you already know. Listen and repeat.

PHONETIC SYMBOL	INITIAL	MEDIAL	FINAL	I.P.A. (WHEN DIFFERENT)
/p/	pen	**op**era	to**p**	
/b/	**b**oy	a**bout**	ro**b**	
/t/	**t**en	a**ft**er	sa**t**	
/d/	**d**ay	**can**dy	ma**d**	
/k/	**c**at	**sec**ond	ne**ck**	
/g/	**g**o	a**gain**	e**gg**	
/f/	**f**ood	be**fore**	kni**f**e	
/v/	**v**oice	**nev**er	be**lieve**	
/s/	**s**ee	**less**on	bu**s**	
/z/	**z**oo	ea**s**y	choo**s**e	
/m/	**m**e	a**mount**	co**m**e	
/n/	**n**o	**an**imal	soo**n**	
/l/	**l**ike	a**l**ive	we**ll**	
/r/	**r**ed	**ver**y	doo**r**	
/w/	**w**alk	a**way**	[1]	
/y/	**y**es	**can**yon	[1]	/j/
/h/	**h**ouse	be**hind**	[1]	

The following symbols are not the same as the letters in the English alphabet. These consonant symbols are more difficult to remember. Listen and repeat.

PHONETIC SYMBOL	INITIAL	MEDIAL	FINAL	I.P.A. (WHEN DIFFERENT)
/θ/	**th**in	**an**y**th**ing	ba**th**	
/ð/	**th**e	**fa**ther	ba**the**	
/ʃ/	**sh**e	ma**chine**	fi**sh**	
/ʒ/	[2]	**pleas**ure	**sab**otage	
/ʧ/	**ch**ild	**teach**er	spee**ch**	
/ʤ/	**j**ob	a**g**ent	pa**g**e	
/ŋ/	[2]	thi**n**k	ki**ng**	

---

[1] This sound does not occur in final position.

[2] This sound does not occur in initial position.

B. Vowel Sounds

Most American English vowels are combinations of sounds. You may need a lot of practice to say them correctly. Listen and repeat.

PHONETIC SYMBOL	INITIAL	MEDIAL	FINAL	I.P.A. (WHEN DIFFERENT)
/iy/	each	re**ceive**	key	/i/
/ɪ/	if	sit	**sunn**y[3]	
/ey/	able	take	pay	/eɪ/
/ɛ/	egg	bread	[4]	
/æ/	**app**le	cat	[4]	
/uw/	ooze	**rul**er	do	/u/
/ʊ/	[5]	book	[4]	
/ow/	own	boat	no	/oʊ/
/ɔ/	all	ball	law	
/ɔy/	oil	noise	boy	/ɔɪ/
/ɑ/	**ar**my	not	Ma	
/ay/	ice	bite	tie	/aɪ/
/aw/	out	house	now	/aʊ/
/ə/	up	cut	**so**da	/ʌ/[6] and /ə/[7]
/ər/	earn	girl	**sis**ter	/ɝ/[8] and /ɚ/[9]

Reminder:
- One letter of the English alphabet may represent several different sounds.
- One sound may represent more than one letter.
- One phonetic symbol represents one sound.

---

[3] When in final position /iy/ and /ɪ/ are heard in standard American English.

[4] This sound does not occur in final position.

[5] This sound does not occur in initial position.

[6] /ʌ/ In the I.P.A. this symbol is used in stressed syllables.

[7] /ə/ In the I.P.A. this symbol is used in syllables that are not stressed.

[8] /ɝ/ In the I.P.A. this symbol is used in stressed syllables.

[9] /ɚ/ In the I.P.A. this symbol is used in syllables that are not stressed.

4. Further Practice

A. Write down the number of letters and sounds in each word. (*Hint:* The vowel letters "ou," "au," "ea," "oi," and "ie" and the consonant letters "th" and "gh" in these one-syllable words are counted as one sound.) Remember to say the words aloud.

		LETTERS	SOUNDS
EXAMPLES:	a. dumb	4	3
	b. cough	5	3
	1. take	_____	_____
	2. field	_____	_____
	3. hour	_____	_____
	4. each	_____	_____
	5. noun	_____	_____
	6. mix	_____	_____
	7. laugh	_____	_____
	8. bath	_____	_____
	9. thought	_____	_____
	10. buy	_____	_____

B. Match these phonetic symbols with the words in which they appear. Remember to say the words aloud.

EXAMPLE:	1. __c__ /f/		a.	house
	2. _____ /iy/		b.	child
	3. _____ /h/		c.	knife
	4. _____ /ð/		d.	most
	5. _____ /ɔ/		e.	just
	6. _____ /tʃ/		f.	ball
	7. _____ /m/		g.	king
	8. _____ /ŋ/		h.	the
	9. _____ /ʤ/		i.	voice
	10. _____ /ɔy/		j.	tea

C. Work with a partner. Compare and discuss your answers. Check your answers with your instructor.

Unit 2

The Speech Mechanism

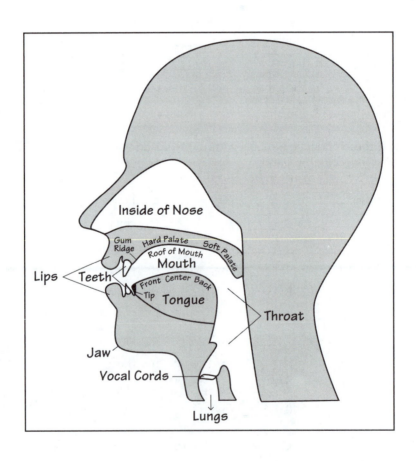

1. Articulators

The figure on page 10 shows the parts of the body that help us make sounds. These are called *articulators* or *speech organs*. They include:

lips	tongue	nose	
teeth	roof of mouth	vocal cords	jaw

These articulators, along with the breath that comes from the lungs, work together to produce consonant and vowel sounds. You will practice articulation in more detail in Part 3 (Vowels) and Part 4 (Consonants).

2. Identify Your Speech Organs

The tongue has four parts: the tip, front, center, and back. The roof of the mouth has three parts: the gum ridge, the hard palate, and the soft palate.

- Place the tip of your tongue in back of your upper front teeth. Do you feel a hard surface? This is your upper gum ridge.
- Now move the tip of your tongue farther back. The roof of the mouth is still hard. You are now touching your hard palate.
- Move your tongue still farther back. You will begin to feel a soft surface—your soft palate.

Your upper jaw does not move, but your lower jaw moves down and up. Together with your lower lip, it opens and closes your mouth. Try opening and closing your mouth. You should feel your lower jaw and lip moving.

3. Voiced and Voiceless Sounds

- Place two fingers on your throat and say the *sound* /s/ (not the letter).
- Now say the sound /z/. Do you feel a difference? When you say /z/, you should feel a vibration of the vocal cords. You should not feel any vibration when you say /s/.

Now say /s/ and /z/ in words and in a sentence: niece   knees

He saw my _____ (niece/knees).

Which word has the voiceless /s/ sound? Which has the voiced /z/ sound? Did he see your relative or a part of your leg? If he saw your relative, it was said with the voiceless /s/ sound; if he saw part of your leg, it was said with the voiced /z/ sound.

Try it again. Place two fingers on your throat and say the sounds /f/ and /v/. (Remember, do not say the names of the letters. Say the *sounds* for the symbols.)

Now try it in words and in a sentence: fan   van

I bought a _____ (fan/van).

Which one did you buy? If you wanted to cool off, then you bought a fan (voiceless /f/). If you wanted an enclosed truck, you bought a van (voiced /v/).

Pronounce voiced sounds, and your vocal cords will vibrate. Pronounce voiceless sounds, and your vocal cords will not vibrate. It is very important to notice the difference between voiced and voiceless sounds. The difference between them can make a difference in the meaning of a word.

4. Consonants

A. The following chart lists all voiced and voiceless consonants and their key words. The paired sounds are made in exactly the same way except that one is voiced, and the other is voiceless. Listen and repeat.

		Voiced		Voiceless	I.P.A. (when different)
Paired	/b/	boy	/p/	pen	
	/d/	day	/t/	ten	
	/g/	go	/k/	cat	
	/v/	voice	/f/	food	
	/z/	zoo	/s/	see	
	/ð/	the	/θ/	thin	
	/ʒ/	**pleas**ure	/ʃ/	she	
	/dʒ/	job	/tʃ/	child	

Handwritten note in left margin:
Voiced =
sonoro
Voiceless
mudo :

	VOICED		VOICELESS		I.P.A. (WHEN DIFFERENT)
NOT PAIRED	/l/	like	/h/	house	
	/r/	red			
	/w/	walk			
	/y/	yes			/j/
	/m/	me			
	/n/	no			
	/ŋ/	king			

B. These pairs of words begin with underlined voiced (Vd.) and voiceless (Vl.) sounds. Listen and repeat.

Vd.	Vl.	Vd.	Vl.
1. Ben	pen	5. thy[2]	thigh[3]
2. do	too	6. zoo	Sue
3. gold	cold	7. jeep	cheap
4. vine[1]	fine		

5. Vowels

A. Listen and repeat. These are the vowel sounds of American English:

/iy/[4]	see	/uw/[4]	do	/ə/[4]	up
/ɪ/	sit	/u/	book	/ər/[4]	sir
/ey/[4]	pay	/ow/[4]	no	/ay/[4]	buy
/ɛ/	met	/ɔ/	all	/aw/[4]	now
/æ/	cat	/ɑ/	not	/ɔy/[4]	boy

---

[1] *vine:* a clinging plant
[2] *thy:* old form of the word "your"
[3] *thigh:* the upper part of a leg
[4] See page 8 for the equivalent I.P.A. symbol.

All vowels are voiced (unless they are whispered). The positions of the jaw, lips, and tongue are very important when you pronounce vowels.[5] Say the sound /iy/ as in "s<u>ee</u>." Then say /ɑ/, as in "n<u>o</u>t." Repeat the sounds: /iy . . . . . ɑ/, /ɑ . . . . . iy/ exaggerating each one.   You should feel your lips and tongue move and your jaw drop lower, then rise again as you go from one sound to the other. Use a mirror to watch your mouth produce the sounds. Can you feel your vocal cords vibrate?

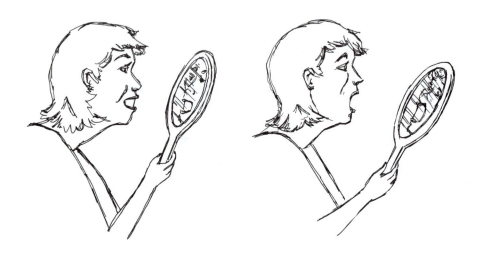

B. When you say these paired words, using a mirror, try to feel the movement of your lips, tongue, and jaw as you say the underlined vowel sounds. Listen and repeat.

1.	<u>ea</u>t	<u>a</u>t	4.	J<u>u</u>ne	J<u>o</u>hn
2.	s<u>ea</u>t	s<u>a</u>t	5.	sh<u>oo</u>t	sh<u>o</u>t
3.	l<u>ea</u>st	l<u>a</u>st	6.	L<u>u</u>ke	l<u>o</u>ck

Reminder:

• There are two groups of sounds in English: vowels and consonants.

• All vowels are voiced.

• Consonants may be voiced or voiceless.

---

[5] Part 3 describes vowel sounds in detail.

6. Further Practice

A. Are the first sounds in these words (represented by the underlined letters) voiced or voiceless? Check yourself by placing two fingers on the side of your throat and saying each word. Do you feel a vibration or no vibration when you make the *first* sound? Write "Vd." (voiced) or "Vl." (voiceless) on the line after each word.

Discuss your answers with a partner. Check with the consonant charts on page 7.

1. <u>b</u>ig _____
2. **<u>v</u>er**y _____
3. <u>p</u>ig _____
4. <u>h</u>e**llo** _____

5. **<u>m</u>on**ey _____
6. <u>d</u>ish _____
7. <u>th</u>is _____
8. **<u>wa</u>**ter _____

9. **<u>c</u>arr**y _____
10. <u>t</u>ell _____
11. <u>g</u>irl _____
12. **<u>s</u>ug**ar _____

B. Look at the consonant charts on page 7 and the vowel chart on page 8. Which sounds are similar to the sounds in your native language? Which are different? Make a list. Discuss them in class.

Consonants that are similar		Consonants that are different	
_____	_____	_____	_____
_____	_____	_____	_____
_____	_____	_____	_____
_____	_____	_____	_____
_____	_____	_____	_____

Vowels that are similar		Vowels that are different	
_____	_____	_____	_____
_____	_____	_____	_____
_____	_____	_____	_____
_____	_____	_____	_____
_____	_____	_____	_____

Part 2

Stress and Intonation

Every language has a system of sounds, stress, and intonation that gives it a rhythm and melody all its own. Non-native speakers say that it is difficult to understand some Americans when they speak English because they "talk too fast." Most likely, one reason is that the stress and intonation patterns of English are not recognized or understood. Although you may be able to pronounce each sound of the language correctly, you need to learn to recognize these stress and intonation patterns when you hear them so that they will be easier for you to understand. You also need to learn to use these patterns if others are to understand you more easily.

Stress refers to the degree of force or loudness you give to a syllable in a word or to a word or words in a phrase or a sentence. Stressing a syllable indicates the importance of that syllable (part of a word). Stressing a word or words in phrases or sentences indicates the importance of those words.

Intonation refers to the various tones of the voice. By using different tones, the speaker gives meaning and expression to the words he or she says. These tones are called *pitches*; they may be low or high pitches; they may be rising or falling pitches. Speaking English can be compared to singing. Stress provides the rhythm of the language, and intonation provides the melody.

Stress, intonation, consonants, and vowels all help to make up the English language. When speaking, these cannot be separated. But, in order to understand them better, you will study them separately. It is important, however, to remember that these parts all go together. In normal conversation one part cannot really exist without the others.

Unit 3

Syllable Stress

1. Identifying Syllables

A syllable is part of a word that contains one vowel sound; it may also contain one or more consonant sounds. In general, the number of vowel sounds in the word determines the number of syllables.

You can think of syllables as the number of "beats" in a word. For example, say the word "heart" while you tap your desk (or clap your hands or tap your foot) once. "Heart" has one syllable: a vowel sound and three consonant sounds (/hɑrt/). Now say "magic" while you tap out the syllables twice, once for each syllable. "Magic" has two vowel sounds and three consonant sounds (/mædʒ-ɪk/).

Now tap and say "India." How many syllables did you count? "India" has three syllables: three vowel sounds and two consonant sounds (/ɪn-diy-ə/).

Counting syllables and practicing syllable stress help you become aware of the rhythm of English.

(*Hint:* Some students find it helpful to count syllables by placing their thumb underneath their chin and counting the number of times their jaw moves while saying the word slowly.)

A. Syllables in Words

Practice these words of one, two, and three or more syllables. The letters for the vowel sound in each syllable are underlined. Listen and repeat.

1. One Syllable

   <u>a</u>ll　　　　　　c<u>u</u>p　　　　　　m<u>a</u>n　　　　　　c<u>a</u>ke

   ch<u>ee</u>se　　　　b<u>oa</u>t　　　　　cr<u>y</u>

2. Two Syllables

   <u>an</u>-sw<u>er</u>　　**st<u>u</u>**-d<u>e</u>nt　　a-**fr<u>ai</u>d**　　de-**gr<u>ee</u>**

3. Three or More Syllables

   r<u>a</u>-di-<u>o</u>　　　po-**t<u>a</u>**-t<u>o</u>　　　de-**p<u>ar</u>t**-m<u>e</u>nt

   d<u>i</u>s-**c<u>o</u>v**-<u>er</u>-<u>y</u>　　v<u>o</u>-**c<u>a</u>b**-<u>u</u>-l<u>ar</u>-<u>y</u>

B. Check Your Listening

Listen to the following words and write down the number of syllables. Check your answers with a dictionary.

1. **sis**ter	_2_	7. **o**ver	_1 → 1._
2. intro**duc**tion	_4_	8. **an**ybody	_3_
3. this	_1_	9. good-**bye**	_2_
4. there	_1_	10. phone	_2 → 1_
5. pro**fess**or	_3_	11. **tel**evision	_5 → 4_
6. **home**work	_3 → 2_	12. **prac**tice	_3 → 2_

2. Syllable Stress

In every word of two or more syllables, one syllable is stressed. That means that the vowel sound in that syllable is said *louder*, is said on a *higher pitch*, and is held *longer* than the other vowel sounds in the same word. This pattern is called *syllable stress*. Each word has one *stressed syllable*.[1] Other syllables (in a word of more than one syllable) are less stressed (not as prominent) or are weak (unstressed) syllables.[2]

level of the voice

---

[1] All one-syllable words, when said in isolation, have primary (the most prominent) stress.

[2] Although words may have secondary (2nd), tertiary (3rd), and weak stresses, for simplification primary stress (also referred to as *syllable stress*) and weak stress (also referred to as *unstressed syllable*) are used in this book.

Say the two-syllable word "afraid" while you tap out the syllables. Do you hear the stress in the second syllable? (a-**fraid**) Now say "radio." Stress the first syllable: **ra**-di-o. Say the word "vocabulary" and tap out the syllables. How many syllables did you count? "Vocabulary" has five syllables. Which syllable did you stress? The second syllable is stressed: vo-**cab**-u-lar-y.

This pattern of stressed and unstressed syllables is characteristic of the English language. It helps identify words we hear. In some other languages (Spanish and French, for example), most syllables receive equal stress. In English this stressing and unstressing creates contrasts between strong and weak syllables; it results in higher and lower pitches. The rhythm of English depends on these contrasts.

> Reminder: In a stressed syllable the vowel sound is louder, is higher in pitch, and is held longer than in the other syllables in the word.

A. Syllable Stress in Words

Tap out the rhythm of the following words and say them with the proper stress. Write down the number of beats each group has. The first group is marked for you.

1. One-Syllable Words   Each word has __1__ beat.

    1. am •   5. low •

    2. make ••   6. do •

    3. have ••   7. thought •

    4. likes ••

2. Two-Syllable Words   Each word has _____ beats.

  a. Stress on first syllable

    1. **ar**-my   4. **den**-tist

    2. **au**-to   5. **plas**-tic

    3. **ba**-by   6. **win**-dow

  b. Stress on second syllable

    1. cam-**paign**   4. per-**haps**

    2. gui-**tar**   5. in-**stead**

    3. de-**sign**   6. an-**tique**

3. Three-Syllable Words   Each word has • • • beats.

   a.   Stress on first syllable

      1. **ac**-ci-dent   4. **dan**-ger-ous

      2. **av**-e-nue   5. **com**-pa-ny

      3. **cit**-i-zen   6. **in**-flu-ence

   b.   Stress on second syllable

      1. sus-**pi**-cious   4. me-**chan**-ic

      2. de-**pos**-it   5. ad-**ven**-ture

      3. lo-**ca**-tion   6. in-**sur**-ance

   c.   Stress on third syllable

      1. dis-a-**ppoint**   4. per-so-**nnel**

      2. en-ter-**tain**   5. un-a-**fraid**

      3. in-tro-**duce**   6. en-gi-**neer**

4. Four-Syllable Words   Each word has _____ beats.

   a.   Stress on first syllable

      1. **cer**-e-mon-y   4. **san**-i-tar-y

      2. **lit**-er-a-ture   5. **tem**-po-rar-y

      3. **nec**-e-ssar-y   6. **sec**-re-tar-y

   b.   Stress on second syllable

      1. a-**rith**-me-tic   4. psy-**chol**-o-gy

      2. e-**mer**-gen-cy   5. se-**cur**-i-ty

      3. ex-**per**-i-ence   6. cer-**tif**-i-cate

   c.   Stress on third syllable

      1. re-cog-**ni**-tion   4. grad-u-**a**-tion

      2. con-ver-**sa**-tion   5. in-for-**ma**-tion

      3. ed-u-**ca**-tion   6. ob-ser-**va**-tion

5. Five- and Six-Syllable Words

Five-syllable words have _____ beats.

Six-syllable words have _____ beats.

1. al-pha-**bet**-i-cal

2. re-**frig**-er-a-tor

3. e-lec-**tric**-i-ty

4. au-to-bi-o-**graph**-ic

5. en-cy-clo-**pe**-di-a

6. re-spon-si-**bil**-i-ty

B. Make up a sentence with one word from each of the above groups. (More than one word from each group may be included in a sentence.) Underline the stressed syllable in the word(s) you select. Tape-record your sentences. When you play the recording back, listen carefully. Do you make the correct syllable stress?

EXAMPLES: a. My <u>bro</u>ther is a <u>den</u>tist in the <u>ar</u>my.
             b. I asked the <u>se</u>cretary for infor<u>ma</u>tion.

3. Check Your Listening

A. Listen to the following list of words. Circle the stressed syllable in each word.

EXAMPLE: (ba)-by

1. med-i-ca-tion

2. ma-chine

3. im-i-tate

4. de-lib-er-ate

5. con-sti-tu-tion

6. com-pu-ter

7. con-cen-trate

8. e-val-u-a-tion

9. reg-is-tra-tion

10. in-tern-al

B. Work with a partner and discuss your answers. Check your answers with a dictionary.

> Reminder: Making the correct syllable stress in a word creates a rhythm that directly affects the pronunciation of that word and its comprehension.

4. Reduced Vowels in Unstressed Syllables

In many words of two or more syllables, the unstressed vowel sounds are reduced to /ə/[3] as in "up" or /ɪ/ as in "sit." When these sounds are used in unstressed syllables, they sound almost alike and may sometimes be interchangeable. There are a large number of unstressed syllables in English. This unstressing (or weakening) of vowel sounds in syllables is extremely important because it helps make up the rhythm pattern of English.

The following words contain /ə/ or /ɪ/ in the unstressed syllables. *The letters for these vowel sounds are underlined.* Which sound do you make, /ə/ or /ɪ/? At times, it may be difficult to hear the difference. However, the important thing is to reduce the vowel sound in the *unstressed* syllable.

A. These two-syllable words have the unstressed vowel in the second syllable. Listen and repeat.

1.	**chil**dren	Where are your **chil**dren?
2.	**bagg**age	They're **watch**ing my **bagg**age.
3.	**car**pet	Did she pay to clean the **car**pet?
4.	**budg**et	No, it's not in her **budg**et.
5.	**hus**band	I would like to meet her **hus**band.
6.	**pri**vate	She has a **pri**vate room.

B. These two-syllable words have the unstressed vowel in the first syllable. Listen and repeat.

1.	a**sleep**	Go to sleep. I was a**sleep.**
2.	a**side**	It's on my side. I said, "Put it a**side.**"
3.	a**way**	Your paper is in the way. Put it a**way.**
4.	a**like**	He's like you; you're both a**like.**
5.	com**pare**	Don't com**pare** him to me.
6.	po**lite**	It's not po**lite** to do so.

C. These three-syllable words have unstressed vowels. Listen and repeat.

1.	pa**ja**mas	He likes to wear pa**ja**mas.
2.	em**barr**ass	Don't em**barr**ass him.

---

[3] The phonetic symbol /ə/, called the *schwa* /ʃwa/, is the most commonly used vowel sound in the English language.

3. **syll**ables   Did you mark the **co**rrect **syll**ables?

4. e**ffici**ent   Yes, I was **ver**y e**ffici**ent.

5. a**part**ment   Did you rent the a**part**ment?

6. **for**tunate   Yes, I was **for**tunate to get it.

5. Check Your Listening

Listen to the following words. Underline the stressed syllable in each word.

EXAMPLES: a.   rel**a**tion   b.   f**ac**tory

1. comm**and**   4. agreement   7. ap**o**strophe

2. supp**ose**   5. ar**i**thmetic   8. commencement

3. c**o**mma   6. p**a**ragraph   9. c**o**mpany

> Reminder: The contrast between stressed and unstressed syllables
>
> 1. aids in the production and comprehension of English;
> 2. is extremely important because it helps to create the rhythm of English.

6. Stress in Words With Prefixes and Suffixes

A. Prefixes

When a prefix is added before the base of a word, the stress pattern of the base word usually remains the same. The meaning of the word, however, changes.

PREFIX	MEANING	BASE WORD	PREFIX ADDED
1. auto-	self	bi**og**raphy	autobi**og**raphy
2. dis-	opposite of	a**gree**	disa**gree**
3. inter-	among, between	**nati**onal	inter**nati**onal
4. re-	again	write	re**write**
5. un-	opposite of, not	**happ**y	un**happ**y

B. Suffixes *the ends of word*

When a suffix is added to the end of a base word, the stress pattern of the word usually changes. The stress usually falls on the syllable that comes immediately before the added suffix.

Suffix	Meaning	Base word	Suffix added
1. -ian	relating to, resembling	**Par**is	Par**i**sian
2. -ic	relating to	**dem**ocrat	demo**crat**ic
3. -ical	relating to	**al**phabet	alpha**bet**ical
4. -ious	quality of, state of	**mys**tery	mys**ter**ious
5. -ity	quality of, state of	**poss**ible	possi**bil**ity
6. -tion	quality of, state of	a**ccuse**	accu**sa**tion

C. Fill in the blanks with words from the above lists that have the added prefixes and suffixes. Circle the stressed syllable. Work with a partner. Take turns reading the sentences. Check each other for correct pronunciation.

> **EXAMPLE:**   We a**gree** to *disagree.*

1. When a **per**son's born in **Par**is, he's called a _Parision_.

2. The **com**pany first went **nati**onal and then _international_.

3. I thought it was **poss**ible to do it, but the _possibility_ never o**ccurred** to them.

4. This is the **Eng**lish **al**phabet; a**rrange** the words in _Alphabetical_ **or**der.

5. He was a**ccused** of **steal**ing, but he de**nied** the _accusation._

6. A bi**og**raphy is the **stor**y of a **per**son's life. An _Autobiography_ is the **stor**y of a **per**son's life **writt**en by that **per**son.

7. He says he's a **Dem**ocrat, but he's not **ver**y _democratic_.

7. Shifts in Stress

Syllable stress in a word does not generally change. However, there is a large group of two-syllable words of paired nouns and verbs that is spelled the same way but is pronounced differently when the stress in the word is changed. This change in stress also changes the meaning of the word. When the wrong syllable is stressed, the speaker may not be understood.

Usually, when the word is a noun, the stress falls on the first syllable. When the word is a verb, the stress falls on the second syllable.

 A. Listen carefully for the shift in stress in the following words and sentences. Listen and repeat.

	Verb	Noun	Example
1.	con**duct**	**con**duct	Con**duct** yourself properly so that your **con**duct will not be questioned.
2.	con**flict**	**con**flict	It may con**flict** with my schedule. If it does, a **con**flict will arise.
3.	con**vert**	**con**vert	When you con**vert** from one religion to another, you are known as a **con**vert.
4.	con**victs**	**con**victs	When the judge con**victs** him, he will join the **con**victs in jail.
5.	de**sert**[4]	**des**ert	Don't de**sert** me when we go into the **des**ert.
6.	ob**ject**	**ob**ject	I ob**ject** to that ugly **ob**ject being in this room.
7.	pre**sent**	**pres**ent	She will pre**sent** you with a **pres**ent on your birthday.
8.	pro**duce**	**pro**duce	The farm will pro**duce** food, and we will sell the **pro**duce in the market.
9.	re**cord**	**rec**ord	He'll re**cord** his voice on the **rec**ord.
10.	sub**ject**	**sub**ject	Don't sub**ject** us to that **sub**ject again because I know all about it.

---

[4] "De**sert**" is a noun when it means an earned reward or punishment, such as "She got her just de**serts** for being so mean." ("De**ssert,**" a noun spelled with a double "s," usually refers to the last course of a meal.)

B. Not all two-syllable noun–verb pairs follow the same stress pattern as those above. In the words below, both nouns and verbs may have the same stress pattern. Listen and repeat.

Verbs	Some nouns pronounced as verbs
1. I'll a**ddress** the envelope.	Put my a**ddress**[5] (**add**ress) on the envelope.
2. Will you per**mit** me to drive?	Do you have a per**mit** (**per**mit) to drive?
3. Does he su**pport** his child?	His su**pport** goes to his child.
4. We'll sur**prise** him with a party.	What a sur**prise** they gave him!
5. He wants to de**fect** from his country.	Don't buy it because it has a de**fect** (**de**fect).[6]

C. Work with a partner.

1. Think of a sentence or sentences for each noun–verb pair. Underline the stressed syllable in the noun <u>once</u> and in the verb <u>twice</u>. Keep in mind that some noun–verb pairs may have the same stress pattern.

2. Each student takes a turn reading a sentence to the class.

	Verb	Noun
Examples:	in<u>crease</u>	<u>in</u>crease
	<u>pro</u>gram	<u>pro</u>gram

a. My profits will in<u>crease</u> the <u>in</u>crease in my sales.
b. Did you <u>pro</u>gram the computer? I already have a <u>pro</u>gram in my computer.

Verb	Noun		Verb	Noun
1. discharge	discharge		3. <u>pro</u>ject	proj<u>ect</u>
2. rebel	rebel		4. digest	digest

---

[5] When this word is used as a noun, meaning a written or a spoken speech, the second syllable always gets the primary stress: "The president will make an inaugural a**ddress**." (An inaugural a**ddress** is a speech that is made by a newly elected president.)

[6] "De**fect**," when used as a noun, can also be pronounced with the stress on the first syllable, "**de**fect." It implies a lack of something; an imperfection. When used as a verb, it means "to leave;" "to de**sert**."

Verb	Noun		Verb	Noun
5. insert	insert		8. progress	progress
6. escort	escort		9. entrance	entrance
7. estimate	estimate		10. export	export

Reminder: Two-syllable words of paired nouns and verbs spelled the same way

1. are pronounced differently when the stress in the word is changed;

2. have different meanings when the stress in the word is changed.

---

8. Stress in Compound Nouns

A compound word may be made up of two or more words that are separate parts of speech, such as nouns, adjectives, or verbs that form a single meaning. A compound word may be written together as one word or as two separate words.

A. Noun + Noun Compounds

When a compound word is made up of two nouns, the primary stress is usually placed on the first noun. Listen and repeat.

1. **base**ball
2. **sales**man
3. post **off**ice
4. **seat**belt
5. sports car
6. **lan**guage lab
7. **coff**ee shop
8. **space**bar
9. **pass**port

B. Compound Proper Nouns

In compound proper nouns the primary stress is usually placed on the second noun. Listen and repeat.

1. Mount **Ev**erest
2. San Fran**cis**co Bay
3. Pa**cif**ic **O**cean
4. U**ni**ted States
5. New York
6. New **Mex**ico

C. Compound Nouns Ending in the Word "Day"

In compound nouns ending in the word "day," the primary stress is usually placed on the first noun. Listen and repeat.

1. New Year's Day
2. Election Day
3. **La**bor Day
4. **Christ**mas Day
5. Thanks**giv**ing Day
6. **Vet**eran's Day

D. Adjective + Noun Compounds

1. Primary stress is usually placed on the adjective. Listen and repeat.

    1. **black**bird   3. **dark**room   5. <u>hot</u> plate

    2. <u>White</u> House   4. **short**stop[7]   6. **short**cut[8]

2. Certain adjective + noun compounds may not function as compounds. It depends on what the speaker means to say. Listen and repeat.

    1a. I saw a **black**bird on the tree. (Type of bird)

    b. I saw a black <u>bird</u> on the tree. (Color of bird)

    2a. The **Pres**ident lives in the <u>White</u> House. (Official residence of the President)

    b. He lives in the white <u>house</u>. (Color of house)

    3a. He de**vel**ops his film in the **dark**room. (A special room for developing film)

    b. He likes to sit in a dark <u>room</u>. (A room with little or no light)

    4a. He plays **short**stop on his team. (A position on field when playing baseball)

    b. She made a short <u>stop</u> at the **traff**ic light. (Foot on the brake)

    5a. She cooks meals on a <u>hot</u> plate. (A small stove used for heating food)

    b. She burned her hand on the hot <u>plate</u>. (A dish that was hot)

    6a. He took a **short**cut to his house. (A shorter way than usual to get home)

    b. He went to the **bar**ber for a short <u>cut</u>. (His hair was cut short)

E. Verb + Noun Compounds

Primary stress is usually placed on the verb. Listen and repeat.

1. **play**boy   4. **swimm**ing pool
2. **hang**man   5. **cross**ing guard
3. **typ**ing **pa**per   6. **flash**light

---

[7] *shortstop:* in baseball, the player who is stationed between second and third base

[8] *shortcut:* a shorter way to a place than usual; a faster way to do something

F. Work with a partner. Each one writes down the answers to the following questions and underlines the stressed part of the compound word. Take turns asking and answering. Compare your answers.

EXAMPLE: What do you call a **bott**le that is filled with hot **wa**ter?
                  a hot-**wa**ter bottle

1. What do you call a card that you use to get **cred**it?

    _____

2. What do you call a card that's green?

    _____

3. What do you call a gun that's held in the hand?

    _____

4. What do you call a plane that flies in the air?

    _____

5. What do you call a watch that's in a **pock**et?

    _____

6. What do you call a **pa**per that **pub**lishes news?

    _____

7. What do you call a light that guides **traff**ic?

    _____

8. What do you call gum that you chew?

    _____

9. What do you call a storm when it rains?

    _____

10. What do you call a board that has keys?

    _____

G. **Days of the Week**

All the days of the week get primary stress on the first syllable. Listen and repeat.

1. **Mon**day
2. **Tues**day
3. **Wednes**day
4. **Thurs**day

5. **Fri**day
6. **Sat**urday
7. **Sun**day

H. **Months of the Year**

The months of the year that have two syllables have primary stress on the first syllable, except for "July." Months of the year that have three syllables have primary stress on the second syllable. Listen and repeat.

1. **Jan**uary
2. **Feb**ruary
3. March

4. **A**pril
5. May
6. June

7. Ju**ly**
8. **Au**gust
9. Sep**tem**ber

10. Oc**to**ber
11. No**vem**ber
12. De**cem**ber

I. Read the following poem aloud.

1. Underline the stressed syllables in *all* words of two or more syllables. Check your work with a partner.

2. Read the passage aloud in class, each student taking one line.

1. Sneeze on a Monday, in January, you sneeze for danger;

2. Sneeze on a Tuesday, in February, you'll kiss a stranger;

3. Sneeze on a Wednesday, in April, you'll sneeze for a letter;

4. Sneeze on a Thursday, in July, for something better.

5. Sneeze on a Friday, in August, you sneeze for sorrow;

6. Sneeze on a Saturday, in September, see your sweetheart tomorrow;

7. Sneeze on a Sunday, in October, your safety seek,

8. For you will have trouble, in November and December, the whole of the week.

9. Further Practice

A. Say each word aloud several times.

1. Write the number of syllables for each word on the line next to the word.

2. Underline the stressed syllable in each word.

3. Place the symbols /ə/ as in "up" or /ɪ/ as in "sit" over the unstressed syllable(s) in each word, wherever applicable.[9]

EXAMPLES: a. applicant   __3__   c. application   __4__

            b. education   __4__   d. polite   __2__

1. define   _____   6. adventure   _____

2. applause   _____   7. emergency   _____

3. silent   _____   8. companion   _____

4. mortgage   _____   9. vacation   _____

5. command   _____   10. circumstantial _____

B. Underline the primary stress in the following compound words.

1. Compare your answers with a partner.

2. Make up a sentence for each of the words. Take turns reading them to the class.

    EXAMPLE: shoelace
                    This shoelace is black; I asked for a white one.

    1. barefoot   5. streetcar

    2. software   6. air conditioner

    3. blueprint   7. crosswalk

    4. handgun   8. railroad

---

[9] *applicable:* wherever it belongs

C. The following sentences contain noun–verb pairs. Underline the stressed syllable in the noun <u>once</u> and in the verb <u>twice</u>.

1. Check your answers with a dictionary.

2. Tape-record the sentences. Listen to the playback. Are you stressing the correct syllables?

   EXAMPLE: When you <u>addict</u> yourself to drugs, you become an <u>add</u>ict.

   1. He said he would contract an illness to get out of his contract.

   2. He will refuse to take out the refuse.

   3. She's very upset at the upset.

   4. I suspect that the suspect will be arrested.

   5. Don't insult me; an insult will not solve anything.

Unit 4

Vowel and Consonant Length

English speakers hold vowel and consonant sounds longer in some words than in others. They do this automatically; it is part of the rhythm of English. (Such changes do not usually take place in the native tongue of the learner of English.) Therefore, comparing and knowing how long a vowel sound or a consonant sound is held in a word is very important. It not only helps the learner acquire a style of speaking similar to native English speakers, but it also helps to make the pronunciation and comprehension of words clearer.

The dictionary's explanation of a "long" vowel, such as /ey/ as in "made," and a "short"vowel, such as /æ/ as in "cat," is concerned with the difference the vowel makes in the meaning of a word.

In linguistics (the study of language), we are concerned with the lengthening and shortening of sounds: their *duration.* By duration we mean the actual length of *time* it takes to make a particular sound.[1] How long you hold a vowel sound or a consonant sound in a word helps identify that word.

1. Lengthening of Vowels Before Consonants

 A. In the following pairs of words the *same* underlined vowel is held longer before *voiced* consonants /b/, /d/, /g/, /v/, and /z/, (column A) than before *voiceless* consonants /p/, /t/, /k/, /f/, and /s/, (column B). Listen and repeat.

---

[1] For in-depth descriptions, see the units on vowels in Part 3 and the units on consonants in Part 4.

A Vd.[2]	B Vl.[3]		A Vd.[2]	B Vl.[3]
1. eyes	ice	7.	rib	rip
2. said	set	8.	side	sight
3. doze	dose	9.	leave	leaf
4. save	safe	10.	pig	pick
5. mob	mop	11.	cub	cup
6. lied	light	12.	log	lock

> **Remember:**
> - Hold a vowel sound longer before a *voiced* consonant than before a *voiceless* consonant.
> - Listen for the difference in the length of the vowel sound to help you identify the word.

B. Work with a partner. Say one of the sentences in each pair below. Your partner must identify it by replying "a" or "b" followed by the sentence. If the answer is incorrect, say it again.

1a. I rode **ev**ery day.
  b. I wrote **ev**ery day.

2a. He needs a cab.
  b. He needs a cap.

3a. Look at his bag.
  b. Look at his back.

✓ 4a. I gave her a tab.
  b. I gave her a tap.

5a. Her side is good.
  b. Her sight is good.

6a. My bed is wide.
  b. My bed is white.

7a. We like to serve.
  b. We like to surf.

8a. The mob is here.
  b. The mop is here.

9a. Can you prove[4] it?
  b. Can you proof[5] it?

10a. Did you buy a log?
  b. Did you buy a lock?

---

[2] *Vd.:* voiced
[3] *Vl.:* voiceless
[4] *prove:* test by experiment
[5] *proof:* make a test of

2. Lengthening of Vowels at the End of Sentences

A. Vowel sounds are usually held longer when they are at the end of a sentence than when they are within a sentence. Listen and repeat.

1a. Let's g<u>o</u>.

  b. Let's g<u>o</u> there.

2a. It's the l<u>aw</u>.

  b. The l<u>aw</u> passed.

> Reminder: Hold a vowel sound longer when it appears in a word that ends a sentence than when it appears within a sentence.

B. In these pairs of sentences the underlined vowel sounds are held longer in the first sentence than in the second. Listen and repeat.

1a. We should g<u>o</u>.

  b. I'll g<u>o</u> **la**ter.

2a. He likes to fl<u>y</u>.

  b. He's going to fl<u>y</u> to **Tex**as.

3a. How well can you s<u>ee</u>?

  b. I can s<u>ee</u> the sign.

4a. Please hand me a tr<u>ay</u>.

  b. Here's the tr<u>ay</u> from the shelf.

5a. Where is my sh<u>oe</u>?

  b. Where is my sh<u>oe</u> with the black strap?

6a. Who likes to dr<u>aw</u>?

  b. I like to dr<u>aw</u> **pic**tures.

7a. Can you do it n<u>ow</u>?

  b. N<u>ow</u> is not the time.

8a. He likes **app**le p<u>ie</u>.

  b. She likes **app**le p<u>ie</u> a la mode.

9a. She bought him a t<u>oy</u>.

  b. He bought him a t<u>oy</u> **sol**dier.

10a. Do you have any gl<u>ue</u>?

  b. I have gl<u>ue</u> for all of us.

3. Lengthening of Consonants at the End of Sentences

A. Say these two sentences. Hold the /s/ in "pri<u>c</u>e" longer than the /z/ in "pri<u>z</u>e." This makes it easier for the listener to understand which word is said.

I like the pri<u>z</u>e.

I like the pri<u>c</u>e.

B. Say these sentences. Hold the voiceless consonant sounds (/s/, /f/, and /ʧ/) that are in the first sentence of each pair longer than the voiced consonant sounds (/z/, /v/, and /ʤ/) that are in the second sentence of each pair. (Voiceless /p/, /t/, and /k/ and voiced /b/, /d/, and /g/, cannot be held.) This makes it easier for the listener to understand which word is being said. Listen and repeat.

1a. He likes the spi<u>c</u>e.

  b. He likes the spie<u>s</u>.

2a. Don't call her Mi<u>ss</u>.

  b. Don't call her M<u>s</u>.[6]

3a. That's a li<u>f</u>e.

  b. That's a**li<u>v</u>e.**

4a. I saw him lun<u>ch</u>.

  b. I saw him lun<u>g</u>e.[7]

> Reminder: Hold *final voiceless* consonant sounds longer than *final voiced* consonant sounds. Exceptions: voiceless /p/, /t/, and /k/ and voiced /b/, /d/, and /g/, which cannot be held.

---

[6] *Ms.* /mɪz/: a title for a woman that does not indicate if she is single or married
[7] *lunge* /ləndʒ/: move forward with sudden force

C. Work with a partner. Take turns. Student A selects to read aloud any sentence "a" or "b." Student B identifies it by replying with the answer and making up a sentence with the underlined word. Can you say and hear the difference in the length of the consonant sounds?

EXAMPLE: Student A: Did you call <u>Mitch</u>?
              Student B: Who's he? I **won**der who <u>Mitch</u> is.

Sentence	Answer
1a. I want my <u>piece</u>.	(**Piz**za)
b. I want my <u>peas</u>.	(**Veg**etable)
2a. Did you get your <u>price</u>?	(I **want**ed more.)
b. Did you get your <u>prize</u>?	(I won an a**ward**.)
3a. Ma**rr**ia saw the <u>place</u>.	(A**part**ment)
b. Ma**rr**ia saw the <u>plays</u>.	(Stage)
4a. They say that's <u>life</u>.	(Who is "they"?)
b. They say that's <u>live</u>.	(**Lob**ster)
5a. Did you call <u>Mitch</u>?	(Who's he?)
b. Did you call <u>Midge</u>?	(Who's she?)
6a. How do you spell "<u>rich</u>"?	(r-i-c-h)
b. How do you spell "<u>ridge</u>"?[8]	(r-i-d-g-e)
7a. Did you hear the <u>bus</u>?	(No, it was **qui**et.)
b. Did you hear the <u>buzz</u>?	(Bee)
8a. He took my <u>batch</u>.[9]	(**Cook**ies)
b. He took my <u>badge</u>.	(I.D.)[10]
9a. I can spell "<u>etch</u>."[11]	(e-t-c-h)
b. I can spell "<u>edge</u>."	(e-d-g-e)
10a. How do you spell "<u>thief</u>"?	(t-h-i-e-f)
b. How do you spell "<u>thieve</u>"?[12]	(t-h-i-e-v-e)

---

[8] *ridge:* a long, narrow, high piece of land
[9] *batch:* a group of things or persons
[10] *I.D.:* a form of identification
[11] *etch:* create a picture by cutting lines in wood, metal, or stone
[12] *thieve:* steal

Reminder:

Vowels:

- A vowel sound is held longer before a *voiced* consonant than before a *voiceless* consonant.
- A vowel sound is held longer when it ends a word that appears at the end of a sentence.

Consonants:

- *Final voiceless* consonant sounds are held longer than *final voiced* consonant sounds except for those that cannot be held (voiceless /p/, /t/, and /k/ and voiced /b/, /d/, and /g/).

4. Further Practice

Work with a partner. Take turns reading each sentence aloud. Discuss with your partner which paired words in each sentence has the longer *vowel* sound and which has the longer *consonant* sound. Underline the longer vowel sound <u>once</u>. Underline the longer consonant sound <u>twice</u>. Explain why to your partner.

EXAMPLE: He wants to l<u>i</u>ve a long li<u>fe</u>.

      "Live" ends in a voiced consonant, so you hold the vowel sound longer. "Life" ends in a voiceless consonant, so you hold the voiceless consonant longer.

1. Is it safe to save it?

2. The price of the prize is ex**pen**sive.

3. I heard the buzz on the bus.

4. I want to eat my peas in peace.

5. Don't leave with**out** the leaf.

6. I saw the rice in the pot rise.

7. She wants to be called Ms., not Miss.

8. It pays to set a pace.

9. The dens were dense with smoke.

10. It's loose, so don't lose it.

Unit 5

Content Words and Function Words

1. Content and Function Words

When talking, speakers of English stress the most important words in a sentence. These words are usually nouns, verbs, adjectives, and adverbs. They are called *content words*, because they express the main idea or content of the phrase or sentence. They are the words that carry the message. Less important words are articles, pronouns, possessives, prepositions, auxiliary verbs, and conjunctions. They are called *function words.* These words are generally not stressed. They connect the content words to form grammatical sentences.

Here are some examples of content and function words.

Content words	
Nouns:	Ma**rie,** book, **pen**cil, chair, **book**case, floor
Verbs:	runs, teach, speak, re**mind,** can't, a**pol**ogize
Adjectives:	sick, **sim**ple, green, hot, **happ**y, big, **ver**y
Adverbs:	**reall**y, **cer**tainly, **al**most, **slow**ly, to**day**

Function words	
Articles:	a, an, the
Pronouns and	
Possessives:	you, your, him, she, he, it, we, our, them
Prepositions:	for, from, by, of, to, at, in, by
Auxiliary Verbs:	am, can, have, were, was, had, has, will
Conjunctions:	and, as, or, but, if, that, than

2. Content Words

During conversations, successful listeners interpret content words to figure out the message. Therefore, it is important that the speaker learn to stress these content words correctly and unstress the function words that are used as grammatical links. This contributes to the understanding of the language.

The following is an example of a message using only content words. The words left out are the function words.

1. Read the words aloud, in the paragraph below, without filling in the blanks. Can you make sense out of it? You probably can, because this is a message using only content words.

2. In the blanks provided, fill in the function words. When you add them to the message, they form grammatical sentences.

3. When you have finished, compare your answers with a classmate. Take turns reading the sentences aloud.

Kathy lost _her_ **hand**bag _in_ _a_ **res**taurant _because_ _she_ _was_ **care**less. _She_ placed _her_ **hand**bag _on_ _the_ floor. _when_ _she_ **fin**ished **eat**ing _dinner_ **com**p**lete**ly for**got** _about the_ _hand_ left _the_ **res**taurant.

3. Function Words

In Unit 3 you practiced vowel sounds in unstressed syllables. For example, the sound /ə/ as in "<u>up</u>" often occurs in words of two or more syllables.

$$\overset{ə}{\text{pa}}\mathbf{ja}\overset{ə}{\text{mas}} \qquad \overset{ə}{\text{a}}\mathbf{sleep}$$

This same sound also occurs in function words. But it occurs only when the word is *unstressed.* Thus, many function words have two pronunciations: a stressed form and an unstressed form. The unstressed form, weakened in conversational speech, is called the *reduced form.* This is because the vowel sound is "reduced," or cut down, to an unstressed form.

A. The following sentences are examples of reduced (unstressed) function words and the use of the stressed function word "can." The stress mark (´) indicates stressed words. Listen and repeat.

1. ~~You~~ can go ~~to the~~ park.   =   You are physically able or have
   ("Can" is stressed; "you,"   permission to go to the park.
   "to," and "the" are
   unstressed.)

2. ~~You can~~ go ~~to the~~ park.   =   The park is one place you
   ("Can" is now unstressed.)   can go.

 B. Listen and repeat the following words and sentences. First you will hear the function word alone. This is its stressed form. Then you will hear a sentence with the unstressed form of the word.

	Stressed form		Unstressed form	
1.	a	/ey/	/ə/	Did you read ~~a~~ good book?
2.	an	/æn/	/ən/	Have ~~an~~ orange.
			or /'n/	
3.	and	/ænd/	/ənd/	We saw Jack ~~and~~ Jill.
			or /'n/	
			or /'nd/	
4.	are	/ɑr/	/ər/	**Mar**y and June ~~are~~ **sis**ters.
5.	as	/æz/	/əz/	You're ~~as~~ sweet ~~as~~ **sug**ar.
6.	be**cause**	/bɪkɔz/	/bɪkəz/	I like it ~~be**cause**~~ it's nice.
7.	can	/kæn/	/kən/	I ~~can~~ do it.
8.	for	/fɔr/	/fər/	Is this ~~for~~ me?
9.	from	/frɑm/	/frəm/	This is ~~from~~ my **broth**er.
10.	had	/hæd/	/həd/	He ~~had~~ been there.
11.	has	/hæz/	/həz/	He ~~has~~ nine **broth**ers.
			or /əz/	
12.	have	/hæv/	/həv/	We should ~~have~~ **wait**ed **long**er.
			or /əv/	
13.	of	/ɑv/	/əv/	I'm **think**ing ~~of~~ you.
14.	or	/ɔr/	/ər/	I want three ~~or~~ four.

	Stressed form		Unstressed form	
15.	th<u>a</u>t	/ðæt/	/ðət/	It's the one ~~that~~ got a**way.**
16.	th<u>a</u>n	/ðæn/	/ðən/	It's **nic**er ~~than~~ yours.
17.	t<u>o</u>	/tuw/	/tə/	Go ~~to~~ school.
18.	w<u>a</u>s	/wɑz/	/wəz/	It ~~was~~ good.

C. You will hear the same sentence twice. The first time the sentence will include the unstressed form of a function word. The second time, the sentence will include the stressed form. Notice the linking of words and the change in the meaning of the sentence. Listen and repeat.

1a.	/'n/	We saw Jack ~~and~~ Jill.	(We saw both Jack and Jill.)
b.	/ænd/	We saw Jack and Jill.	(Jill was there too, but we didn't expect to see her.)
2a.	/ər/	**Ma**ry ~~and~~ June ~~are~~ **sis**ters.	(Simple information.)
b.	/ar/	**Ma**ry ~~and~~ June áre **sis**ters.	(They are sisters, but we thought they weren't.)
3a.	/wəz/	The food ~~was~~ good.	(Simple statement of opinion.)
b.	/wɑz/	The food wás good.	(It was good, and I was rather surprised.)
4a.	/kən/	I ~~can~~ do it.	(Simple statement of fact.)
b.	/kæn/	I cán do it.	(Of course I can do it. Did you think I couldn't?)
5a.	/həd/	He ~~had~~ been here.	(He was here at an earlier time.)
b.	/hæd/	He hád been here.	(It was a surprise to learn that he was here. Or the meaning could be an accusation: You told me he hadn't been here, but that wasn't true.)

Reminder:

- Content words that are stressed are held longer than function words that are not stressed.
- Function words are not stressed unless they are important to the meaning of the message.

rule.
to be.

4. Check Your Listening

As you listen to the sentences, draw a line through the unstressed function words you hear.

1. I think Tom ~~and~~ Lee went home.

2. The **par**ty ~~was~~ fun.

3. You ~~can~~ pass ~~the~~ test.

4. We ~~have~~ been here ~~all~~ day.

5. Yes, ~~we are~~ **com**ing home now.

6. Do ~~as~~ I say, not ~~as~~ I do.

7. I think ~~of~~ you all ~~the~~ time.

8. They ~~have~~ more ~~than~~ they need.

9. He ~~was a~~ good **teach**er.

10. I eat it be**cause** ~~it's~~ **heal**thy.

Correct ←

5. Function Words in Phrases and Sentences

In the following exercises you will practice the reduced form of function words. Connect the function word with the other words of the phrase and say the phrase with a smooth rhythm.

A. Articles: "a," "an," and "the"

Listen to and repeat the following phrases and sentences.

1. Pronounce the word "a" as /ə/ before words beginning with a consonant.

   a. ~~a~~ drink   Have ~~a~~ drink.

   b. ~~a~~ **num**ber   Take ~~a~~ **num**ber.

   c. ~~a~~ **mov**ie   See ~~a~~ **mov**ie.

2. Pronounce the word "an" as /ən/ before words beginning with a vowel sound.

   a. ~~an~~ **au**to   Buy ~~an~~ **au**to.

   b. ~~an~~ egg   Boil ~~an~~ egg.

   c. ~~an~~ **off**er   Make me ~~an~~ **off**er.

3. Pronounce the word "the" as /ðə/ before words beginning with consonants.

   a. t̶h̶e̶ má̶p   Get t̶h̶e̶ máp.

   b. t̶h̶e̶ cláss   Take t̶h̶e̶ cláss.

   c. t̶h̶e̶ bóy   Meet t̶h̶e̶ bóy.

4. Pronounce the word "the" as /ðiy/ before words beginning with a vowel sound.

   a. t̶h̶e̶ **ór**der   Take t̶h̶e̶ **ór**der.

   b. t̶h̶e̶ **én**trance   Near t̶h̶e̶ **én**trance.

   c. t̶h̶e̶ ex**ám**ple   Use t̶h̶e̶ ex**ám**ple.

B. **Pronouns and Possessives: "you," "your," "he," "him," and "her"**

1. Reduce "you" to /yə/. "You" is usually not reduced when it ends a sentence. (It may be reduced in some expressions.)

   a. Did y̶o̶u̶ sée Mike?

   b. I saw y̶o̶u̶ **dánc**ing.

   c. Was it **réal**ly you?

   d. Hi, how are y̶o̶u̶?

2. Reduce "your" to /yər/.[1]

   a. Here's y̶o̶u̶r̶ hát.

   b. He took y̶o̶u̶r̶ pláce.

   c. Tell y̶o̶u̶r̶ bóss.

3. Reduce "he" to /iy/. "He" at the beginning of a sentence is usually not reduced.

   a. Where did h̶e̶ gó?

   b. What does h̶e̶ wánt?

   c. He said h̶e̶ wóuld.

4. Reduce "him" to /əm/ or /'m/.

   a. Give h̶i̶m̶ a bréak.

   b. I saw h̶i̶m̶ to**dáy.**

   c. Do you like h̶i̶m̶?

---

[1] Some speakers do not pronounce the final /r/.

5. Reduce "her" to /ər/.[2]

    a. It's ~~her~~ **broth**er.

    b. What's ~~her~~ name?

    c. Give it to ~~her~~.

C. Prepositions: "of," "to," "at," and "for"

1. Reduce "of" to /əv/ or /ə/.

    a. Tired ~~of~~ **work**ing?

    b. All ~~of~~ the time.

    c. It's a lot ~~of~~ **mon**ey.

    d. A cup ~~of~~ **cof**fee.

2. Reduce "to" to /tə/. Do not reduce it at the end of a sentence.

    a. He went ~~to~~ **coll**ege.

    b. Give it ~~to~~ me.

    c. Does he have to?

    d. He wants to.

3. Reduce "at" to /ət/. Do not reduce it at the end of a sentence.

    a. I'm ~~at~~ school.

    b. Come ~~at~~ once.

    c. What's he **look**ing at?

4. Reduce "for" to /fər/.[2] Do not reduce it at the end of a sentence.

    a. Get it ~~for~~ me.

    b. Ask ~~for~~ change.

    c. What are you **look**ing for?

    d. What's the bill for?

D. Auxiliary Verbs: "am," "was," and "can"

1. Reduce "am" to /əm/ or /'m/. Do not reduce it at the end of a sentence.

    a. Where ~~am~~ I **go**ing?

    b. ~~Am~~ I **fin**ished?

---

[2] Some speakers do not pronounce the final /r/.

    c. I think I am.

    d. I know I am.

2. Reduce "was" to /wəz/. In some expressions it may be reduced at the end of a sentence.

    a. I ~~was~~ right.

    b. ~~Was~~ it **rain**ing?

    c. Yes, it was.

    d. They showed me where it ~~was~~.

3. Reduce "can" to /kən/. Do not reduce it at the end of a sentence.

    a. He ~~can~~ read.

    b. ~~Can~~ I talk?

    c. Yes, you can.

    d. He'll come when he can.

E. Conjunctions: "and," "as," and "or"

1. Reduce "and" to /ən/ or /'n/

    a. Come ~~and~~ see me.

    b. They're **sis**ter ~~and~~ **broth**er.

    c. I'd like **ba**con ~~and~~ eggs.

2. Reduce "as" to /əz/.

    a. He's ~~as~~ old ~~as~~ Ann.

    b. It's ~~as~~ white ~~as~~ snow.

    c. It's ~~as~~ good ~~as~~ gold.

3. Reduce "or" to /ər/ or /ə/.[3]

    a. Take it ~~or~~ leave it.

    b. I'll take one ~~or~~ two.

    c. It's now ~~or~~ **nev**er.

Reminder: Use the stressed form of a function word

- when you say the word by itself;
- when the function word is important to the meaning of the sentence.

---

[3] Some speakers do not pronounce the final /r/.

6. Rhythm of English

Every language has its own rhythm. Unlike many other languages in the world, English depends on the correct pronunciation of stressed and unstressed or weakened syllables recurring in the same phrase or sentence. Mastering the rhythm of English makes speaking more effective.

A. The following four sentences take about the same length of time to say. Tap out a beat for each of the three content words: *men, fight, wars.* Keep the beat the same for all four sentences. Stress the content words. Reduce the function words by saying them quickly. Variation of words or syllables that have strong stress with those that have weaker or reduced stress is typical and contributes to the rhythm of English. You should be able to say sentences 2, 3, and 4 to the same three beats you tapped for sentence 1. Listen and repeat.

1. Men fight wars.

2. ~~The~~ men fight wars.

3. ~~The~~ men ~~will~~ fight wars.

4. ~~The~~ men ~~will~~ fight ~~the~~ wars.

B. The same is true for longer sentences. Those below are divided into phrases, indicated by the symbol (/). Each phrase should take about the same time to say. Draw a line through the function words. Read the sentences aloud in class.

1. **Us**ing the com**pu**ter / I can co**rrect** / all my **spell**ing **err**ors.

2. The **oth**er day / I saw my **cous**in / who is **ver**y sick.

C. Saying nursery rhymes, poems, and ballads[4] aloud is one way of getting the feel of the rhythm of English. In the rhyme below, pay attention to the stressed content words and the reduced function words. How many beats does each line have?

It's quick and **qui**et   It's **spinn**ing, it's **spinn**ing,
It's soft and it's light.   It makes quite a show.
It's free—you can't buy it.   What is it? . . . in **win**ter?
It just comes in white.   Does **an**yone know?

What is it?

---

[4] *ballad:* a poem or song that tells a story with simple words

> Reminder: The unstressed function words are said quickly in order to get them out in time to maintain the rhythm of English.

7. More Reductions

We have seen how stressing content words and unstressing or reducing function words can change pronunciation and meaning. There are further reductions that speakers make in their everyday conversational speech. You may find it uncomfortable, and you may even hesitate to use these reductions in your speech. However, it is important that you recognize these reductions when you hear them, so that you can understand better what native speakers are saying. These changes in pronunciation, as spelled out below, are not considered incorrect or sloppy speech, but are considered proper to use in informal, conversational speech.

A. The spellings of words you see below, in the left-hand column, are not found in written English. Listen and repeat.

CONVERSATIONAL	WRITTEN
(Friend meets friend)	
1. Hi, how**ar**ya?	Hi, how are you?
2. Ahm **hun**gry.	I'm **hun**gry.
3. **Din**cha eat?	**Did**n't you eat?
4. No, did**jou?**	No, did you?
5. Yeah. I **hadd**a **ba**con 'n egg **san**wich.	Yes, I had a **ba**con and egg **sand**wich.
6. **Would**ja come with me ta the **coff**ee shop?	Would you come with me to the **coff**ee shop?
7. I'll **mee**tcha there.	I'll meet you there.
(Later, at the coffee shop)	
8. Whut **would**ja like ta eat?	What would you like to eat?
9. Ahdu**nno.** I **haf**ta eat **some**thing.	I don't know. I have to eat **some**thing.
10. **Can**tcha find **any**thing on the **men**u?	Can't you find **any**thing on the **men**u?

CONVERSATIONAL	WRITTEN
11. Well, that's the **prob**lem. There's **lots**a food here 'n I can't de**cide.**	Well, that's the **prob**lem. There's a lot of food here and I can't de**cide.**
12. Well, **would**ja like souper**sal**ad?	Well, would you like soup or **sal**ad?
13. What's a souper**sal**ad?	What's a souper**sal**ad?
14. Ya know, soup or **sal**ad.	You know, soup or **sal**ad.
15. Oh, is that **wha**cha mean? I'll**av**a **sal**ad.	Oh, is that what you mean? I'll have a **sal**ad.

B. Decode the following expressions, writing English sentences in the blanks provided.

1. Tape-record the expressions.

2. Listen to the playback. Discuss your feelings in class about speaking informal, conversational speech.

EXAMPLE: **Did**ja eat **break**fast?   *Did you eat breakfast?*

1. **Whad**ja **wann**a drink?

   _____

2. I du**nno.**

   _____

3. **Wach**a **haf**ta drink?

   _____

4. Cokea**coff**ee.

   _____

5. **Don**cha have milk?

   _____

6. Sure, 'n **whut**'ll 'e have?

   _____

7. Give 'im the check.

   _____

8. Yer friend says ta give ya the check.

_____

9. Did 'e say that?

_____

10. Yeah. That's whut 'e said.

_____

11. OK. I guess I'm **gonn**a **haf**ta pay it.

_____

8. Further Practice

1. Work with a partner. Take turns reading the following sentences to each other.

2. Draw a line through the function words that you reduce and place the symbol /ə/ above the letter or letters that represent this sound. (You may want to use /'n/ for "and," where appropriate.)

3. As you decide the markings, discuss your reasons for doing so.

4. Tape-record the sentences. Listen to the playback. Do you hear the function words reduced?

EXAMPLES: a. **Or**der bread ~~and~~ **butt**er ~~with the~~ ham ~~and~~ eggs.

                        b. ~~I can~~ give ~~you a~~ map ~~for your~~ trip.

1. He's an **hon**or **stu**dent.

2. Your **broth**er is as old as I am.

3. Was your **girl**friend at home?

4. I'm sick and tired of **clean**ing the house.

5. Ann is **stud**ying to be a **sec**retary.

6. My **sis**ter can read **En**glish, but not **ver**y well.

7. **Soon**er or **lat**er the work will have to be done.

8. She goes to school **dur**ing the day and works at night.

9. My friend and I ate lunch in the cafe**ter**ia.

10. He's **stud**ying to be an e**lec**trical engi**neer.**

Unit 6

Word Stress and Phrasing

1. Word Stress in Sentences

In Unit 3 you practiced syllable stress in words. In this unit you will practice word stress in phrases and sentences.

Word stress means:

- stressing the most important words in a sentence.
- saying them with more force and loudness than other words.
- holding them longer and saying them on a higher pitch.

Word stress is very important. It gives meaning to the words you say. The following exercises contain content words that are stressed and function words that are unstressed and reduced. This alternating pattern of stressing and unstressing is typical of English and is very important to the rhythm of English. (Remember, the content words are the words that carry the most information.)

A. The following sentences are examples of word stress. Listen and repeat.

1. I'm **stud**ying at the Uni**ver**sity.
2. What's your **ma**jor?
3. **Sci**ence.
4. Who's your pro**fess**or?
5. **Mor**gan, and he's great!

B. Work with a partner. In the following sentences, place a stress mark over the most important content words. Read the sentences aloud to your partner and compare your answers.

    EXAMPLES: a. I read the book.

                        b. I was **jogg**ing in the park.

1. He's **go**ing to the **off**ice.
2. He's **work**ing at his com**pu**ter.
3. He's on the **In**ternet.
4. Did you go to the **mov**ies?
5. What time did you go?

6. What **mov**ie did you see?
7. *Gone with the Wind.*
8. Where's my va**lise?** Noor
9. I put it on the floor.
10. Do you have the key?

> Reminder: The contrast between stressed content words and unstressed function words is important to the rhythm of English.

2. Phrasing and Linking

In normal conversation we do not pronounce words one at a time. Instead, we form our thoughts and say them with words that are joined and blended together to make a phrase (a thought group). We say the words in the phrase smoothly, connecting the sound of the last word to the beginning sound of the next word without stopping after each word. This joining and blending of words is called linking.

A. In the exercise below, you can get the feel of linking words together in a phrase by comparing the individual words to the corresponding phrases. The words in each phrase are said as if they were one long word. Both have the same rhythm and the same number of beats (third column). The connecting lines indicate linking. Listen and repeat.

	WORD	PHRASE OR SENTENCE	NUMBER OF BEATS
EXAMPLE:	con**fus**ing	I'm **us**ing. (Im**us**ing)	3
1.	ad**vice**	He's **nice.**	2
2.	**di**et	**Try** it.	2
3.	to**day**	It's **May.**	2
4.	**sweet**er	**Need** her.	2
5.	inse**cure**	It's for **sure.**	3
6.	volun**teer**	It's my **ear.**	3
7.	com**pu**ter	I'll **sue** her.	3
8.	reco**mmend**	It's the **end.**	3

B. Each phrase of linked words usually has one main idea and one stressed word. Remember that many times one phrase may sound like one long word. A slash (/) marks the end of a phrase. Listen and repeat.

1. I have to go / to the **book**store.   (Ihaftago / tathe**book**store.)

2. What for?   (What**for?**)

3. Buy a book / for my ESL class.   (Buya**book** / formy**ESL**class.)

4. What's the name / of the book?   (Whatsthe**name** / ofthe**book**?)

5. **Dic**tionary / of A**mer**ican   (**Dic**tionary /

    English.   ofA**mer**ican**En**glish.)

C. Many times a final consonant in a word is followed by a word that begins with the same sound. Say this sentence: "My bo<u>ss s</u>ent me." The /s/ sound at the end of "bo<u>ss</u>" and the /s/ at the beginning of "<u>s</u>ent" are not said separately. The sounds are combined to form one long consonant sound.[1] Listen and repeat.

EXAMPLE: My bo<u>ss s</u>ent me.

1. My frien<u>d d</u>id it.   6. I ca<u>n **nev**</u>er go.

2. Go to the fa<u>r r</u>ight.   7. He did it the fir<u>st t</u>ime.

3. The des<u>k c</u>ame.   8. A big game was pláyed.

4. The thie<u>f fl</u>ed.   9. Keep pea<u>ce</u> in the house.

5. Wear a fre<u>sh sh</u>irt.   10. A do<u>ll l</u>ay on the ground.

D. Say the following linked words aloud. Write a sentence for each one. Record them on tape and have your instructor listen to your sentences. Be prepared to read them in class.

EXAMPLES: a. o<u>ne n</u>ight   *I stayed at the motel only one night.*
              b. th<u>e e</u>nd   *This is the end of the story.*

1. say a prayer   6. lab book

2. English ship   7. call long distance

3. fool around   8. both thought

4. bus stop   9. leave on time

5. car ride   10. sing a song

---
[1] except the sounds /p/, /b/, /t/, /d/, /k/, and /g/, which cannot be held.

3. Phrasing and Pausing

A pause is a short break or stop in speaking. In written English, punctuation marks such as commas and periods indicate pauses. However, in spoken English you punctuate with your voice. Pauses may differ from speaker to speaker depending on the meaning and the situation. Phrasing, linking of words, and pausing make speaking more effective.

Notice how placement of pauses changes the meaning of the following sentences.

1. Mark the important content words and indicate the phrases.

2. Take turns reading to the class the question and sentences. Members of the class must answer either "a" or "b" and then repeat that sentence.

EXAMPLE: Which is more flattering to the waitress?   *b*

　　　　a.　A **pret**ty young **wait**ress served us.

　　　　b.　A **pret**ty, young **wait**ress served us.

1. In which sentence is the secretary late?

　　a.　The **sec**retary said, "The boss was late."

　→ b.　"The **sec**retary," said the boss, "was late."

2. Both are slang greetings, but which is insulting?

　　a.　What's the **lat**est dope?[2]

　→ b.　What's the **lat**est, dope?

3. In which sentence is the woman a beast? The man?

　→ a.　**Wom**an, with**out** her man, is a beast.

　　b.　**Wom**an, with**out** her, man is a beast.

---

[2] *dope:* a slang expression that has at least two meanings. One refers to a stupid person; the other refers to factual information.

4. In which sentence should John fear for his life?

a. We're **go**ing to eat John.

b. We're **go**ing to eat, John.

5. Which one is the neurotic[3] personality?

    a. She too **ea**gerly a**waits** the spring.

    b. She, too, **ea**gerly a**waits** the spring.

6. Which is a warning to drivers?

    a. Go slow—**chil**dren.

    b. Go slow, **chil**dren.

7. Which is easier for children?

    a. In the pa**rade** will be **sev**eral **hun**dred **chil**dren **carr**ying flags, and **man**y im**por**tant of**fici**als.

    b. In the pa**rade** will be **sev**eral **hun**dred **chil**dren, **carr**ying flags and **man**y im**por**tant of**fici**als.

8. In which sentence does the woman have a pool?

    a. She has a car, pool, and three **chil**dren.

    b. She has a **car**pool and three **chil**dren.

9. Who had the fruitcake, a or b?

    a. We bought fruit, cake, and ice cream.

    b. We bought **fruit**cake and ice cream.

10. Which one had the **dish**pan in the **kitch**en?

    a. We saw a dish, pan, and sink in the **kitch**en.

    b. We saw a **dish**pan and sink in the **kitch**en.

Reminder:
- The linking of words in the same phrase leads to a smooth passing from one word to the next.
- If words in a phrase are not linked properly, the rhythm of speech is broken, and the result is choppy or unconnected speech.
- If proper pauses are not used, the message may not be understood.

---

[3] *neurotic:* A neurotic person may have an unreasonable fear of something.

4. Numbers

Whole numbers, fractions, and addresses are sometimes not understood because of improper word stress, and/or poor linking and phrasing.

A. Tens and Teens

Numbers from thirteen to nineteen are called the "teens," and from twenty to ninety are called the "tens."[4] Listen and repeat the following examples.

1. Syllable Stress

   The "ten" numbers always receive syllable stress on the *first* syllable:

   twenty, **thir**ty, **for**ty, and so on.

   The "teen" numbers may have syllable stress on *either* syllable:

   thirteen/thir**teen; four**teen/four**teen; fif**teen/fif**teen, and so on.

   However in order not to confuse the "teens" with the "tens," the last syllable in the "teens" should be stressed.

1. thir**teen**	**thir**ty	5. seven**teen**	**seven**ty
2. four**teen**	**for**ty	6. eigh**teen**	**eigh**ty
3. fif**teen**	**fif**ty	7. nine**teen**	**nin**ety
4. six**teen**	**six**ty		

2. Word Stress

   When the number ends a phrase or a sentence, *word* stress falls on the noun.

1. We've thir**teen doll**ars.	We've thir**teen.**
2. I've fif**teen** maga**zines.**	I've fif**teen.**
3. **Dian**a has **twen**ty books.	**Dian**a has **twen**ty.
4. This book has **thir**ty-six **u**nits.	This book has **thir**ty-six.

B. Dates

In the United States the month, date, and year are usually said and written in that order. Write the dates down, in numbers, as you listen and repeat them.

1. I was born on March the eigh**teenth,** nine**teen sev**enty-five.

_____

---

[4] Cardinal numbers (thirteen, fourteen, etc.) and ordinal numbers (thirteenth, fourteenth, etc.) are dealt with in the same manner.

2. My **birth**day is on June four**teenth,** nine**teen six**ty-nine.

My birthday is on may thirty nineteen

C. Fractions

When saying fractions or long numbers, the last part of the fraction or number receives the *word* stress. Write the fractions down, in numbers, as you listen and repeat the sentences.

1. My **an**swer is thir**teen** and a **quar**ter. (Or thir**teen** and one-fourth.)

   _____

2. My room is seven**teen** and a half by **twen**ty-two and a third. (Or

   seven**teen** and one-half by **twen**ty-two and one-third.)

   _____

Fractions written with decimal points may also be read in different ways.

3. My **frac**tion is fif**teen** and six-tenths. (Or fif**teen** point six.)

   _____

4. My **frac**tion is fif**teen** and **twen**ty-six **hun**dredths. (Or fif**teen** point

   two six.)

   _____

D. Telephone Numbers

In the United States, telephone numbers usually consist of seven digits preceded by an area code. The first three numbers of the area code are said as one phrase; the first three digits of the phone number are also said as one phrase. The four numbers following may be divided into two phrases or said as one. In a series of numbers the last number in a phrase receives the *word* stress. Write the numbers down as you listen and repeat the sentences.

1. My **num**ber is two one two, / five **sev**en eight, / three five, / nine

   four. (Or two one two, / five **sev**en eight, / three five nine four.)

   _____

2. Her phone **num**ber is **ar**ea code three **zer**o[5] three, / nine two

   six, / one eight, / three four. (Or three **zer**o three, / nine two six, / one

   eight three four.)

   _____

_____
[5] "Oh" may be used in place of "zero."

E. Addresses

In the United States, addresses usually consist of a number, street name, city, state, and zip code. Make certain that you say the name of the places clearly before the stressed words. Write the numbers down as you listen and repeat.

A. Native speakers use word stress on "**boul**evard," "**av**enue," "road."

1. Mel Smith lives at **fif**ty-five dash **thir**ty-six Bell **Boul**evard, **Bay**side, New York one one three, six **zer**o.

   _____

2. The **Pres**ident lives at six**teen hun**dred Pennsyl**van**ia **Av**enue, **Wash**ington, D.C. two oh five, oh two.

   _____

3. My friend lives at **eigh**ty-four **Up**land Road, **Cleve**land, **Ohi**o four four two, two eight.

   _____

B. When "street" is part of the address and comes at the end of a phrase, the word or number before it is stressed.

1. Brad lives at fif**teen twen**ty-three Park Street, **Boul**der, Colo**rad**o eight oh three, oh two.

   _____

2. Juan lives at twelve **thir**ty-nine **Se**cond Street, **Brook**lyn, New York one one three, two nine.

   _____

5. Further Practice

A. After you mark the stressed words and phrases in the following questions, ask a native speaker to answer them. Write the answers down after hearing them *only one time*. Read them aloud in class.

1. What's your zip code?

2. What's your **ar**ea code?

3. What are the last four **dig**its of your **tel**ephone **num**ber?

4. What month and day were you born?

5. What year is this?

B. Work with a partner. In the proverbs[6] below, place a stress mark (✎) over the words you think are important. Mark your phrases. Exchange your papers and read each other's sentences. Listen for word stress and phrasing. Discuss the meanings of the sentences in class.

EXAMPLE: Háste makes wáste.

1. Look be**fore** you leap.

2. All's well that ends well.

3. **Bett**er late than **nev**er.

4. All good things come to an end.

5. Where there's smoke, there's fire.

6. No news is good news.

7. A stitch in time saves nine.

8. You are what you eat.

9. **Ab**sence makes the heart grow **fond**er.

10. **See**ing is be**liev**ing.

C. Many proverbs are universal. Write five proverbs you are familiar with in your native language and translate them into English. Mark word stress and phrasing. Read the proverbs to your class.

Reminder:
- Word stress in a sentence gives meaning to the content of that sentence.
- Words that are linked together in a phrase should flow smoothly.
- Syllable stress, word stress, and linking words in a phrase all help to create the rhythm of English.

---

[6] *proverb:* a short meaningful saying

Unit 7

Intonation

1. Rising and Falling Intonation

Intonation creates the melody of the language we speak. (Each language has its very own melody.) Our voices rise and fall in tones like notes in a musical scale, from high to low or low to high. The different notes we produce are called pitches. This upward and downward movement of the voice produces the melody. Different pitches may indicate different meanings for the same utterance.[1] Different pitches help us express our feelings: happiness, sadness, curiosity, surprise, annoyance, anger, and so on. Intonation makes speech meaningful.

English has two basic intonation patterns: *rising* and *falling*.

Rising Intonation	Falling Intonation

Is Mr. Jones in?

No, he's not in.

___
[1] *utterance:* an oral expression that may be one word, a phrase, or a sentence

"Is Mr. Jones in?" has rising intonation. The pitch of the voice goes up at the end of the utterance. The speaker is asking a question. "No, he's not in" has falling intonation. The pitch of the voice goes down at the end of the utterance. The speaker is answering a question.

2. Falling Intonation

Intonation and stress work together to express meaning. Usually, the last word or the next to last word in an utterance is stressed. The pitch of your voice goes down at the end of an utterance. But, before it goes down (or glides[2] down), it rises on the vowel sound of the most important word that is stressed.

A. Use falling intonation with statements and commands. A downward arrow (⌒) indicates falling intonation. Listen and repeat.

EXAMPLES: a. He wants some **chick**en.

                   b. I said to do it.

1. I'm **stud**ying.
2. I'm **stud**ying **En**glish.
3. Do it to**day.**
4. Do it **lat**er to**day.**

5. She's **go**ing home.
6. She's **go**ing home to**morr**ow.
7. I'll call the **doc**tor.
8. I'll call Dr. Chen.

B. Use falling intonation with *wh*-questions. *Wh*-questions begin with such words as "when," "what," "where," "why," "how," "who," "whose," and "which." Listen and repeat.

1. Who's **com**ing to **dinn**er?
2. Where is it **be**ing held?
3. Why are we **go**ing there?
4. When should we be **read**y?

5. How do we get to the place?
6. Where should we wait?
7. Who's **giv**ing us a ride?
8. Whose car is it?

> Reminder: The speaker's voice rises with the most important stressed word and falls at the end of the utterance. This rising–falling pattern is very common in American English.

---

[2] *glide:* move easily and quickly over a surface

3. Rising Intonation

[handwritten: Yes o no question]

A. Use rising intonation at the end of an utterance when you ask *yes–no* questions. Yes–no questions require "yes" or "no" for an answer. Here, the pitch of the voice goes up (or glides up) at the end of the utterance. It rises on the vowel sound (of the stressed syllable) of the most important word and continues to rise. Listen and repeat.

EXAMPLES: a.   Did you see him?   *[handwritten: Yes or not ↑]*

b.   Do you like the shirt?

1. Is it new?
2. Do you like it?
3. Do I have to tell you?
4. Can I tell you **la**ter?

5. Is it **snow**ing?
6. Is it **snow**ing hard?
7. Do you go out in the snow?
8. Would you like to make a **snow**man?

B. Use rising intonation when naming items on a list or when offering choices, except for the last item or choice. For the last item or choice, use falling intonation. Listen and repeat.

[handwritten: choices ↑]

1. He went to **En**gland, France, Spain, and **Rus**sia.
2. The **chil**dren want pens, **pen**cils, **pa**per, and glue.
3. Do you want **wa**ter or **so**da?
4. You can come with us, or you can stay home.
5. I'd like blue, red, brown, and **yel**low **cray**ons.
6. He spoke with John, **Mar**y, Tom, and Steve.
7. I took out the **gar**bage and fed the cat.
8. I'm **stud**ying phi**los**ophy, bi**ol**ogy, **cal**culus, and **En**glish.

Reminder:
- Use *rising intonation* when you ask *yes–no* questions.
- Use *rising intonation* when you list items or when you give choices. For the last item or choice, use *falling intonation.*

2 Kings — sure.
         — insure

4. Tag Questions

A tag question is a short question that is added to a statement. Many times it is used to start a conversation. Use falling intonation when the speaker expects the listener to agree. Use rising intonation when the speaker may not be sure of the answer he or she will get. Listen and repeat.

agree.ed
↑

	SPEAKER IS SURE LISTENER WILL AGREE.	SPEAKER IS NOT SURE LISTENER WILL AGREE.
EXAMPLES:	Nice day, **is**n't it?	Nice day, **is**n't it?
1.	They're rich, aren't[3] they?	They're rich, aren't they?
2.	He's **funn**y, **is**n't he?	He's **funn**y, **is**n't he?
3.	You re**mem**ber her, don't you?	You re**mem**ber her, don't you?
4.	The **mov**ie be**gins** at eight, **does**n't it?	The **mov**ie be**gins** at eight, **does**n't it?
5.	She talks a lot, **does**n't she?	She talks a lot, **does**n't she?

Reminder:

• When you make a statement and follow it with a short question, and you expect the listener to agree, use *falling* intonation.

• When you make a statement and follow it with a short question, and you may not be sure of the answer, use *rising* intonation.

5. Check Your Listening

Listen to each of the following sentences.   Mark the rising or falling intonation with arrows (⤴ ⤵). (Remember to listen for tag questions and lists of items or choices offered.)

EXAMPLES: a.   She went **shopp**ing for gloves.

b.   What time is it?

c.   Are you **com**ing home, or are you **go**ing to the **off**ice?

d.   You're **com**ing home, aren't you?

---
[3] "Aren't" has two pronunciations: /ɑrnt/ and /ɑrənt/.

1. You're **com**ing to my **part**y, aren't you?

2. Yeah, sure. What are you **cel**ebrating?

3. I moved to a new a**part**ment.

4. Oh, you're **hav**ing a **house**warming?[4]

5. Yeah. Do me a **fa**vor, will you?

6. Sure. No **prob**lem. I'd be glad to.

7. Please get some **app**les, **or**anges, ba**nan**as, and a de**ssert.**

8. Would you like **app**le pie or **choc**olate cake?

9. I'd like **app**le pie, **would**n't you?

10. Well, not **real**ly. I like **choc**olate cake.

> Reminder: Stress and intonation work together to express meaning.

6. Speaker Attitude

A. In the sentences below, the same words are spoken but communicate different meanings. A stress mark (´) indicates the important word in each sentence. Listen and repeat.

SENTENCE	MEANING

EXAMPLE:

a. John loves me. (John does, not Paul.)

---

[4] *housewarming:* a party given when someone moves in to a new apartment or house

b. John loves me.　　　　(Me, not you.)

c. John loves me.　　　　(Is it really true?)

1a. I speak **En**glish.　　　(I do, but he doesn't.)

b. I speak **En**glish.　　　(But I don't read it.)

c. I speak **En**glish.　　　(Not another language.)

2a. Who wants to go?　　　(Who?)

b. Who wants to go?　　　(Who really wants to?)

c. Who wants to go?　　　(Normal question.)

3a. Don't go there.   (Do not.)

b. Don't go there.   (Any place but there.)

c. Don't go there?   (Why not?)

B. A Broadway producer is auditioning actors for a play. The only thing he asks you to do is to say the word "hello" five different ways. Take turns saying the words below five different ways. Some of the emotions you may want to express are disgust, doubt, surprise, disbelief, happiness, sadness, uncertainty, or anger. Students in the class have to guess what emotion the speaker is expressing.

1. Yes   2. No   3. Oh   4. OK   5. Hello

C. Work with a partner.

1. Place a stress mark over the most important word in each sentence.

2. Indicate the intonation pattern with arrows (⌣ ⌐) for rising and falling intonation.

3. Write *your* meaning for each statement.

4. Take turns reading the sentences and asking your partner to guess what you mean.

Sentence	Meaning
1. I told him I was **go**ing.	_____
2. I told him I was **go**ing.	_____
3. I told him I was **go**ing.	_____
4. I told him I was **go**ing.	_____
5. I told him I was **go**ing.	_____
6. I told him I was **go**ing.	_____
7. I told him I was **go**ing?	_____

D. Work with a partner. Place a stress mark over the most important word(s) in each sentence and indicate the intonation pattern with arrows (⌣ ⌐) for rising and falling intonation.

1. Read the sentences in each column aloud. All the sentences in column A have *falling* intonation; all the sentences in column B have *rising* intonation.

2. Compare the sentences in column A with those in column B. Discuss how they differ in meaning.

A Falling intonation	B Rising intonation
1. The man's **craz**y.	The man's **craz**y?
2. He'd like a drink.	He'd like a drink?
3. They'll take the bus.	They'll take the bus?
4. She'd like some **coff**ee.	She'd like some **coff**ee?
5. When are they **com**ing?	When are they **com**ing?

7. Dialog

Work with a partner taking turns reading the telephone conversation Maria and Manuel are having. Mark the intonation patterns for each sentence with arrows (╱ ╲), indicating rising or falling intonation. Do you both have the same interpretation?

1. **Man**uel: He**llo,** Ma**ri**a?

2. Ma**ri**a: Yes. **Man**uel? Is that you? We have a **terr**ible co**nnec**tion.

3. **Man**uel: Yeah. I can **hard**ly hear you.

4. Ma**ri**a: Where are you?

5. **Man**uel: Home.

6. Ma**ri**a: Are you **call**ing from a **cord**less phone?

7. **Man**uel: Yeah. I'm out in the back. I don't want my **sis**ter to **lis**ten in.

8. Ma**ri**a: Oh. Well, try **chang**ing the **chann**el, will you?

9. **Man**uel: Is this OK? This is **bett**er, **is**n't it?

10. Ma**ri**a: Not much. **Lis**ten, I can't stand this **stat**ic.[5] Next time call me when your **sis**ter **is**n't home.

---

[5] *static:* a noise caused by some type of interference

8. Further Practice

Each of these sentences has a different meaning. Read the sentences and their meanings. Mark the sentences for stress and intonation. Use a stress mark (´) for stressed words and arrows (⟋ ⟍) for rising and falling intonation.

SENTENCE	MEANING
1. I like my job.	(Normal statement of fact.)
2. I like my job.	(You may not like yours, but I like mine.)
3. I like my job.	(I didn't say I didn't like it!)
4. I like my job.	(I don't know about you, but I do.)
5. I like my job.	(Now, whatever gave you that idea?)

B. Work with a partner. Take turns reading the above sentences at random. Your partner has to guess which one you are saying.

C. Below is part of a famous old passage about a man named Esau Wood (pronounced /iysɔ wʊd/). In order to make sense out of this "play on words,"[6] correct stress must be made on certain words. In addition, sentences should be divided into pauses (thought groups).

The first five sentences are marked for you. A stress mark (´) indicates stressed words; a slash mark (/) indicates short pauses.

1. Esau Wood /sawed[7] wood.[8] / Esau Wood / would saw[9] wood. /
2. All the wood / Esau Wood saw / Esau Wood / would saw. / In **oth**er
3. words, / all the wood / Esau saw to saw / Esau sought to saw. / Oh, the
4. wood / Wood would saw! / And oh, the **wood**-saw[10] with which Wood
5. would saw wood. But one day Wood's **wood**-saw would saw no wood,
6. and thus the wood Wood sawed was not the wood Wood would saw
7. if Wood's **wood**-saw would saw wood. I **nev**er saw a **wood**-saw
8. that would saw as the **wood**-saw Wood saw would saw un**til** I saw
9. Esau saw wood. Now Wood saws wood with the **wood**-saw Wood
10. saw saw wood.

---

[6] *play on words:* words that sound alike but have different meanings

[7] *sawed:* past tense of the verb "to saw" (to cut)

[8] *wood:* refers to lumber

[9] *saw:* present tense of the verb "to saw"; past tense of the verb "to see"

[10] *wood-saw:* a cutting tool, with teeth, that cuts wood

Unit 8

Using a Dictionary for Pronunciation

1. Dictionary Pages

You can get a great deal of information about pronouncing words, their definitions, and examples of how they are used from your dictionary. The guide below and the sample pages that follow are from *The Newbury House Dictionary of American English*. Use this information to complete the activities in this unit.

GUIDE TO PRONUNCIATION SYMBOLS

Vowels			Consonants		
Symbol	Key Word	Pronunciation	Symbol	Key Word	Pronunciation
/ɑ/	hot	/hɑt/	/b/	boy	/bɔɪ/
	far	/fɑr/	/d/	day	/deɪ/
/æ/	cat	/kæt/	/dʒ/	just	/dʒʌst/
/aɪ/	fine	/faɪn/	/f/	face	/feɪs/
/aʊ/	house	/haʊs/	/g/	get	/gɛt/
/ɛ/	bed	/bɛd/	/h/	hat	/hæt/
/eɪ/	name	/neɪm/	/k/	car	/kɑr/
/i/	need	/nid/	/l/	light	/laɪt/
/ɪ/	sit	/sɪt/	/m/	my	/maɪ/
/oʊ/	go	/goʊ/	/n/	nine	/naɪn/
/ʊ/	book	/bʊk/	/ŋ/	sing	/sɪŋ/
/u/	boot	/but/	/p/	pen	/pɛn/
/ɔ/	dog	/dɔg/	/r/	right	/raɪt/
	four	/fɔr/	/s/	see	/si/
/ɔɪ/	toy	/tɔɪ/	/t/	tea	/ti/
/ʌ/	cup	/kʌp/	/tʃ/	cheap	/tʃip/
/ɜr/	bird	/bɜrd/	/v/	vote	/voʊt/
/ə/	about	/əˈbaʊt/	/w/	west	/wɛst/
	after	/ˈæftər/	/y/	yes	/yɛs/
			/z/	zoo	/zu/
			/ð/	they	/ðeɪ/
			/θ/	think	/θɪŋk/
			/ʃ/	shoe	/ʃu/
			/ʒ/	vision	/ˈvɪʒən/

Stress

/ˈ/	city	/ˈsɪti/

used before a syllable to show primary (main) stress

/ˌ/	dictionary	/ˈdɪkʃəˌnɛri/

used before a syllable to show secondary stress

Note: See pages 7 and 8 for the phonetic symbols equivalent to the I.P.A. symbols used in this dictionary.

71

me·tal·lic /məˈtælɪk/ *adj.* related to metal (iron, steel, copper, etc.): *He painted his car with metallic paint.*

met·al·lur·gy /ˈmɛtl̩ˌɜrdʒi/ *n.* [U] the study of metals, the extraction of them from ores and their preparation for use: *Metallurgy is a field of engineering.* *-n.* **metallurgist.**

met·al·work /ˈmɛtl̩ˌwɜrk/ *n.* [U] metal shaped for particular uses, such as ventilation ducts, or decorative shapes, such as wrought iron fences *-n.* [U] **metalworker; metalworking.**

met·a·mor·pho·sis /ˌmɛtəˈmɔrfəsɪs/ *n.* [U] **-ses 1** (in biology) a dramatic change from one stage of life to another, as in the butterfly's change from a cocoon to a winged insect: *Ancient people believed that humans could undergo metamorphosis from human form to animal form.* **2** [C] *fig.* a dramatic change in character, appearance, etc.: *He underwent a real metamorphosis in his teenage years from a weak boy to a strong young man.* *-v.* **metamorphose** /ˌmɛtəˈmɔrˌfoʊz/.

met·a·phor /ˈmɛtəˌfɔr/ *n.* [C;U] a figure of speech that suggests similarity between one thing and another: *"All that glitters is not gold" is a metaphor for saying that things are not always what they appear to be.* *-adj.* **metaphorical** /ˌmɛtəˈfɔrɪkəl, -ˈfɑr-/.

met·a·phys·ics /ˌmɛtəˈfɪzɪks/ *n.* [U] *pl.* used with a *sing.v.* (in philosophy) the study of the nature of reality and knowledge: *Metaphysics is a difficult and deep field of study.* *-adj.* **metaphysical.**

me·tas·ta·size /məˈtæstəˌsaɪz/ *v.* **-sized, -sizing, -sizes** usu. of cancer, to spread from a local tumor throughout an organism: *Her cancer has metastasized from the lungs all through her body.* *-n.* [U] **metastasis** /məˈtæstəsɪs/.

mete /mit/ *v.* **meted, meting, metes** to give out, (*syn.*) to dispense: *The father meted out punishment when his son came home late at night.*

me·te·or /ˈmitiər, -ˌɔr/ *n.* a small body of matter from outer space that burns up when it enters the earth's atmosphere: *On clear nights, meteors often can be seen streaking across the sky.*

me·te·or·ic /ˌmitiˈɔrɪk, -ˈɑr-/ *adj.* **1** related to meteors: *Geologists found pieces of meteoric rock in a field.* **2** *fig.* speedy, rapid: *He had a meteoric rise in politics, from local mayor to President.*

me·te·or·ite /ˈmitiəˌraɪt/ *n.* a small meteor that lands on Earth: *Meteorites have been found and studied by scientists.*

me·te·or·ol·o·gy /ˌmitiəˈrɑlədʒi/ *n.* [U] the study of the earth's atmosphere and weather conditions: *Meteorology includes the study of weather.* *-n.* **meteorologist;** *-adj.* **meteorological** /ˌmitiərəˈlɑdʒɪkəl/.

me·ter /ˈmitər/ *n.* **1** a linear measurement of 39.37 inches (3.37 inches more than a yard): *Most countries measure distance in meters and kilometers.* **2** a machine that measures things, such as the use of water, electricity, and gas: *A parking meter shows how much time a car can stay in a parking space.* **3** the rhythmic pattern of music or poetry: *Poetry is written in different meters.*
—v. to measure with a meter: *The use of electricity is metered in each house.*

meter maid *n.* a civil employee (often female) who checks parking meters and writes tickets if the meter is not paid: *Meter maids walk up and down the streets looking for parking violations.*

meth·a·done /ˈmɛθəˌdoʊn/ *n.* [U] a substitute for heroin that can help cure drug addiction: *She takes methadone in a program to stop using drugs.*

meth·ane /ˈmɛˌθeɪn/ *n.* [U] a colorless, odorless, flammable gas: *Methane is widely used for cooking and heating.*

meth·a·nol /ˈmɛθəˌnɔl/ *n.* wood alcohol, a colorless liquid used for fuel and as a solvent: *Methanol is a very flammable liquid.*

meth·od /ˈmɛθəd/ *n.* a way of doing s.t., a means, technique: *That business uses trucks as its method of moving goods.*

me·thod·i·cal /məˈθɑdɪkəl/ *adj.* systematic, careful, in a step-by-step manner: *He is very methodical in his work habits.*

meth·od·ol·o·gy /ˌmɛθəˈdɑlədʒi/ *n.* the manner in which tasks are performed, methods as a group: *Teachers use different methodologies to teach language to students.* *-adj.* **methodological** /ˌmɛθədəˈlɑdʒəkəl/.

me·tic·u·lous /məˈtɪkyələs/ *adj.* careful and thorough, painstaking: *She is meticulous in spelling every word correctly in her papers.*

me·tier /mɛˈtyeɪ, meɪ-/ *n.frml.* (French for) one's occupation, specialty: *Her metier is painting portraits of children.*

met·ric /ˈmɛtrɪk/ *adj.* **1** related to the metric system: *Most of the world uses the metric system of measurement.* **2** related to a rhythmic pattern of poetry: *Iambic pentameter is a metric pattern in much of Shakespeare's poetry.*

metric system *n.* the system of measurement based on the meter, kilogram, and second: *The metric system is based on the use of decimals and is easier to use than the English system.*

met·ro /ˈmɛtroʊ/ *adj.infrml.* short for metropolitan, referring to a city and its surrounding area: *Rain showers will cross the metro area today.*
—n. **-ros** (French for) subway: *People in Paris go to work on the metro.*

me·trop·o·lis /məˈtrɑpəlɪs/ *n.frml.* a large, important city: *New York City is a metropolis.*

met·ro·pol·i·tan /ˌmɛtrəˈpɑlətən/ *adj.* related to a city and its suburbs: *Metropolitan Miami covers a much larger area than the city of Miami itself.*

met·tle /ˈmɛtl/ *n.* [U] courage and endurance, character: *She takes the hardest courses that she can to test her mettle as a good student* -*adj.* **mettlesome** /ˈmɛtlsəm/.

mew /myu/ *n.v. var. of* meow: *The kitten <v.> mews when it is hungry.*

mez·za·nine /ˈmɛzəˌnin, ˌmɛzəˈnin/ *n.* the floor or balcony above the main floor in a store or hotel: *Business offices of the hotel are located on the mezzanine.*

mgr /ˈmænɪdʒər/ *n.abbr. for* manager: *She signs her letters, Jane Wong, General Mgr.*

mica /ˈmaɪkə/ *n.* [U] a mineral found in thin layers, used as insulating material

mice /maɪs/ *n.pl. of* mouse

mi·crobe /ˈmaɪˌkroʊb/ *n.* germs, bacteria, or viruses too small to be seen without a microscope: *Microbes cause disease.*

mi·cro·bi·ol·o·gy /ˌmaɪkroʊbaɪˈɑlədʒi/ *n.* [U] the study of microorganisms: *Biology students must take at least one course in microbiology.*

mi·cro·chip /ˈmaɪkroʊˌtʃɪp/ *n.* a tiny integrated circuit used in computers and other electrical equipment: *Microchips are manufactured in Silicon Valley, California.*

mi·cro·com·puter /ˈmaɪkroʊkəmˌpyutər/ *n.* a category of small computers smaller than minicomputers: *Microcomputers are used in many businesses.*

mi·cro·cosm /ˈmaɪkroʊˌkazəm/ *n.* a small, complete version of s.t. larger, a sample: *The style of life in Pittsburgh is a microcosm of how people live in America in general.*

mi·cro·ec·o·nom·ics /ˌmaɪkroʊˌɛkəˈnɑmɪks, -ˌikə-/ *n.* [U] *v.* the study of types of businesses in an economy, rather than the overall economy: *The study of microeconomics is done with computers and mathematics. See:* macroeconomics.

mi·cro·fiche /ˈmaɪkrəˌfiʃ/ *n.* [C;U] the photographic reduction, storage, and retrieval of information, esp. copies of printed documents on film: *Our business has all our old accounting documents on microfiche.*

mi·cro·film /ˈmaɪkrəˌfɪlm/ *n.* [C;U] a small film of highly reduced images of things: *In spy novels, secret documents are saved on microfilm.*

mi·cro·man·age /ˌmaɪkroʊˈmænɪdʒ/ *v.* **-aged, -aging, -ages** to tell s.o. else what to do step-by-step: *Her boss micromanages every task he gives her to do.*

mi·crom·e·ter /maɪˈkrɑmətər/ *n.* a machine used to measure distances in fractions of an inch: *A micrometer can measure the accuracy of parts of a machine.*

mi·cro·or·ga·nism /ˌmaɪkroʊˈɔrgəˌnɪzəm/ *n.* a tiny creature, such as viruses and bacteria, so small that it can be seen only under a microscope: *There are many thousands of kinds of microorganisms.*

mi·cro·phone /ˈmaɪkrəˌfoʊn/ *n.* an electronic device that changes sound into electric current, usu. for recording on magnetic or digital tape, or for making the sound louder through amplifiers and speakers: *The rock singer picked up a microphone and started to sing.*

microphone

mi·cro·proc·es·sor /ˈmaɪkroʊˌprɑsɛsər/ *n.* a computer chip that performs the basic calculations and processing of a computer: *Microprocessors are used in digital wristwatches, as well as computers.*

mi·cro·scope /ˈmaɪkrəˌskoʊp/ *n.* an optical instrument that uses lenses to make small objects appear larger: *Under the microscope, the students could see tiny organisms. -n.* [U] **microscopy** /maɪˈkrɑskəpi/.

microscope

mi·cro·scop·ic /ˌmaɪkrəˈskɑpɪk/ *adj.* very small, visible only with a microscope: *Viruses are microscopic in size.*

mi·cro·sur·ger·y /ˈmaɪkroʊˌsɜrdʒəri/ *n.* [U] surgery done with small instruments and laser beams while the doctor views the process on a television screen: *Microsurgery reduces the size of the wound created when the surgeon cuts the skin.*

mi·cro·wave /ˈmaɪkrəˌweɪv/ **1** a short frequency electromagnetic wave: *Radar uses microwaves.* **2** a microwave oven —*v.* **-waved, -waving, -waves** to cook with a microwave oven: *She microwaved her dinner when she came home from work. See:* nuke, USAGE NOTE.

mid or **mid-** /mɪd/ *prefix* referring to the middle of s.t.: *The temperature was in the mid-90s.‖She paused in mid-sentence.*

mid·air /mɪdˈɛr/ *n.* a location in the air: *Two airplanes hit each other in midair.*

mid·day /ˈmɪdˌdeɪ/ *adj.* around noon, the middle of the day: *The man eats a midday meal.*

mid·dle /ˈmɪdl/ *n.* **1** the center of s.t.: *The core of an apple is in its middle.* **2** *infrml.* the

2. Recognizing Syllables

The dictionary shows the number of syllables in a word. It uses dots (•) to separate the syllables in the entry word.

EXAMPLE: met•ro•pol•i•tan

The word "metropolitan" has five syllables.

Write the number of syllables in each word below. Then look at the dictionary entries on pages 72–73 and check your answers.

WORD	NUMBER OF SYLLABLES	WORD	NUMBER OF SYLLABLES
1. meter	_____	6. microscope	_____
2. methodical	_____	7. microprocessor	_____
3. methanol	_____	8. microwave	_____
4. mezzanine	_____	9. midday	_____
5. mice	_____	10. middle	_____

3. Recognizing the Stressed Syllable

The dictionary puts a stress mark (') before the syllable that has primary stress.

EXAMPLE: met•ro•pol•i•tan /ˌmɛtrəˈpɑlətən/

The third syllable of the word "metropolitan" has primary stress.

Underline the stressed syllable in each word below. Then look at the dictionary entries to check your answers.

EXAMPLE: metro<u>pol</u>itan

1. meteor	4. meter	7. method
2. microbiology	5. microeconomics	8. microphone
3. microwave	6. midday	9. middle

4. Recognizing Primary Stress

Two words in each group below have the primary stress on the same syllable.
One word has the stress on a different syllable. Circle the word that is different.

EXAMPLE: metro   (metaphysics)   methadone

1. metaphor   meteor   methodical
2. microbe   microbiology   microfilm
3. microbiology   microscopic   micromanage

5. Grouping by Parts of Speech

In the dictionary, parts of speech are given as abbreviations— *n.* for noun, *v.* for
verb, and *adj.* for adjective.

EXAMPLE: met•ro•pol•i•tan /ˌmɛtrəˈpɑlətən/ *adj.* related to a city
            and its suburbs: *Metropolitan Miami covers a much larger*
            area than the city of Miami itself.

Group the words below according to noun, verb, and adjective. Then underline
the stressed syllable in each word.

microwave	metered	methodical
mezzanine	micromanage	microscopic
midday	microscope	metamorphose

	Noun	Verb	Adjective
EXAMPLE:	<u>mi</u>crochip	me<u>tas</u>tasize	me<u>tic</u>ulous
	_____	_____	_____
	_____	_____	_____
	_____	_____	_____

6. Recognizing Vowel Sounds

The dictionary uses symbols to show you how to pronounce words.

EXAMPLE: me•tal•lic /məˈtælɪk/

Do the *underlined* letters in the exercise below have the same vowel sound or a different sound? Look on pages 72–73 to find the phonetic symbols for each pair of words. Check your answers.

			SAME	DIFFERENT
EXAMPLES:	a. microbe	microscope	**X**	_____
	b. mice	middle	_____	**X**
	1. metallic	metallurgy	_____	_____
	2. meteor	meter	_____	_____
	3. metric	metro	_____	_____
	4. microfilm	midday	_____	_____
	5. midair	middle	_____	_____

7. Recognizing Phonetic Symbols for Vowels

Look on pages 72–73 to find the phonetic symbol for the underlined vowel for each word below. Then find another word on the page with the *same* vowel sound in the last syllable.

EXAMPLE: microchip /ɪ/ *microeconomics*

1. metaphor   /_____/   _____

2. methadone   /_____/   _____

3. metropolis   /_____/   _____

4. microfiche   /_____/   _____

5. midday   /_____/   _____

8. Further Practice

Use the dictionary symbols on pages 72–73 or the phonetic symbols on pages 7 and 8 to find the words represented by the symbols below. Write the words in the crossword puzzle below.

PRONUNCIATION SYMBOLS USED IN DICTIONARY	PHONETIC SYMBOLS USED IN TEXT

ACROSS

1.	/'mitiər/	/miytiər/
2.	/'maikrəfɪlm/	/maykrəfɪlm/
4.	/mə'tɪkyələs/	same
5.	/'mɛtroʊ/	/mɛtrow/
6.	/maɪs/	/mays/

DOWN

1.	/'mɪdl/	/mɪdl̩/
2.	/maɪ'krɑmətər/	/maykrɑmətər/
3.	/'maɪkroʊtʃɪp/	/maykrowtʃɪp/
4.	/'mɛθəd/	same

Part 3

Vowel Sounds

The vowel sounds of American English are shown in the chart below.

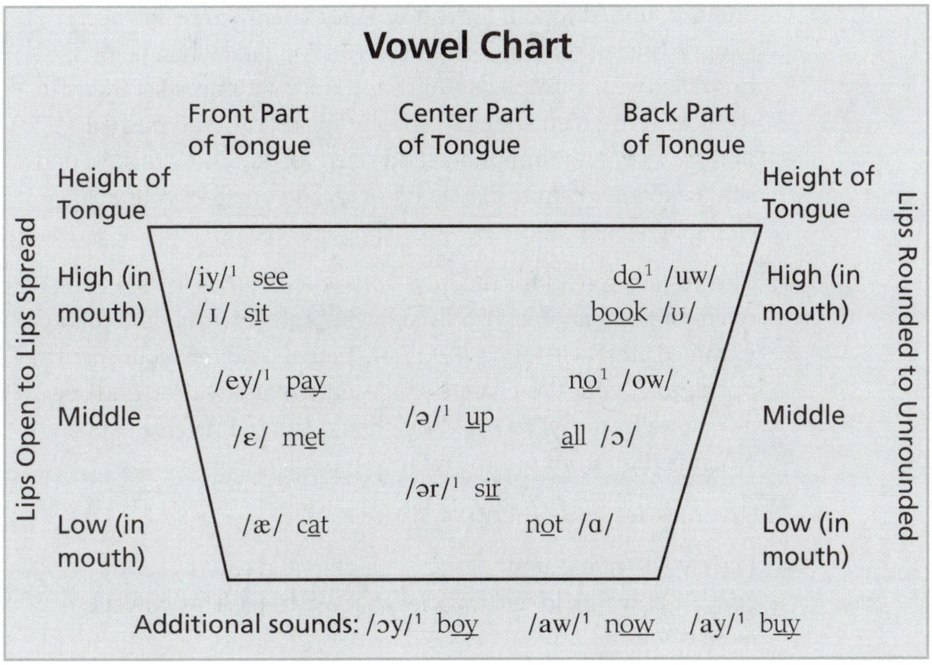

Vowel Chart

	Front Part of Tongue	Center Part of Tongue	Back Part of Tongue	
Height of Tongue				**Height of Tongue**
High (in mouth)	/iy/[1] s<u>ee</u> /ɪ/ s<u>i</u>t		d<u>o</u>[1] /uw/ b<u>oo</u>k /ʊ/	**High (in mouth)**
Middle	/ey/[1] p<u>ay</u> /ɛ/ m<u>e</u>t	/ə/[1] <u>u</u>p /ər/[1] s<u>ir</u>	n<u>o</u>[1] /ow/ <u>all</u> /ɔ/	**Middle**
Low (in mouth)	/æ/ c<u>a</u>t		n<u>o</u>t /ɑ/	**Low (in mouth)**

Lips Open to Lips Spread (left side)   *Lips Rounded to Unrounded* (right side)

Additional sounds: /ɔy/[1] b<u>oy</u>   /aw/[1] n<u>ow</u>   /ay/[1] b<u>uy</u>

---

[1] See page 8 for the equivalent I.P.A. symbols.

Things to consider when producing vowels sounds:

1. What is the height of the tongue (in the mouth), and which part of the tongue helps shape the vowel sound?

   The tongue is divided into four parts, as follows.

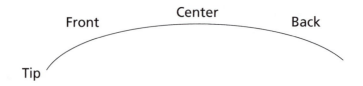

   a. Say /uw/ as in "fool." It's the back part of the tongue, held in a high position at the back of the mouth, which is mainly involved in producing the sound.

   b. Say /iy/ as in "see." It's the front part of the tongue, held in high position at the front of the mouth.

2. What is the shape of the lips? Are they rounded, spread, or wide open?

   a. The lips are rounded for the *high back* vowel /uw/ as in "fool" and unrounded (open) for the *low back* vowel /ɑ/ as in "not." (This is the sound the doctor asks you to make when he or she examines your throat.) Say /uw/ and follow it immediately with the sound /ɑ/. You should feel your lips round (and pushed out) for /uw/ and unrounded and open for /ɑ/. Now reverse and say /ɑ/ followed immediately by /uw/. Did you feel your lips changing shape (and your jaw falling and rising)?

   b. The lips are spread for the *high front* vowel /iy/ as in "see" and open for the *low front* vowel /æ/ as in "cat." Say /iy/ and follow it immediately with the sound /æ/. You should feel your mouth open more, your lips change shape, and your jaw drop and rise as you go from /iy/ to /æ/. You should feel the reverse happen when you go from /æ/ to /iy/.

3. Are the muscles tense (tight) or lax (relaxed)?

   a. Place your thumb underneath your chin and say /ey/ as in "pay." You should feel muscles that are tight. This vowel is a *tense* vowel.

   b. Keep your thumb in the same place and say /ɛ/ as in "met." The muscles are relaxed. This vowel is a *lax* vowel.

4. All vowels are voiced (unless they are whispered).

   Say /ɑ/ as in "n<u>o</u>t" while placing two fingers on the side of your throat. Your vocal cords are vibrating. When you feel vibration, sounds are voiced.

5. All vowels are continuants: you can say and hold the vowel sound for any length of time.

   Say /ɑ/ as in "n<u>o</u>t." You can hold the vowel sound for as long as your breath holds out.

Note: Linguists (those who study the science of language) agree that descriptions of the movements and positions of the tongue, the lips, the jaw, and the amount of tension involved in producing vowels are not exact. (However, they disagree about the number of distinct vowel sounds in the language as well as about which phonetic symbols to use.)

You will hear variations in the pronunciation of some vowels. For example, the word "marry" may be pronounced /mæriy/ or /mɛriy/, depending on which dialect of American English you hear. When vowel sounds vary significantly, as in the above example, it will be noted.

The vowel sounds in the following units are described in general terms and according to how they relate to one another.

Reminder:
- All vowels are voiced.
- All vowels can be held continuously.
- The height of one part of the tongue is important in the production of vowel sounds.
- The position of the lips is important in the production of vowel sounds.
- Vowel sounds can be tense or lax.

Unit 9

/iy/ as in *see*
/ɪ/ as in *sit*

1. Producing /iy/

EXAMPLES: <u>ea</u>t, <u>ea</u>st, re**ceive,** be**lieve, peo**ple, sw<u>ee</u>t, b<u>e</u>, sk<u>i</u>, k<u>e</u>y

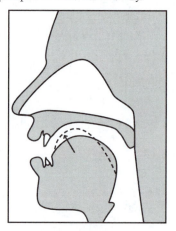

- Hold the *front* part of your tongue *high* in your mouth, close to the roof.
- Press the sides of your tongue against the upper back teeth. The muscles of your tongue should be *tense*.
- Spread your lips.
- As you begin to say this *long* vowel sound, move the front part of your tongue forward and up.
- Place your thumb underneath your chin to feel the *tense* muscles.

2. Producing /ɪ/

EXAMPLES: h<u>i</u>t, l<u>i</u>p, h<u>i</u>m, b<u>ee</u>n, b<u>ui</u>ld, **bus**y, **wom**en, **sys**tem

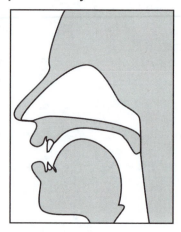

- Hold the *front* part of your tongue *high* in your mouth, but lower than for /iy/.
- Place the sides of your tongue against the upper back teeth, but *do not press*. The muscles of your tongue should be *lax*.
- The lips are a little less spread than for /iy/.
- The tongue does not move as you say this *short* vowel sound.
- Place your thumb underneath your chin. You should feel no tense muscles; the muscles are re-laxed.

3. Contrast: /iy/ and /ɪ/

A. Many students of English as a second language do not hear the difference between /iy/ as in "s_ee_" and /ɪ/ as in "s_i_t." Practice these two sounds, first normally, then with exaggeration,[1] then normally. Listen and repeat.

     1. /iy/   /iy . . ./   /iy/

     2. /ɪ/   /ɪ . . ./   /ɪ/[2]

B. Now practice these sounds in words. Notice the phonetic spelling. Listen and repeat each word twice.

     1. kn_ee_   /niy/   kn_ee_

     2. b_e_   /biy/   b_e_

     3. b_ea_t   /biyt/   b_ea_t

     4. _ea_t   /iyt/   _ea_t

     5. _i_t   /ɪt/   _i_t

     6. _i_ll   /ɪl/   _i_ll

     7. h_i_m   /hɪm/   h_i_m

     8. b_i_g   /bɪg/   b_i_g

4. Check Your Listening

You will hear words with the sounds /iy/ and /ɪ/. First, cover the words in the following list with a piece of paper. Then listen to each word. Concentrate on the sound, not the spelling. Which vowel sound do you hear? Place a check mark in the correct column.

		/iy/ as in "s_ee_"	/ɪ/ as in "s_i_t"
tr_ee_	1.	√	√
m_ea_n	2.	√	
s_i_ck	3.		√

---

[1] Whenever you do contrasts, s-t-r-e-t-c-h out the sound to get the "feel" of it.

[2] When you cover your ears with the palms of your hands, you can hear the distinction between the vowels better.

		/iy/ as in "s<u>ee</u>"	/ɪ/ as in "s<u>i</u>t"
d<u>i</u>d	4.		✓
sh<u>ee</u>p	5.	✓	
sh<u>i</u>p	6.	✓	✓
h<u>e</u>	7.	✓	
thr<u>ee</u>	8.	✓	✓
th<u>i</u>n	9.	✓	✓
h<u>i</u>s	10.	✓	✓

5. Practice the Contrast: /iy/ as in "s<u>ee</u>" with /ɪ/ as in "s<u>i</u>t"

A. Practice these contrasting sounds. Listen and repeat each word pair.

	/iy/	/ɪ/		/iy/	/ɪ/
1.	<u>ea</u>t	<u>i</u>t	11.	s<u>ee</u>k	s<u>i</u>ck
2.	<u>ea</u>ch	<u>i</u>tch	12.	p<u>ea</u>k	p<u>i</u>ck
3.	r<u>ea</u>ch	r<u>i</u>ch	13.	l<u>ea</u>k	l<u>i</u>ck
4.	s<u>ea</u>t	s<u>i</u>t	14.	h<u>ea</u>p	h<u>i</u>p
5.	f<u>ee</u>t	f<u>i</u>t	15.	t<u>ea</u>m	T<u>i</u>m
6.	b<u>ea</u>t	b<u>i</u>t	16.	s<u>ee</u>n	s<u>i</u>n
7.	h<u>ea</u>t	h<u>i</u>t	17.	r<u>ea</u>d	r<u>i</u>d
8.	l<u>ea</u>st	l<u>i</u>st	18.	h<u>ea</u>l[3]	h<u>i</u>ll
9.	d<u>ee</u>p	d<u>i</u>p	19.	st<u>ea</u>l[3]	st<u>i</u>ll
10.	l<u>ea</u>p	l<u>i</u>p	20.	**C<u>ae</u>**sar's	**sc<u>i</u>ss**ors

---

[3] When /iy/ is followed by /l/, it usually helps to add the vowel /ə/ as in "<u>u</u>p" before /l/: /hiyəl/; /stiyəl/.

B. Now practice the contrasting sounds in sentence pairs. The first sentence of each pair has the sound /iy/, and the second has the sound /ɪ/. Pay attention to stressed words, function words, phrasing, and intonation patterns.

1a. **heat**ing   I'm **heat**ing the pán.

 b. **hitt**ing   I'm **hitt**ing the pán.

2a. sl<u>ee</u>p   Did you sl<u>ee</u>p on the floor?

 b. sl<u>i</u>p   Did you sl<u>i</u>p on the floor?

3a. b<u>ea</u>ds   The b<u>ea</u>ds look quite good.

 b. b<u>i</u>ds [4]   The b<u>i</u>ds look quite good.

4a. sh<u>ee</u>p   Who found the sh<u>ee</u>p?

 b. sh<u>i</u>p   Who found the sh<u>i</u>p?

----

[4] *bid:* offer of a price or of a fee

5a. p<u>ea</u>ch   It was a good p<u>ea</u>ch.

b. p<u>i</u>tch   It was a good p<u>i</u>tch.

6a. l<u>ea</u>ve   When did she l<u>ea</u>ve?

b. l<u>i</u>ve   When did she l<u>i</u>ve?

7a. l<u>ea</u>d[5]   I'm **tak**ing the l<u>ea</u>d.

b. l<u>i</u>d[6]   I'm **tak**ing the l<u>i</u>d.

8a. f<u>ee</u>l   Did you f<u>ee</u>l the box?

b. f<u>i</u>ll   Did you f<u>i</u>ll the box?

9a. **h<u>ea</u>t**er   Where did the **h<u>ea</u>t**er go?

b. **h<u>i</u>tt**er   Where did the **h<u>i</u>tt**er go?

10a. **b<u>ea</u>t**en   The boy was **b<u>ea</u>t**en.

b. **b<u>i</u>tt**en   The boy was **b<u>i</u>tt**en.

---

[5] *lead* /liyd/: go first; take first place or position. (The spelling of this word is the same for the noun /lɛd/, a heavy soft metal.)

[6] *lid:* a movable cover

6. Stress and Intonation

The sentences below contain the vowel sounds /iy/ and /ɪ/.

1. Before you listen to the tape, place the appropriate phonetic symbol above the underlined letters.

2. Now listen to the tape and repeat the sentences. Pay attention to stressed words, function words, and phrasing. The intonation patterns are marked.

EXAMPLES:

                /iy/   /ɪ/

a. They heal the sick.

                /iy/   /ɪ/

b. Are they **meet**ing for **dinn**er?

1. Did you heat the milk?

2. It's a cheap watch, isn't it?

3. When did you see my in**struc**tor?

4. Who needs to sleep on two **pill**ows?

5. My **litt**le **broth**er can't sit still for a **min**ute.

6. Let's have a dish of **choc**olate chip ice cream.

7. I'll have a **ba**gel with cream cheese, please.

8. Ann, you want to try the pink **lip**stick, don't you?

9. Why don't you put the **dish**es in the sink?

10. Do you need a sheet for your **queen**-size bed?

7. Further Practice

A. Write /iy/ as in "see" or /ɪ/ as in "sit" for the underlined sound in each word. Say each word aloud several times. Use a dictionary to help you with any new words. Work with a partner. Compare your answers.

ExAMPLES: a. drill   /ɪ/

               b. meet   /iy/

1. bill	/____/		11. fish	/____/	
2. rip	/____/		12. pinch	/____/	
3. him	/____/		13. **vi**sion	/____/	
4. beans	/____/		14. sweet	/____/	
5. dish	/____/		15. kill	/____/	
6. cheap	/____/		16. build	/____/	
7. did	/____/		17. **mi**ster	/____/	
8. think	/____/		18. **syr**up	/____/	
9. meal	/____/		19. **mirr**or	/____/	
10. mean	/____/		20. in**stead**	/____/	

B. Think of a sentence for five of the above words. Write down your sentences and be prepared to read them in class.

C. Read the following (anonymous) poem aloud to yourself.

1. Draw a <u>single</u> line underneath the letters representing the sound /iy/ as in "see" and a <u>double</u> line for /ɪ/ as in "sit."

2. Mark the poem for stress and intonation.

3. There are eight lines and a title line in the poem. Make a list below of the words on each line, in the appropriate column, that contain the sounds /iy/ as in "see" and /ɪ/ as in "sit." The title and first line are marked for you. (*Hint:* There is a total of 26 words, 22 with /ɪ/ and 4 with /iy/. They include the title, the first line of the poem, and words that are repeated.)

4. After you finish, compare your answers with your partner. Take turns reading the poem aloud.

1.   **Fi**sherman's Love

2.   When the wīnd īs īn th<u>e</u> East

3.   It's **nei**ther[8] good for man nor beast

4.   When the wind is in the North

5.   The **skill**ful **fish**erman goes not forth.

6.   When the wind is in the South

7.   It blows the bait[9] in the fish's mouth.

8.   When the wind is in the West

9.   Then it is at its **ver**y best.

/iy/	/ɪ/
1. _____	Fisherman's _____
2. the, East_____	wind, is, in_____
3. _____	_____
4. _____	_____
5. _____	_____
6. _____	_____
7. _____	_____
8. _____	_____
9. _____	_____

---

[8] *neither* /niyðər/ or /nayðər/: This word has two pronunciations; the first is more common.
[9] *bait:* something that is used to attract animals or people

Unit 10

/ey/ **as in _pay_**
/ɛ/ **as in _met_**

1. Producing /ey/

EXAMPLES: a̲im, e̲i̲ght, ta̲ke,[1] wa̲it, va̲in, bre̲a̲k, sa̲y, the̲y

- Hold the *front* part of your tongue in the middle of your mouth, a little lower than for /iy/ and /ɪ/.
- Press the sides of your tongue against the upper back teeth. The muscles of your tongue should be *tense.*
- Lower your jaw and open your lips more than for /iy/ and /ɪ/.
- As you begin to say this *long* vowel sound, raise your jaw slightly and move the front part of your tongue forward and up.
- Place your thumb under your chin to feel the tense muscles.

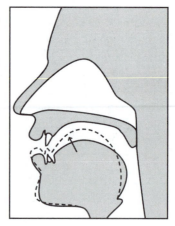

---

[1] The final "e" in words such as "take," "date," and "age" signals the /**ey**/ pronunciation for the letter "a." Compare "hat" /hæt/ with "hate" /heyt/.

2. Producing /ɛ/

EXAMPLES: end, friend, get, guess, says, said, bread, **bury**[2]

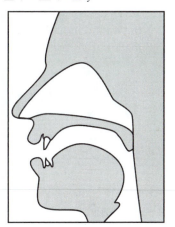

- Hold your tongue in the same position as for /ey/, but a little lower in your mouth.
- Place the sides of your tongue against the upper back teeth, but _do not press._ The muscles of your tongue should be _lax._
- Open your lips slightly more than for /ey/.
- Your jaw and tongue do not move as you make this _short_ vowel sound.
- Place your thumb underneath your chin. You should feel no tense muscles; the muscles are _relaxed._

3. Contrast: /ey/ and /ɛ/

Some students confuse the sound /ey/ as in "p<u>ay</u>" with the sound /ɛ/ as in "m<u>e</u>t."

A. Practice these two sounds, first normally, then with exaggeration, then normally. Listen and repeat.

1. /ey/   /ey . . . /   /ey/
2. /ɛ/   /ɛ . . . /   /ɛ/

B. Now practice these sounds in words. Notice the phonetic spelling. Listen and repeat each word twice.

1. <u>eigh</u>t   /eyt/   <u>eigh</u>t
2. s<u>ay</u>   /sey/   s<u>ay</u>
3. h<u>a</u>te   /heyt/   h<u>a</u>te
4. <u>e</u>gg   /ɛg/   <u>e</u>gg
5. g<u>ue</u>ss   /gɛs/   g<u>ue</u>ss
6. n<u>e</u>ck   /nɛk/   n<u>e</u>ck
7. d<u>a</u>te   /deyt/   d<u>a</u>te
8. r<u>e</u>d   /rɛd/   r<u>e</u>d

---

[2] _bury:_ (verb) hide something; put a dead person in a grave. "Berry" (noun), a small fruit, is pronounced the same way.

4. Check Your Listening

You will hear words with the sounds /ey/ and /ɛ/. First, cover the words in the following list with a piece of paper. Then listen to each word. Concentrate on the sound, not the spelling. Which vowel sound do you hear? Place a check mark in the correct column.

		/ey/ as in "pay"	/ɛ/ as in "met"
age	1.	✓	
edge	2.		✓
met	3.	✓	✓
main	4.	✓	
pen	5.		✓
let	6.		✓
wait	7.	✓	
they	8.	✓	
when	9.		✓
steak	10.	✓	

5. Practice the Contrast: /ɛ/ as in "met" with /ey/ as in "pay"

A. Practice these contrasting sounds. Listen and repeat each word pair.

	/ɛ/	/ey/		/ɛ/	/ey/
1.	Bess	base[3]	6.	get	gate
2.	chess	chase	7.	fed	fade
3.	met	mate	8.	red	raid
4.	wet	wait	9.	bled	blade
5.	west	waste	10.	led	laid

---

[3] *base:* the lowest part or bottom of a thing; a foundation. (A different spelling but pronounced the same way is the word "bass" /beys/, which refers to a deep tone; an instrument. "Bass," pronounced /bæs/, refers to a type of fish.)

/ɛ/	/ey/		/ɛ/	/ey/
11. l<u>e</u>t	l<u>a</u>te	16. y<u>e</u>ll	Y<u>a</u>le[4]
12. **l<u>e</u>tt**er	**l<u>a</u>t**er	17. d<u>e</u>n	D<u>a</u>ne
13. b<u>e</u>ll	b<u>ai</u>l[4]	18. m<u>e</u>n	m<u>ai</u>n
14. t<u>e</u>ll	t<u>ai</u>l[4]	19. s<u>e</u>nt	s<u>ai</u>nt
15. f<u>e</u>ll	f<u>ai</u>l[4]	20. r<u>e</u>st	r<u>a</u>ced

B. Now practice the contrasting of sounds in sentence pairs. The first sentence of each pair has the sound /ɛ/, and the second has the sound /ey/. Listen and repeat, using the same stress and intonation patterns. (Pay attention to contractions and function words.)

1a. <u>e</u>dge   Is it the <u>e</u>dge of the chair?

b. <u>a</u>ge   Is it the <u>a</u>ge of the chair?

2a. <u>E</u>d   Can you find <u>E</u>d in the **off**ice?

b. <u>ai</u>d   Can you find <u>ai</u>d in the **off**ice?

3a. l<u>e</u>ss   Do you want l<u>e</u>ss on the shirt?

b. l<u>a</u>ce   Do you want l<u>a</u>ce on the shirt?

4a. b<u>e</u>t   Who's **tak**ing the b<u>e</u>t to**morr**ow?

b. b<u>ai</u>t   Who's **tak**ing the b<u>ai</u>t to**morr**ow?

---

[4] When /ey/ is followed by /l/, it usually helps to add the vowel sound /ə/ as in "<u>u</u>p" before /l/: "b<u>ai</u>l" /beyᵊl/, "t<u>ai</u>l" /teyᵊl/, "Y<u>a</u>le" /yeyᵊl/.

5a. d<u>e</u>bt   We're **talk**ing a**bout** my d<u>e</u>bt.

b. d<u>a</u>te   We're **talk**ing a**bout** my d<u>a</u>te.

6a. p<u>e</u>st[5]   The p<u>e</u>st is all **o**ver me.

b. p<u>a</u>ste   The p<u>a</u>ste is all **o**ver me.

7a. t<u>e</u>st   The t<u>e</u>st was **prett**y good.

b. t<u>a</u>ste   The t<u>a</u>ste was **prett**y good.

8a. s<u>e</u>ll   I would like to s<u>e</u>ll my boat.

b. s<u>ai</u>l   I would like to s<u>ai</u>l my boat.

9a. p<u>e</u>n   His p<u>e</u>n is **aw**ful, **is**n't it?

b. p<u>ai</u>n   His p<u>ai</u>n is **aw**ful, **is**n't it?

---

[5] *pest:* an annoying person or thing; a nuisance

10a. **pepp**er   The **pepp**er was passed **around**
                         to all of us.

 b. **pa**per   The **pa**per was passed a**round**
                         to all of us.

6. Stress and Intonation

1. The first underlined vowel sound in a word of each of the following
   sentences is /ey/ as in "pa**y**." The second underlined vowel sound of
   the word in the same sentence is /ɛ/ as in "m**e**t."

2. Mark the stressed words you hear with a stress mark (ʹ).

3. Pay attention to function words, phrasing, and intonation that is
   already marked. Listen and repeat.

EXAMPLES: a.   I think the tr**ai**n is b**e**st.

          b.   Did you f**ai**l the math t**e**st?

          c.   He p**ai**d the b**e**t, **did**n't he?

1. He taught the dog to pl**a**y d**ea**d.

2. Does Sp**ai**n have good **weath**er now?

3. Do you have time to m**ai**l the **lett**er?

4. I **tast**ed the br**ea**d, and it was de**lici**ous.

5. I told him I have a p**ai**n in my n**e**ck.

6. Do you pl**a**y **tenn**is with your **part**ner at night?

7. If you w**ai**t there, you'll get all w**e**t.

8. You have **mon**ey to p**a**y the r**e**nt, don't you?

9. Did you see the br**a**ve m**e**n do their work?

10. You **did**n't put the pl**a**te on the d**e**sk last night, did you?

7. Further Practice

A. Write /ey/ as in "pa̲y" or /ɛ/ as in "me̲t" for the underlined sound in each word. Say each word aloud several times. Work with a partner. Compare your answers.

EXAMPLES: a.   bre̲ath   /ɛ/

b.   ja̲il   /ey/

1. che̲ss	/ɛ/		11. **ra̲il**road	/ey/	
2. **sta̲**tion	/ey/		12. **e̲x**it	/ɛ/	
3. tra̲y	/ey/		13. stra̲ight	/ey/	
4. **ve̲r**y	/ɛ/		14. **me̲a**sure	/ey/	
5. **bu̲r**y	/ɛ/		15. na̲il	/ey/	
6. pre̲ss	/ɛ/		16. re**me̲m**ber	/ɛ/	
7. sha̲pe	/ey/		17. ce̲nt	/ɛ/	
8. de̲sk	/ɛ/		18. stra̲nge	/ey/	
9. pla̲ce	/ey/		19. thre̲ad	/ɛ/	
10. sca̲le	/ey/		20. ska̲te	/ey/	

B. Work with a partner. Say sentence a or b, below, at random. Your partner must identify the correct sentence by saying "a" or "b" and repeating it. Take turns. Can you hear the difference between the vowel sounds?

1a. The sha̲de is in the back of the house.

b. The she̲d[6] is in the back of the house.

2a. I'm con**cern**ed a**bout** the wa̲ste.

b. I'm con**cern**ed a**bout** the We̲st.

3a. Did you ta̲ste it be**fore** I came?

b. Did you te̲st it be**fore** I came?

---

[6] *shed:* a small structure built for storage

4a. Do you have a p<u>ai</u>n in your hand?

  b. Do you have a p<u>e</u>n in your hand?

5a. Did you b<u>ai</u>t him with the five **doll**ars?

  b. Did you b<u>e</u>t him with the five **doll**ars?

6a. Please don't tr<u>ea</u>d[7] there a**gain.**

  b. Please don't tr<u>a</u>de there a**gain.**

7a. How much was the b<u>ai</u>l?

  b. How much was the b<u>e</u>ll?

8a. He put the r<u>a</u>ke[8] in the back**yard.**

  b. He put the wr<u>e</u>ck in the back**yard.**

9a. We l<u>ai</u>d it there for a **pur**pose.

  b. We l<u>e</u>d it there for a **pur**pose.

10a. We all want to see the D<u>a</u>ne.[9]

  b. We all want to see the d<u>e</u>n.

---

[7] *tread:* walk on

[8] *rake:* a tool with wooden or metal teeth and a long handle, often used to collect fallen leaves, stones, etc.

[9] *Dane:* a native of Denmark

Unit 11

/æ/ **as in c<u>a</u>t**

1. Producing /æ/[1]

EXAMPLES: <u>a</u>m, <u>a</u>t, **<u>a</u>n**swer, b<u>a</u>d, b<u>a</u>nk, l<u>au</u>gh, b<u>a</u>t

• Hold the front and back parts of your tongue *low* in your mouth.
• Touch your lower front teeth lightly with the tip of your tongue.
• Lower your jaw; your lips are wide open.
• The muscles in your tongue should not be tense; they should be *relaxed*.

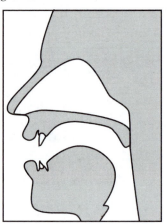

2. Contrast: /æ/ and /ɛ/

Some students confuse the sound /æ/ as in "c<u>a</u>t" with the sound /ɛ/ as in "m<u>e</u>t."

A. Practice these two sounds, first normally, then with exaggeration, then normally. Listen and repeat.

   1. /æ/   /æ . . . /   /æ/

   2. /ɛ/   /ɛ . . . /   /ɛ/

---

[1] This vowel may be replaced by /ɛ/, as in "m<u>e</u>t," when it comes before /r/ depending on which dialect of American English you hear. For example: "parrot" /pɛrət/ for /pærət/; "carry" /kɛriy/ for /kæriy/.

B. Now practice these sounds in words. Notice the phonetic spelling. Listen and repeat each word twice.

1.	c<u>a</u>t	/kæt/	c<u>a</u>t
2.	<u>a</u>nd	/ænd/	<u>a</u>nd
3.	m<u>a</u>n	/mæn/	m<u>a</u>n
4.	g<u>a</u>s	/gæs/	g<u>a</u>s
5.	g<u>ue</u>ss	/gɛs/	g<u>ue</u>ss
6.	b<u>e</u>t	/bɛt/	b<u>e</u>t
7.	<u>a</u>dd	/æd/	<u>a</u>dd
8.	bl<u>a</u>ck	/blæk/	bl<u>a</u>ck

3. Check Your Listening

You will hear words with the sounds /æ/ and /ɛ/. First, cover the words in the following list with a piece of paper. Then listen to each word. Concentrate on the sound, not the spelling. Which vowel sound do you hear? Place a check mark in the correct column.

		/æ/ as in "c<u>a</u>t"	/ɛ/ as in "m<u>e</u>t"
b<u>a</u>t	1.	✓	
b<u>e</u>st	2.		✓
l<u>a</u>nd	3.	✓	
b<u>e</u>t	4.		✓
<u>a</u>sk	5.	✓	
<u>e</u>nd	6.		✓
m<u>e</u>n	7.		✓
s<u>a</u>d	8.	✓	
h<u>ea</u>d	9.	✗	✓
m<u>a</u>n	10.	✓	

4. Practice the Contrast: /æ/ as in "cat" with /ɛ/ as in "met"

A. Practice these contrasting sounds. Listen and repeat each word pair. (Remember to lower your jaw for /æ/.)

/æ/	/ɛ/		/æ/	/ɛ/
1. mat	met	6.	bad	bed
2. sat	set	7.	and	end
3. add	Ed	8.	band	bend
4. sad	said	9.	had	head
5. Dad	dead	10.	bag	beg

B. Now practice the contrasting sounds in sentence pairs. The first sentence of each pair has the sound /ɛ/, and the second has the sound /æ/. Listen and repeat, using the same stress, phrasing, and intonation patterns. (Listen for contractions and function words.)

1a. bet	Did you hear a**bout** the bet I made?
b. bat	Did you hear a**bout** the bat I made?

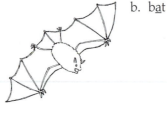

2a. pen	I bought a pen **yes**terday.
b. pan	I bought a pan **yes**terday.

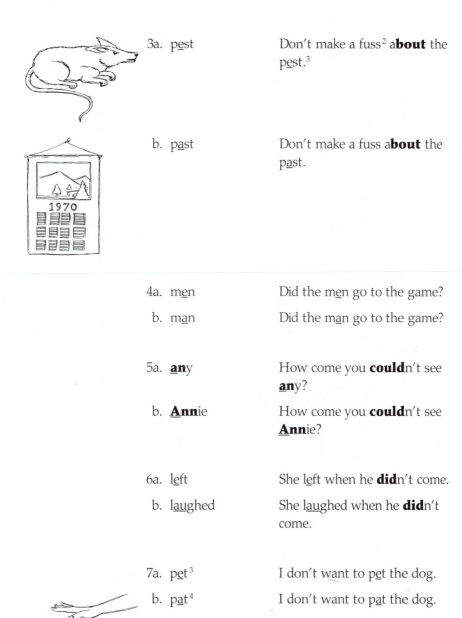

3a. p_est Don't make a fuss[2] a**bout** the p_est.[3]

b. p_ast Don't make a fuss a**bout** the p_ast.

4a. m_en Did the m_en go to the game?

b. m_an Did the m_an go to the game?

5a. **an**y How come you **could**n't see **an**y?

b. **Ann**ie How come you **could**n't see **Ann**ie?

6a. l_eft She l_eft when he **did**n't come.

b. l_aughed She l_aughed when he **did**n't come.

7a. p_et[3] I don't want to p_et the dog.

b. p_at[4] I don't want to p_at the dog.

---

[2] *fuss:* a show of great concern over something unimportant
[3] *pet:* stroke lightly with the hand; a tame animal or favorite person
[4] *pat:* tap gently with the hand

8a. s<u>e</u>nd   He'll s<u>e</u>nd the **fur**niture down.

b. s<u>a</u>nd[5]   He'll s<u>a</u>nd the **fur**niture down.

9a. **kett**le   I found the **kett**le in the barn.[6]

b. **catt**le[7]   I found the **catt**le in the barn.

10a. m<u>e</u>ss   What a mess!

b. m<u>a</u>ss[8]   What a mass!

---

[5] *sand:* smooth a rough surface with a rough paper or a machine
[6] *barn:* usually a building found on a farm in which animals and food are kept
[7] *cattle:* cows, bulls, and oxen as a group
[8] *mass:* a large number or quantity

5. Stress and Intonation

A. This selection focuses on the production of the front vowels:

/iy/ as in "s<u>ee</u>"   /ey/ as in "p<u>ay</u>"   /æ/ as in "c<u>a</u>t"

/ɪ/ as in "s<u>i</u>t"   /ɛ/ as in "m<u>e</u>t"

1. Before listening to the tape, read the following passage aloud, (to yourself) to become familiar with the words.

2. Listen carefully to the pronunciation of words, phrasing, and intonation. (Pay attention to the function words.)

3. Mark the stressed words you hear.

EXAMPLE: I'm de**scrib**ing the flag of the U**nit**ed States.

The Flag of the U**nit**ed States

1. In the be**ginn**ing, the U**nit**ed States con**sist**ed of thir**teen A**mer**ican states.

2. Their **mott**o[9] was "In **Un**ion there is Strength."

3. The first flag had thir**teen** stripes: **sev**en red, six white, and a white star for each state.

4. Each time a state joined the **Un**ion, a star was **add**ed to the flag.

5. As the **coun**try grew, more and more stars were **add**ed.

6. There are now **fif**ty stars on the flag repre**sent**ing the **fif**ty states.

7. How**ev**er, the thir**teen** stripes re**main.**

8. They were **nev**er changed be**cause** they repre**sent** the o**rig**inal thir**teen** states.

B. Describe the symbols and colors of the flag from your native country. Draw a picture of that flag. Explain what you know of the history of that flag. Be prepared to discuss it in class.

---

[9] *motto:* a saying, proverb

6. Further Practice

A. The words listed below have these sounds:

/iy/ as in "s<u>ee</u>"   /ey/ as in "p<u>ay</u>"   /æ/ as in "c<u>a</u>t"

/ɪ/ as in "s<u>i</u>t"   /ɛ/ as in "m<u>e</u>t"

First, say the word. Then write the word in the column that corresponds to the sound of the *underlined* letter or letters. For example, the word "s<u>ee</u>" goes in the /iy/ column, the word "s<u>i</u>t" in the /ɪ/ column, the word "p<u>ay</u>" in the /ey/ column, and so on. (*Hint:* There are seven words for each sound.)

1. ch<u>ee</u>se	11. **<u>el</u>**bow	21. **<u>bus</u>**iness
2. **t<u>ea</u>ch**er	12. <u>a</u>xe	22. a**w<u>a</u>ke**
3. **w<u>i</u>n**dow	13. s<u>ay</u>s	23. ch<u>a</u>nce
4. tr<u>i</u>p	14. **l<u>i</u>q**uor	24. t<u>a</u>x
5. s<u>ai</u>d	15. sh<u>a</u>ve	25. <u>eigh</u>t
6. m<u>a</u>tch	16. wh<u>i</u>ch	26. ch<u>e</u>ss
7. **c<u>a</u>n**dle	17. **<u>e</u>n**vy	27. be**l<u>ie</u>ve**
8. m<u>a</u>de	18. ch<u>ea</u>t	28. **c<u>a</u>l**endar
9. w<u>eigh</u>	19. **s<u>ea</u>**son	29. **h<u>i</u>s**tory
10. **r<u>a</u>**dio	20. ma**ch<u>i</u>ne**	30. m<u>ea</u>nt

	/iy/	/ɪ/	/ey/	/ɛ/	/æ/
EXAMPLES:	"s<u>ee</u>"	"s<u>i</u>t"	"p<u>ay</u>"	"m<u>e</u>t"	"c<u>a</u>t"
	_____	_____	_____	_____	_____
	_____	_____	_____	_____	_____
	_____	_____	_____	_____	_____
	_____	_____	_____	_____	_____
	_____	_____	_____	_____	_____
	_____	_____	_____	_____	_____

B. Think of five sentences with five of the above words, one from each column. (More than one of the above words can be in each sentence.) Be prepared to read them in class.

Unit 12

/ɑ/ **as in _nòt_**

1. Producing /ɑ/[1]

EXAMPLES: <u>a</u>h, **occ**upy, c<u>a</u>lm, h<u>o</u>t, **fa**ther, **coll**ege, M<u>a</u>

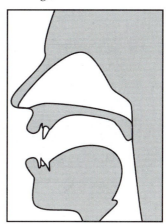

- Hold the _back_ part of your tongue _low_ in your mouth, _lower_ than for any other sound.
- Touch the lower front teeth lightly with the tip of the tongue.
- Lower your jaw; lips are open wide.
- The muscles of your tongue should be _relaxed_.
- Say "ahhh." Imagine that a doctor wants to look at your throat.

2. Contrast: /ɑ/, /æ/, **and** /ɛ/

Some students confuse the sound /ɑ/ as in "n<u>o</u>t" with the sound /æ/ as in "c<u>a</u>t" or /ɛ/ as in "m<u>e</u>t."

A. Practice these sounds, first normally, then with exaggeration, then normally. Listen and repeat.

1. /ɑ/   /ɑ . . . /   /ɑ/

2. /æ/   /æ . . . /   /æ/

3. /ɛ/   /ɛ . . . /   /ɛ/

---

[1] This vowel may vary depending on which dialect of American English you hear. For example: before voiceless /θ/ and /f/, "path" /pæθ/ may be heard as /pɑθ/; "half" /hæf/ may be heard as /hɑf/, etc.

B. Now practice these sounds in words. Notice the phonetic spelling. Listen and repeat each word twice.

1. arm	/ɑrm/	arm
2. not	/nɑt/	not
3. clock	/klɑk/	clock
4. am	/æm/	am
5. laugh	/læf/	laugh
6. map	/mæp/	map
7. met	/mɛt/	met
8. sell	/sɛl/	sell
9. less	/lɛs/	less

3. Check Your Listening

You will hear words with sounds /ɑ/, /æ/, and /ɛ/. First, cover the words in the following list with a piece of paper. Then listen to each word. Concentrate on the sound, not the spelling. Which vowel sound do you hear? Place a check mark in the correct column.

		/ɑ/ as in "not"	/æ/ as in "cat"	/ɛ/ as in "met"
mop	1.	✓		
leg	2.			✓
land	3.	✗	✓	
calm	4.	✓		
odd	5.	✓		
end	6.			✓
said	7.		✓	
sad	8.	✓		
on	9.	✓		
map	10.	✓		

4. Practice the Contrast: /ɑ/ as in "n*o*t," /æ/ as in "c*a*t," and /ɛ/ as in "m*e*t"

A. Practice these contrasting sounds. Listen and repeat each group of three words.

/ɑ/	/æ/	/ɛ/
1. p*o*t	p*a*t	p*e*t
2. *o*dd	*a*dd	*E*d
3. b*o*nd	b*a*nd	b*e*nd
4. *o*n	*a*n	"n"
5. D*o*n	D*a*n	d*e*n
6. S*o*l	S*a*l	s*e*ll
7. l*o*g	l*a*g	l*e*g
8. r*o*ck	r*a*ck	wr*e*ck
9. *o*x	*a*xe	"x"
10. **f*o*ll**ow	**f*a*ll**ow[2]	**f*e*ll**ow

B. Now practice the contrasting sounds in sentence pairs. The first sentence in each pair has the sound /ɑ/, and the second has the sound /æ/. Pay attention to contractions and function words. Listen and repeat.

1a.	c*o*t	I've a c*o*t in my room.
b.	c*a*t	I've a c*a*t in my room.

2a.	b*o*x	I can see their b*o*x from a **dis**tance.
b.	b*a*cks	I can see their b*a*cks from a **dis**tance.

---

[2] *fallow:* Farmland that is not planted with crops lies fallow.

3a. p<u>o</u>t   She gave me a p<u>o</u>t.

b. p<u>a</u>t   She gave me a p<u>a</u>t.

4a. m<u>o</u>p   I need a new m<u>o</u>p for my **off**ice.
b. m<u>a</u>p   I need a new m<u>a</u>p for my **off**ice.

5a. S<u>o</u>l   She came with her friend S<u>o</u>l.
b. S<u>a</u>l   She came with her friend S<u>a</u>l.

6a. c<u>o</u>p   Is the c<u>o</u>p in the house?
b. c<u>a</u>p   Is the c<u>a</u>p in the house?

7a. m<u>o</u>sque   The m<u>o</u>sque was new five years **ago.**

b. m<u>a</u>sk   The m<u>a</u>sk was new five years **ago.**

8a. s<u>o</u>ck   There's a hole in the s<u>o</u>ck.
b. s<u>a</u>ck   There's a hole in the s<u>a</u>ck.

9a. <u>o</u>x [3]   Does he have an <u>o</u>x on his ranch?

b. <u>a</u>xe   Does he have an <u>a</u>xe on his ranch?

10a. **p<u>o</u>ck**et   It's been in my **p<u>o</u>ck**et all day.

b. **p<u>a</u>ck**et [4]   It's been in my **p<u>a</u>ck**et all day.

C. The first sentence of each pair has the sound /ɑ/, and the second has the sound /ɛ/. Pay attention to contractions and function words. Listen and repeat.

1a. p<u>o</u>t   I bought a p<u>o</u>t for my **moth**er.

b. p<u>e</u>t   I bought a p<u>e</u>t for my **moth**er.

2a. J<u>o</u>hn   Did you <u>see</u> John to**day?**

b. J<u>e</u>n   Did you see Jen to**day?**

3a. r<u>o</u>ck   He's sure he saw the r<u>o</u>ck.

b. wr<u>e</u>ck   He's sure he saw the wr<u>e</u>ck.

4a. d<u>o</u>t   The d<u>o</u>t was on my **pa**per.

b. d<u>e</u>bt   The d<u>e</u>bt was on my **pap**er.

5a. g<u>o</u>t   I g<u>o</u>t it from my **sis**ter.

b. g<u>e</u>t   I g<u>e</u>t it from my **sis**ter.

[3] *ox:* a large cow-like animal
[4] *packet:* a small package

preposition reduced

the last word
got to be stressed

✓ 6a. st**o**p   Where's the st**o**p su**pposed** to be?

b. st**e**p   Where's the st**e**p su**pposed** to be?

7a. **o**dd   Did you think that was **o**dd?

✓ b. **E**d   Did you think that was **E**d?

8a. bl**o**nd   We all like the bl**o**nd.

✓ b. bl**e**nd   We all like the bl**e**nd.

5. Stress and Intonation

The words below begin with the letter "o" and are followed by sentences. In these words, "o" represents the sound /ɑ/ as in "n**o**t."

1. Place a stress mark over the stressed words you hear.

2. Pay attention to the marked pauses, intonation patterns, and function words. Listen and repeat.

EXAMPLE: oppor**tu**nity

He was **giv**en / an oppor**tu**nity to **tra**vel.

1. **ob**ject   The **ob**ject of the game / is to win.

2. **ob**ligated   I'm **ob**ligated / to my boss.

extara

3. **o**dd   It looks **o**dd, / **does**n't it?

4. **oc**topus   It looks / like an **oc**topus.

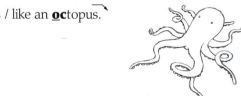

5. **ob**vious   The dent in the car / was quite **ob**vious.

6. <u>o</u>ccu**pa**tion   What's your <u>o</u>ccu**pa**tion?

7. <u>O</u>c**to**ber   She'll **vis**it him / in <u>O</u>c**to**ber.

8. **ob**stinate   Don't be **ob**stinate. / Do it!

9. **occ**upy   My **sis**ter / will **occ**upy the house.

10. **ob**stacle   The **ob**stacle course / was **dif**ficult.

6. Dialogs

You will hear eight short dialogs. The first sentence of each dialog contains words with /ɑ/ as in "n<u>o</u>t," the second contains words with /æ/ as in "c<u>a</u>t," and the third has words with /ɛ/ as in "m<u>e</u>t." Discuss any new vocabulary with your teacher and classmates.

1. Listen for the vowel sounds /ɑ/, /æ/, and /ɛ/.

2. Place a stress mark over the stressed words you hear. Pay attention to the function words.

3. Mark the intonation patterns you hear.

The first sentence is marked for you. Listen and repeat.

1. M<u>a</u>rk: It's in the glove com**part**ment of the c<u>a</u>r.

2. **Sall**y: I thought it was in the b<u>a</u>ck.

3. M<u>a</u>rk: L<u>e</u>t me g<u>e</u>t it for you.

4. **Ar**thur: <u>A</u>re there two c<u>a</u>rs in your ga**rage**?

5. **Pa**trick: Yeah. The bl<u>a</u>ck **Ca**dillac be**longs** to **Sall**y.

6. **Ar**thur: And the r<u>e</u>d **Chev**rolet be**longs** to <u>E</u>d?

7. Mr. P<u>a</u>rk: Did the **ar**tist **cop**y the car**toon?**

8. Ms. **Tann**er: No, he de**mand**ed **mon**ey in ad**vance.**

9. Mr. P<u>a</u>rk: W<u>e</u>ll, wh<u>e</u>n I g<u>e</u>t the time, I'll do it my**self.**

10. **Mar**cy: Does he play rock on his gui**tar?**

11. Ann: I don't think he can; ask him.

12. **Mar**cy: No, I just met him **yes**terday.

13. Bob: What do you want?

14. Ralph: A ham **sal**ad **sand**wich.

15. Bob: Well, I'd like some eggs for **break**fast.

16. Charles: Are you **shopp**ing at the **mark**et to**morr**ow?

17. **Al**ice: I need ba**nan**as, a half **gall**on of **app**le juice, and a **can**ta-loupe.⁵

18. Charles: Well, don't for**get** to get the **straw**berries, **jell**y, bread, **lem**ons, and **pret**zels.

19. John: Did you solve the **prob**lem?

20. Sam: The one we had in math class? Yeah.

21. John: Great! Let's get a**noth**er one.

22. Don: Why is the car in the **bod**y shop?

23. **An**dy: It was **dam**aged in the **ac**cident.

24. Don: Will we get it be**fore W**ednes**day?

7. Further Practice

A. Circle the word that has the same vowel sound as the word in the model column. *Reminder:* Say all the words aloud.

	Model		
EXAMPLE:	hat	sock	met	(black)

---

⁵ *cantaloupe:* a round melon with rough skin and sweet, light-orange insides

MODEL			
1. can	cent	cat	calm
2. dead	laugh	large	head
3. wet	what	when	was
4. math	men	mess	mass
5. **pen**cil	**par**ty	past	pest
6. **an**y	art	plan	friend
7. said	sad	**read**y	calm
8. sell	solve	help	**Sat**urday
9. wash	**coll**ar	wreck	catch
10. have	head	heart	hand
11. **hon**est	**coll**ege	ham	hell
12. **app**le	says	match	arm

B. Make up six short sentences with six different words selected from the column marked "Model." Underline the word in your sentence. Be prepared to read the sentences in class.

EXAMPLE: The hat her mother wore to the wedding looked beautiful.

Unit 13

/ay/ **as in _buy_**

1. Producing /ay/[1]

EXAMPLES: i̲ce, e̲y̲e, mi̲ne, hei̲ght, gui̲de, rhy̲me, my̲, di̲e

- The first part of this sound is similar to /ɑ/ as in "n̲o̲t."
- Hold your tongue low in your mouth.
- Touch the lower front teeth lightly with the tip of your tongue.
- As you begin to say this _long_ sound, open your lips wide and lower your jaw.
- To complete the sound, raise your jaw with your lips closing a little as you raise the front part of your tongue forward and up.
- Tongue muscles are _relaxed_.

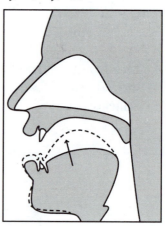

2. Contrast: /ay/ **and** /æ/

Some students confuse the sound **/ay/** as in "b̲u̲y̲" with the sound **/æ/** as in "c̲a̲t."

A. Practice these two sounds, first normally, then with exaggeration, then normally. Listen and repeat.

1. /ay/   /ay . . . /   /ay/

2. /æ/   /æ . . . /   /æ/

---

[1] The final "e" in words such as "gu̲i̲de," "rhy̲me," and "hi̲de" signals the /ay/ pronunciation for the first vowel sound. Compare "hi̲d" /hɪd/ with "hi̲de" /hayd/. But in words such as "ice," the final "e" marks the "c" as /s/.

B. Now practice these sounds in words. Notice the phonetic spelling. Listen and repeat each word twice.

1.	ice	/ays/	ice
2.	die	/day/	die
3.	hide	/hayd/	hide
4.	back	/bæk/	back
5.	had	/hæd/	had
6.	sand	/sænd/	sand
7.	fine	/fayn/	fine
8.	fly	/flay/	fly

3. Check Your Listening

You will hear words with the sounds /ay/ and /æ/. First, cover the words in the following list with a piece of paper. Then listen to each word. Concentrate on the sound, not the spelling. Which vowel sound do you hear? Write a check mark in the correct column.

		/ay/ as in "buy"	/æ/ as in "cat"
fly	1.	✓	
sigh	2.	✓	
mice	3.	✓	
hat	4.		✓
man	5.		✓
height	6.	✓	
wife	7.	✓	
crash	8.	✓	✓
side	9.	✓	
sand	10.		✓

4. Practice the Contrast: /ay/ as in "b<u>u</u>y" with /æ/ as in "c<u>a</u>t"

A. Practice these contrasting sounds. Listen and repeat each word pair.

/ay/	/æ/		/ay/	/æ/
1. r<u>igh</u>t	r<u>a</u>t		7. m<u>igh</u>t	m<u>a</u>t
2. h<u>i</u>de	h<u>a</u>d		8. f<u>igh</u>t	f<u>a</u>t
3. s<u>i</u>de	s<u>a</u>d		9. m<u>i</u>ce	m<u>a</u>ss
4. d<u>ie</u>d	D<u>a</u>d		10. m<u>i</u>ne	m<u>a</u>n
5. b<u>i</u>ke	b<u>a</u>ck		11. f<u>i</u>ne	f<u>a</u>n
6. h<u>eigh</u>t	h<u>a</u>t		12. l<u>i</u>ke	l<u>a</u>ck

B. Now practice the contrasting sounds in sentence pairs. The first sentence of each pair has the sound /ay/, and the second has the sound /æ/. Listen and repeat.

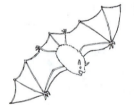

1a. b<u>i</u>te   It was a big b<u>i</u>te.

b. b<u>a</u>t   It was a big b<u>a</u>t.

2a. h<u>i</u>de   They **al**ways h<u>i</u>de it in the **clos**et.

b. h<u>a</u>d   They **al**ways h<u>a</u>d it in the **clos**et.

3a. f<u>i</u>ne   It was a large f<u>i</u>ne, **was**n't it?

b. f<u>a</u>n   It was a large f<u>a</u>n, **was**n't it?

4a. m*i*ne   The old m*i*ne looks **prett**y good.

b. m*a*n   The old m*a*n looks **prett**y good.

5a. b*i*ke   Can you see the b*i*ke from here?

b. b*a*ck   Can you see the b*a*ck from here?

6a. s*i*gned   I think it was s*i*gned.

b. s*a*nd   I think it was s*a*nd.

5. Stress and Intonation

1. Listen for the vowel sound /ay/ as in "b*u*y."

2. Mark the stressed words with a stress mark (ʼ).

3. Mark the falling or rising intonations. Pay attention to the function words and phrasing.

EXAMPLES: a.   I'd like to eat r*i*ce to**night.**

b.   Did he say he **want**ed to try the French fr*i*es?

1. You're qu*i*te r*i*ght to do that.

2. The br*i*de cr*i*ed as she walked down the a*i*sle.

3. I was de**ligh**ted with the r*i*pe **pine**apple.

4. The **is**land of **Ice**land is qu*i*te n*i*ce.

5. **Fly**ing to **Chi**na is ex**cit**ing.

6. Why did the wh*i*te dog b*i*te **I**da?

7. Did you see the **high**way sign?

8. When did you re**mind** him to get the ice?

9. The bright lights were **shin**ing.

10. Did the su**ppli**es a**rri**ve on time?

6. Further Practice

The following poem is an old rhyme that contains a riddle.[2]

1. Read it with a partner. You can use a dictionary to help you with the pronunciation of new words.

2. Draw a <u>single</u> line under all letters representing the sound /**ay**/ as in "b<u>uy</u>" and a <u>double</u> line under all letters representing the sound /æ/ as in "c<u>a</u>t."

3. The important stressed words are marked. Remember to monitor the reduced forms and the phrasing.

EXAMPLE: I met a man with **sev**en wives.

1.   As I Was **Go**ing to St. Ives[3]

2.   As I was **go**ing to St. Ives,

3.   I met a man with **sev**en wives,

4.   Each wife had **sev**en sacks,

5.   Each sack had **sev**en cats.

6.   Each cat had **sev**en kits,[4]

7.   Kits, cats, sacks, and wives,

8.   How **man**y were **go**ing to St. Ives?

Can you answer the last question of the rhyme? How many *were* going to St. Ives?

---

[2] *riddle:* a puzzle
[3] *St. Ives:* a town in England
[4] *kit:* an old word for "kitten"

Unit 14

/aw/ **as in *now***

1. Producing /aw/[1]

EXAMPLES: ouch, out, cloud, house, town, **vow**el, how, cow

- The first part of this sound is similar to /ɑ/ as in "n<u>o</u>t."
- Hold your tongue low in your mouth.
- Touch the lower front teeth lightly with the tip of the tongue.
- As you begin to say this *long* sound, open your lips and lower your jaw.
- To complete the sound, move the back part of your tongue toward the roof (soft palate) of your mouth (but do not touch it). Raise your jaw and round your lips.

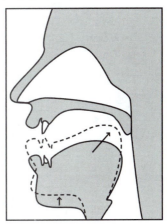

2. Contrast: /aw/ and /ɑ/

Students do not usually have a problem pronouncing the sound /aw/ as in "n<u>ow</u>." However, they may confuse it with /ɑ/ as in "n<u>o</u>t."

A. Practice these two sounds, first normally, then with exaggeration, then normally. Listen and repeat.

   1. /aw/   /aw . . . /   /aw/

   2. /ɑ/   /ɑ . . . /   /ɑ/

---

[1] In Canada and in some Southern states this sound, when it comes before voiceless consonants, may be replaced by the sound /əw/. For example, "about" /əbawt/ may be replaced by /əbəwt/.

119

Now practice these sounds in words. Notice the phonetic spelling. Listen and repeat each word twice.

1.	<u>ou</u>t	/awt/	<u>ou</u>t
2.	p<u>ou</u>nd	/pawnd/	p<u>ou</u>nd
3.	d<u>ou</u>bt	/dawt/	d<u>ou</u>bt
4.	p<u>o</u>nd[2]	/pand/	p<u>o</u>nd
5.	d<u>o</u>t	/dat/	d<u>o</u>t
6.	f<u>a</u>r	/far/	f<u>a</u>r
7.	h<u>ow</u>	/haw/	h<u>ow</u>
8.	br<u>ow</u>n	/brawn/	br<u>ow</u>n

3. Check Your Listening

You will hear words with the sounds /aw/ and /a/. First, cover the words in the following list with a piece of paper. Then listen to each word. Concentrate on the sound, not the spelling. Which vowel sound do you hear? Write a check mark in the correct column.

		/aw/ as in "n<u>ow</u>"	/a/ as in "n<u>o</u>t"
t<u>ow</u>n	1.	√	
<u>ah</u>	2.		√
h<u>ou</u>r	3.	√	
<u>a</u>re	4.		√
T<u>o</u>m	5.		√
cl<u>ou</u>d	6.	√	
<u>ou</u>ch	7.		
g<u>o</u>t	8.		√
d<u>ow</u>n	9.		
sh<u>ou</u>t	10.		

---

[2] *pond:* a body of water smaller than a lake

4. Practice the Contrast: /aw/ **as in "now" with** /ɑ/ **as in "n_ot_"**

A. Practice these contrasting words. Listen and repeat each word pair.

/aw/	/ɑ/		/aw/	/ɑ/
1. <u>ow</u>	<u>ah</u>	6. sp<u>ou</u>t[3]	sp<u>o</u>t
2. p<u>ou</u>nd	p<u>o</u>nd	7. d<u>ow</u>n	D<u>o</u>n
3. t<u>ow</u>n	T<u>o</u>m	8. f<u>ou</u>nd	f<u>o</u>nd
4. d<u>ou</u>bt	d<u>o</u>t	9. br<u>ow</u>ns	br<u>o</u>nze
5. sh<u>ou</u>t	sh<u>o</u>t	10. sc<u>ou</u>ts	Sc<u>o</u>ts

B. Now practice the contrasting sounds in sentence pairs. The first sentence of each pair has the sound /aw/, and the second has the sound /ɑ/. Listen and repeat.

1a.	<u>ow</u>	Did she say "<u>ow</u>"?
b.	<u>ah</u>	Did she say "<u>ah</u>"?
2a.	sh<u>ou</u>t	A sh<u>ou</u>t came from the back.
b.	sh<u>o</u>t	A sh<u>o</u>t came from the back.
3a.	sc<u>ou</u>ts	All sc<u>ou</u>ts know this song.
b.	Sc<u>o</u>ts	All Sc<u>o</u>ts know this song.

---

[3] *spout:* an opening from which liquid comes out

| | 4a. | doubt | I doubt it **ev**ery time. |
| | b. | dot | I dot it **ev**ery time. |

| | 5a. | spout | Did you see the spout on the sink? |
| | b. | spot | Did you see the spot on the sink? |

| | 6a. | pound[4] | The dog is in the pound. |
| | b. | pond | The dog is in the pond. |

| | 7a. | down | Did you call down from up**stairs?** |
| | b. | Don | Did you call Don from up**stairs?** |

| | 8a. | found | He said the word is "found." |
| | b. | fond | He said the word is "fond." |

| | 9a. | town | I went to town last night. |
| | b. | Tom | I went to Tom last night. |

| | 10a. | browns | I'd like them in browns. |
| | b. | bronze[5] | I'd like them in bronze. |

---

[4] *pound:* a place where lost or unwanted dogs and cats are kept by a town until somebody claims them

[5] *bronze:* a gray to reddish-brown metal made of tin and copper

5. Stress and Intonation

1. Before you listen to the tape, draw a <u>single</u> line under the letters that represent the sound /aw/ as in "n<u>ow</u>" and a <u>double</u> line under the letters that represent /ɑ/ as in "n<u>o</u>t."

2. Now listen to the tape and repeat the sentences. Mark the falling or rising intonation patterns. (_Reminder:_ Monitor the stressed words, reduced forms, and the phrasing.)

EXAMPLES: a.   It's **p<u>o</u>ss**ible to pro**nounce** all the **vow**el s<u>ou</u>nds

n<u>ow</u>.

b.   Do you **prom**ise to show me h<u>ow</u>?

1. The cl<u>o</u>ck in t<u>ow</u>n broke d<u>ow</u>n.

2. The job I **want**ed is in a**not**her town.

3. It's a**pprox**imately one <u>ou</u>nce.

4. Is that **prop**er to a**nnounce?**

5. The **cock**roach crept into the spout.

6. The **ser**geant got up with a shout.

7. Is it **poss**ible to take a **show**er?

8. Yes, if the a**larm** goes off at an **ear**ly h<u>ou</u>r.

9. My **mon**ey **mark**et a**ccount** is **doubt**ful.

10. That **sound**ed like a **mouth**ful.

6. Further Practice

A. Read the following old rhyme aloud. You can use a dictionary to help you with the pronunciation of new words.

    1. Draw a line under all the letters that represent the sound /aw/ as in "n<u>ow</u>." (Hint: There are 14 different words. Words that are repeated should be counted once only.)

    2. Mark the important stressed words and the pauses. The first sentence is marked for you.

1.	The <u>ow</u>l / looked d<u>ow</u>n / with his great / r<u>ou</u>nd eyes
2.	At the **low**ering⁶ clouds and the dark skies,
3.	"A good night for **scout**ing," ⁷ says he,
4.	"With **nev**er a s<u>ou</u>nd I'll go **prowl**ing⁸ a**round.**
5.	A m<u>ou</u>se or two may be f<u>ou</u>nd on the ground
6.	Or a fat little bird in a tree."
7.	So d<u>ow</u>n he flew from the old church **tow**er,
8.	The m<u>ou</u>se and the **bird**ie cr<u>ou</u>ch⁹ and **cow**er.¹⁰
9.	Back he flies in half an h<u>ou</u>r,
10.	"A **ver**y good **supp**er," says he.

B. Work with a partner. Record the above passage. Help each other with the correct sounds, stress, and intonation.

---

⁶ *lowering* /laʊərɪŋ/: threatening or seeming to threaten
⁷ *scouting:* exploring
⁸ *prowling around:* searching here and there
⁹ *crouch:* bend down
¹⁰ *cower:* crouch in fear

Unit 15

/ə/ as in _up_

1. Producing /ə/[1]

EXAMPLES: <u>u</u>s, **<u>um</u>**pire, **<u>Sun</u>**day, bl<u>oo</u>d, **tr<u>ou</u>b**le, <u>a</u>**bout**, <u>o</u>**ppose,**
ba**<u>nan</u>**a, **prec<u>i</u>**ous, **co**<u>ma</u>

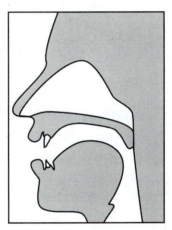

- Hold the _front_ part of your tongue low in your mouth.
- Touch the lower front teeth lightly with the tip of your tongue.
- Lower your jaw and open your lips slightly.
- Raise the _center_ part of your tongue toward the roof (hard palate) of your mouth (but do not touch it).
- Native speakers often use this sound when they are hesitating. It is usually written "uh."

2. Contrast: /ə/, /ɑ/, /æ/, and /ɛ/

Some students confuse the sound /ə/ as in "<u>u</u>p" with other sounds. These sounds include /ɑ/ as in "n<u>o</u>t," /æ/ as in "cat," and /ɛ/ as in "m<u>e</u>t."

A. Practice these sounds, first normally, then with exaggeration, then normally. Listen and repeat.

1. /ə/	/ə . . . /	/ə/
2. /ɑ/	/ɑ . . . /	/ɑ/
3. /æ/	/æ . . . /	/æ/
4. /ɛ/	/ɛ . . . /	/ɛ/

---

[1] This vowel is called the _schwa_ /ʃwɑ/, the most commonly used sound in the English language.

B. Now practice these sounds in words. Notice the phonetic spelling. Listen and repeat each word twice.

1. u̱p	/əp/	u̱p
2. lo̱ve	/ləv/	lo̱ve
3. cu̱t	/kət/	cu̱t
4. no̱t	/nɑt/	no̱t
5. clo̱ck	/klɑk/	clo̱ck
6. mo̱b	/mɑb/	mo̱b
7. ca̱t	/kæt/	ca̱t
8. ha̱ve	/hæv/	ha̱ve
9. ba̱g	/bæg/	ba̱g
10. me̱t	/mɛt/	me̱t
11. de̱ad	/dɛd/	de̱ad
12. e̱nd	/ɛnd/	e̱nd

3. Check Your Listening

You will hear words with the sounds /ə/, /ɑ/, /æ/, and /ɛ/. First, cover the words in the following list with a piece of paper. Then listen to each word. Concentrate on the sound, not the spelling. Which vowel sound do you hear? Write a check mark in the correct column.

		/ə/ as in "u̱p"	/ɑ/ as in "no̱t"	/æ/ as in "ca̱t"	/ɛ/ as in "me̱t"
cu̱p	1.	_____	✓	_____	_____
su̱n	2.	_____	_____	_____	_____
✗ ca̱n	3.	_____	✓	_____	_____
✓ se̱t	4.	_____	✓	_____	✓
✗ sho̱p	5.	✓	✓	_____	_____
✓ le̱g	6.	_____	_____	_____	✓
◡ po̱t	7.	_____	✓	_____	_____

		/ə/ as in "up"	/ɑ/ as in "not"	/æ/ as in "cat"	/ɛ/ as in "met"
✗ gum	8.	✓____	✓____	____	____
✓ sad	9.	____	____	✓____	____
lunch	10.	✓____	____	____	____

4. Practice the Contrast: /ə/ as in "u̱p" with /æ/ as in "ca̱t"

A. Practice these contrasting sounds. Listen and repeat each word pair.

/ə/	/æ/		/ə/	/æ/
1. lu̱ck	la̱ck	6.	stu̱ck	sta̱ck
2. su̱ck	sa̱ck	7.	mu̱d	ma̱d
3. so̱me	Sa̱m	8.	to̱n	ta̱n
4. fu̱n	fa̱n	9.	du̱mb	da̱m
5. bu̱t	ba̱t	10.	mu̱ch	ma̱tch

B. Now practice the contrasting sounds in sentence pairs. The first sentence of each pair has the sound /ə/, and the second has the sound /æ/. Listen and repeat.

1a.	cu̱p	I found the cu̱p in the **clos**et.
b.	ca̱p	I found the ca̱p in the **clos**et.
2a.	cu̱t	I've a small cu̱t that needs **atten**tion.
b.	ca̱t	I've a small ca̱t that needs **atten**tion.
3a.	bu̱g	Did you see that bu̱g?
b.	ba̱g	Did you see that ba̱g?

4a. h<u>u</u>t   I found the **pic**ture of the h<u>u</u>t.

b. h<u>a</u>t   I found the **pic**ture of the h<u>a</u>t.

5a. tr<u>u</u>cks   The tr<u>u</u>cks were seen here.

b. tr<u>a</u>cks   The tr<u>a</u>cks were seen here.

6a. **un**cle   Did you see my **un**cle?

b. **an**kle   Did you see my **an**kle?

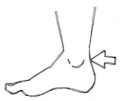

5. Practice the Contrast: /ə/ as in "**up**" with /ɛ/ as in "m**e**t"

A. Practice these contrasting sounds. Listen and repeat each word pair.

/ə/	/ɛ/		/ə/	/ɛ/
1. b<u>u</u>t	b<u>e</u>t	5. fl<u>oo</u>d	fl<u>e</u>d
2. t<u>o</u>n	t<u>e</u>n	6. b<u>u</u>g	b<u>e</u>g
3. d<u>o</u>ne	d<u>e</u>n[2]	7. m<u>u</u>st	m<u>e</u>ssed
4. bl<u>oo</u>d	bl<u>e</u>d	8. b<u>u</u>nch	b<u>e</u>nch

---
[2] *den:* the home of certain animals

B. Now practice the contrasting sounds in sentence pairs. The first sentence of each pair has the sound /ə/, and the second has the sound /ɛ/. Listen and repeat.

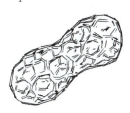

1a. n<u>u</u>t The n<u>u</u>t is on the **ta**ble.

b. n<u>e</u>t The n<u>e</u>t is on the **ta**ble.

2a. r<u>u</u>st We want to see the r<u>u</u>st.

b. r<u>e</u>st We want to see the r<u>e</u>st.

3a. d<u>u</u>ck[3] We saw the d<u>u</u>ck much **lat**er.

b. d<u>e</u>ck[4] We saw the d<u>e</u>ck much **lat**er.

4a. h<u>u</u>m[5] Fix the h<u>u</u>m on the ma**chine.**

b. h<u>e</u>m[6] Fix the h<u>e</u>m on the ma**chine.**

---

[3] *duck:* a type of water bird
[4] *deck:* a wooden platform attached to a house
[5] *hum:* a continuous sound; an annoying noise
[6] *hem:* the lower edge of a piece of cloth, turned up and sewn

5a. b<u>u</u>st   He would b<u>u</u>st it if he could.

b. b<u>e</u>st   He would b<u>e</u>st it if he could.

6a. **m<u>o</u>n**ey   Do you have **m<u>o</u>ney read**y?

b. **m<u>a</u>n**y   Do you have **m<u>a</u>ny read**y?

6. Practice the Contrast: /ə/ as in "<u>u</u>p" with /ɑ/ as in "n<u>o</u>t"

A. Practice these contrasting sounds. Listen and repeat each word pair.

/ə/	/ɑ/		/ə/	/ɑ/
1. c<u>u</u>p	c<u>o</u>p	5. d<u>u</u>ck	d<u>o</u>ck[7]
2. sh<u>u</u>t	sh<u>o</u>t	6. d<u>u</u>ll	d<u>o</u>ll
3. r<u>u</u>b	r<u>o</u>b	7. b<u>u</u>m	b<u>o</u>mb
4. f<u>u</u>nd	f<u>o</u>nd	8. st<u>u</u>ck	st<u>o</u>ck

B. Now practice the contrasting sounds in sentence pairs. The first sentence of each pair has the sound /ə/, and the second has the sound /ɑ/. Listen and repeat.

1a. c<u>u</u>t   I saw the small c<u>u</u>t.

b. c<u>o</u>t   I saw the small c<u>o</u>t.

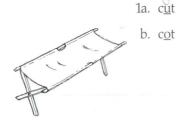

2a. h<u>u</u>t   How do you spell "h<u>u</u>t"?

b. h<u>o</u>t   How do you spell "h<u>o</u>t"?

3a. c<u>o</u>me   We were all told to c<u>o</u>me down.

b. c<u>a</u>lm   We were all told to c<u>a</u>lm down.

---

[7] *dock:* a pier at which boats or ships stop

4a.	luck	My luck seems to be **hold**ing out.[8]
b.	lock	My lock seems to be **hold**ing out.
5a	nut	Did you find the nut?
b.	knot	Did you find the knot?
6a.	duck	I can see the duck from here.
b.	dock	I can see the dock from here.

7. /ə/ in Unstressed Syllables

A. Words Ending With "-ous"

Some words end with the sounds /əs/ in an unstressed syllable. These sounds are represented by the letters "ous." Listen and repeat these words and sentences.

1.	**cau**tious	He's **cau**tious when he's **spend**ing his own **mon**ey.
2.	**con**scious	Was he **con**scious when he fell?
3.	con**tin**uous	Our brain needs a con**tin**uous su**pply** of blood.
4.	**cour**teous	The sales clerk was not **ver**y **cour**teous.
5.	**cur**ious	She's **cur**ious about my **boy**friend.
6.	**dan**gerous	Do you think **roll**er **coast**ers are **dan**gerous?
7.	e**nor**mous	He paid an e**nor**mous sum of **mon**ey for it.
8.	**hu**morous	Did you hear that **hu**morous **stor**y?
9.	**fa**mous	He's **fa**mous for **play**ing **Ham**let.
10.	**jeal**ous	Do you think he's a **jeal**ous man?

---

[8] *holding out:* not giving way; lasting

B. **Dropping /ə/ in Unstressed Syllables**

In some words, /ə/ occurs as an unstressed syllable between two consonant sounds. Many speakers, in informal speech, do not produce the /ə/ in such words. (Sometimes the syllables are so short that they tend to disappear.) Listen and repeat these examples.

1. acci**den**tally	13. **fam**ily	25. re**cov**ery
2. **bach**elor	14. **gall**ery	26. **ref**erence
3. **bak**ery	15. **gen**eral	27. **sal**ary
4. **bev**erage	16. **groc**ery	28. satis**fact**ory
5. **cam**era	17. **his**tory	29. **sev**eral
6. **choc**olate	18. **in**terested	30. **slipp**ery
7. **com**fortable[9]	19. **lab**oratory	31. **tem**perature
8. **diff**erent	20. **lib**eral	32. **trav**eler
9. dis**cov**ery	21. **mem**ory	33. **veg**etable
10. ele**men**tary	22. **mys**tery	34. **vet**eran
11. **ev**ery	23. **op**era	35. **won**dering
12. **fac**tory	24. **priv**ilege	

8. Stress and Intonation

1. Think of a sentence for each of the phrases below. They include the vowel sound /ə/.

2. Mark the words you think are important to stress.

3. Mark the falling or rising intonation patterns. (Remember to monitor your phrasing and function words.)

4. Work with a partner or in a small group. Check each other for pronunciation and intonation.

---

[9] The sound /r/ in this word is also omitted.

EXAMPLE: come up

Will you come up to see me today?

1. some fun
2. **stud**y on **Mon**day
3. lunch on **Sun**day
4. **cinn**amon buns

5. arrive **hun**gry
6. **doub**le my **mon**ey
7. **di**et **so**da
8. love the **pupp**y

I'll go to casino and then I'll double my money

9. Further Practice

The vowel sound /ə/ as in "up" is spelled different ways in the following list of words. Sometimes it is stressed, and sometimes it is unstressed. Draw a line through the letters representing /ə/ in unstressed syllables. Put a stress mark above the letters for the /ə/ sound that are stressed.

EXAMPLES: a. comma (unstressed)

b. touch (stressed)

1. us
2. alarm
3. announce
4. ugly
5. compete

6. won
7. justice
8. island
9. support
10. coma

11. does
12. punish
13. tough
14. Canada
15. discuss

16. data
17. mustang
18. complain
19. cousin
20. dynasty

Unit 16

/ər/ **as in _sir_**

1. Producing /ər/[1]

EXAMPLES: <u>ur</u>ge, **ear**ly, ch<u>ur</u>ch, h<u>ear</u>d, sh<u>ir</u>t, w<u>or</u>m, **per**son, **jour**nal, **pleas**<u>ure</u>, h<u>er</u>, **sug**<u>ar</u>, **wat**<u>er</u>

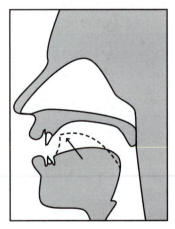

- This sound is a combination of /ə/ and /r/. The result is a single sound that can be represented by the letters "er."
- Hold the _front_ part of your tongue low in your mouth.
- Lower your jaw and open your lips slightly.
- As you begin to say the sound, raise the _center_ part of your tongue toward the roof (hard palate) of your mouth (but do not touch it).
- Move the tongue tip up, toward the upper gum ridge (but do not touch it) as you move your jaw up slightly.
- The muscles in your tongue should be _tense_.

---

[1] The /r/ sound, when it appears in final position, may not be pronounced, depending on which dialect of American English you hear. For example: "f<u>ar</u>" /fɑr/ may be replaced by /fɑ/; "after" may be replaced by /æftə/. However, /r/ is usually pronounced when it is followed by a word that begins with a vowel sound and it is linked to that sound. For example, far away; after eight.

2. Contrast: /ər/ and /ɑr/

Some students confuse the sound /ər/ as in "si̲r" with /ɑr/ as in "fa̲r."

A. Practice these sounds, first normally, then with exaggeration, then normally. Listen and repeat.

1. /ər/   /ər . . . /   /ər/
2. /ɑr/   /ɑr . . . /   /ɑr/

B. Now practice these sounds in words. Notice the phonetic spelling. Listen and repeat each word twice.

1. ea̲rn   /ərn/   ea̲rn
2. bi̲rd   /bərd/   bi̲rd
3. si̲r   /sər/   si̲r
4. a̲rt   /ɑrt/   a̲rt
5. ha̲rd   /hɑrd/   ha̲rd
6. fa̲r   /fɑr/   fa̲r

3. Check Your Listening

You will hear words with the sounds /ər/ and /ɑr/. First, cover the words in the following list with a piece of paper. Then listen to each word. Concentrate on the sound, not the spelling. Which vowel sound do you hear? Write a check mark in the correct column.

		/ər/ as in "si̲r"	/ɑr/ as in "fa̲r"
tu̲rn	1.	✓	
hea̲rd	2.		
ba̲r	3.		✓
ha̲rd	4.		✓
fa̲rm	5.		✓
shi̲rt	6.	✓	
ta̲r	7.		✓
bu̲rn	8.	✓	

	/ər/ as in "si̱r"	/ɑr/ as in "fa̱r"
ve̱rb	9. ✓	_____
ca̱rd	10. _____	✓

4. Practice the Contrast: /ər/ as in "si̱r," /ɑr/ as in "fa̱r," and /ə/ as in "u̱p"

A. Practice the contrasting sounds /ər/ and /ɑr/ in sentence pairs. The first sentence of each pair has the sound /ər/, and the second has the sound /ɑr/. Listen and repeat.

1a. fu̱r   It's fu̱r from the U.S.A.

b. fa̱r   It's fa̱r from the U.S.A.

2a. fi̱rm   Is the fi̱rm well **man**aged?

b. fa̱rm   Is the fa̱rm well **man**aged?

3a. hu̱rt   Did you say "hu̱rt"?

b. he̱art   Did you say "he̱art"?

4a. h<u>ear</u>d   Spell the word "heard."

  b. h<u>ar</u>d   Spell the word "hard."

5a. **cur**tain   Which **cur**tain did she buy?

  b. **car**ton   Which **car**ton did she buy?

B. Now practice the contrasting sounds /ər/ and /ə/. The first sentence of each pair has the sound /ər/, and the second has the sound /ə/. Listen and repeat.

1a. t<u>ur</u>n   We thought we had a t<u>ur</u>n.

  b. t<u>o</u>n[2]   We thought we had a t<u>o</u>n.

2a. sh<u>ir</u>t   Can you spell "sh<u>ir</u>t"?

  b. sh<u>u</u>t   Can you spell "sh<u>u</u>t"?

3a. h<u>ur</u>t   We can see you're h<u>ur</u>t.

  b. h<u>u</u>t   We can see your h<u>u</u>t.

---

[2] *ton:* a unit of weight, in the U.S.A. 2,000 lbs.

4a. bu<u>r</u>n   Did you see the bu<u>r</u>n on the **ta**ble?

b. bu<u>n</u>[3]   Did you see the bu<u>n</u> on the **ta**ble?

5a. s<u>ear</u>ch   How can you say "s<u>ear</u>ch"?

b. s<u>u</u>ch   How can you say "s<u>u</u>ch"?

5. Spelling of /ər/

The sound /ər/ as in "s<u>ir</u>" is represented by seven different spellings. Examples of each spelling are in the words and sentences below. The sound /ər/ occurs in both stressed and unstressed syllables. Listen and repeat each word and sentence.

A.   "ir" Spelling

Listen and repeat.

1. th<u>ir</u>d   It's the th<u>ir</u>d one.

2. **cir**cle   I have a **cir**cle of friends.

3. g<u>ir</u>l   That g<u>ir</u>l is **tall**er than I am.

4. **dir**ty   The floor is **dir**ty.

5. sk<u>ir</u>t   She bought a sk<u>ir</u>t in the store.

B.   "ear" Spelling

Listen and repeat.

1. <u>ear</u>th   The <u>ear</u>th is round.

2. <u>ear</u>n   I can <u>ear</u>n a lot of **mon**ey.

3. **ear**nest   He said it in **ear**nest.

4. p<u>ear</u>ls   Those pink pearls are **beau**tiful.

5. l<u>ear</u>n   Can we l<u>ear</u>n it by heart?

---

[3] *bun:* a small rounded bread

C. "or" Spelling

Listen and repeat.

1. w<u>or</u>k   We w<u>or</u>k all day long.

2. w<u>or</u>d   Look up the new w<u>or</u>d.

3. w<u>or</u>se   It's w<u>or</u>se than I thought.

4. w<u>or</u>ld   Let's take a trip a**round** the w<u>or</u>ld!

5. a**tto**rney   I could use a good a**ttor**ney.

D. "ur" Spelling

Listen and repeat.

1. **ur**gent   Is it **ur**gent that we go with you?

2. p<u>ur</u>se   I lost my p<u>ur</u>se.

3. **pur**pose   What's the **pur**pose of that?

4. **sur**face   That has a smooth **sur**face.

5. re**turn**   Did you re**turn** my book?

E. "er" Spelling

Listen and repeat.

1. s<u>er</u>ve   Will you s<u>er</u>ve meat for **dinn**er?

2. n<u>er</u>ve   You need a lot of n<u>er</u>ve to do that.

3. **cer**tain   Is there a **cer**tain song you like?

4. de**ter**mine   We have to de**ter**mine the **out**come.

5. re**served**   Is that seat re**served?**

F. "ar" Spelling

Listen and repeat.

1. **doll**<u>ar</u>   Can you spare a **doll**<u>ar</u>?

2. **coll**<u>ar</u>   The **coll**<u>ar</u> on the coat is **dir**ty.

3. **sug**<u>ar</u>   Do you take **sug**<u>ar</u> in your **coff**ee?

4. **gramm**ar To**day,** we're **stud**ying **gramm**ar.

5. **cow**ard A **cow**ard is a **per**son with**out cour**age.

G. "our" Spelling

Listen and repeat.

1. **jour**nal I write in my **jour**nal **ev**ery day.

2. **jour**ney She went on a long **jour**ney.

3. ad**journ**[4] The judge **want**ed to ad**journ** the case.

4. **cour**age He had a lot of **cour**age to go on.

5. **glam**our **Holl**ywood is a **cit**y of **glam**our.

6. Stress and Intonation

A. The underlined letters in the words below represent the sound /ər/.

 1. As you listen to and repeat the sentences, place a stress mark (´) over the stressed words you hear.

 2. Pay attention to phrasing, function words, and intonation.

EXAMPLE: W<u>e</u>re you **ev**er h<u>ur</u>t in an **ac**cident?

 1. I had the w<u>or</u>st luck to**day.**

 2. I fell in ch<u>ur</u>ch and t<u>ur</u>ned my **an**kle.

 3. It h<u>ur</u>t so much I went to the e**mer**gency room in the **hos**pital.

 4. The n<u>ur</u>se said she would have to take an **X**-ray . . . you know . . . a **pic**t<u>ur</u>e, to see if there was a **frac**t<u>ur</u>e.

 5. I had to wait an e**ter**nity for the re**sults.**

 6. I be**came** quite con**cer**ned.

 7. How**ev**er, the n<u>ur</u>se told me not to be **ner**vous and con**cer**ned.

 8. **Fi**nally, I got the w<u>or</u>d!

 9. It was a bad sprain, no **frac**t<u>ur</u>e.

 10. It's too bad I don't have to re**turn;** there was a cute **in**t<u>er</u>n I had my eye on.

---

[4] *adjourn:* stop for a time

B. Work with a partner. Compare your copy with your partner. Did you stress the same words? Take turns reading alternate sentences. Monitor each other for correct stressing, use of function words, phrasing, and intonation.

7. Further Practice

A. Read the following story aloud. You can use a dictionary to help you with the meaning and pronunciation of new words.

   1. Underline all words that contain the sound /ər/. (*Hint:* There are 17 *different* words.)

   2. Place a stress mark over words you think are important.

   3. Record your reading. Monitor your stress, function words, phrasing, and intonation patterns. The first sentence is marked for you.

1. Last **Thurs**day, while I was **stand**ing on the **cor**ner of Third

2. **Av**enue and Thir**teenth** Street, I felt a **burn**ing sen**sa**tion in the palm

3. of my hand. I **did**n't know what had **happ**ened. **Sudd**enly I **re**alized

4. that I had been stung by a bee. My palm be**gan** to hurt and swell up.

5. My friend urged me to go to a **doc**tor. Since it was **Sun**day, I knew

6. that no **doc**tor would be in, so I de**cid**ed to go to the e**mer**gency

7. room of Uni**ver**sity **Hos**pital. **Man**y **peo**ple were there before me,

8. so I had to wait my turn. **Af**ter I had **wait**ed a long time, an **in**tern

9. **fi**nally looked at my hand. But, by that time, the pain had gone away

10. and the **swell**ing had gone down. I went home, **won**dering why I

11. **ev**er **both**ered **go**ing to the e**mer**gency room!

B. Did you or anyone you know ever have an emergency? Relate your experience to the class.

Unit 17

/ɔy/ **as in boy**

1. Producing /ɔy/

    EXAMPLES: <u>oi</u>l,[1] **<u>oy</u>s**ter, c<u>oi</u>n, s<u>oi</u>l, **r<u>oy</u>**al, en**<u>joy</u>**, t**<u>oy</u>**, em**<u>ploy</u>**ment

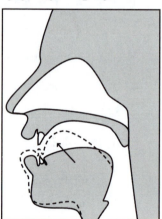

- Hold the front part of your tongue low in your mouth. Raise the *back* part toward the roof (soft palate) of the mouth (but do not touch it).
- Touch the lower front teeth lightly with the tip of the tongue.
- Drop your jaw and round your lips a little, protruding them (pushing them out) slightly.
- As you begin to say the sound, raise your jaw slightly as the front part of your tongue moves forward and up. Move your lips back slightly as you complete the sound.

2. Practice the Sound

    Students usually have no problem pronouncing the sound /ɔy/ as in "b<u>oy</u>."

A.   Practice the sound, first normally, then with exaggeration, then normally. Listen and repeat.

        /ɔy/   /ɔy . . . /   /ɔy/

---

[1]When /ɔy/ is followed by /l/, it usually helps to add the vowel /ə/ as in "<u>u</u>p" before /l/: /ɔyᵊl/, /bɔyᵊl/.

B. Now practice the sound in words. Notice the phonetic spelling. Listen and repeat each word twice.

     1. oil   /ɔyl/   oil

     2. boil   /bɔyl/   boil

     3. toy   /tɔy/   toy

     4. noise   /nɔyz/   noise

C. Practice the contrasting sounds /ɔy/ and /ay/. The first word in each pair has the sound /ɔy/ as in "boy," and the second has the sound /ay/ as in "buy." Listen and repeat.

     1a. toy   /tɔy/   toy

      b. tie   /tay/   tie

     2a. oil   /ɔyl/   oil

      b. aisle /ayl/   aisle

     3a. toil   /tɔyl/   toil

      b. tile   /tayl/   tile

     4a. points /pɔynts/ points

      b. pints /paynts/ pints

3. Check Your Listening

You will hear words with the sounds /ɔy/ and /ay/. First, cover the words in the following list with a piece of paper. Then listen to each word. Concentrate on the sound, not the spelling. Which vowel sound do you hear? Write a check mark in the correct column.

		/ɔy/ as in "boy"	/ay/ as in "buy"
file	1.	_____	_____
noise	2.	_____	_____
boil	3.	_____	_____

	/ɔy/ as in "b<u>oy</u>"	/ay/ as in "b<u>uy</u>"
t<u>ie</u>	4. _____	_____
b<u>oy</u>	5. _____	_____
m<u>i</u>ce	6. _____	_____
v<u>oi</u>ce	7. _____	_____
v<u>i</u>ce	8. _____	_____
c<u>oi</u>n	9. _____	_____
<u>oi</u>l	10. _____	_____

4. Practice the Contrast: /ɔy/ as in "b<u>oy</u>" with /ay/ as in "b<u>uy</u>"

Now practice the contrasting sounds /ɔy/ and /ay/ in sentence pairs. The first sentence in each pair has the sound /ɔy/ and the second has the sound /ay/. Listen and repeat.

1a. t<u>oy</u>   That's a nice t<u>oy</u> you bought.

 b. t<u>ie</u>   That's a nice t<u>ie</u> you bought.

2a. p<u>oi</u>nts   How **man**y p<u>oi</u>nts did you get?

 b. p<u>i</u>nts   How **man**y p<u>i</u>nts did you get?

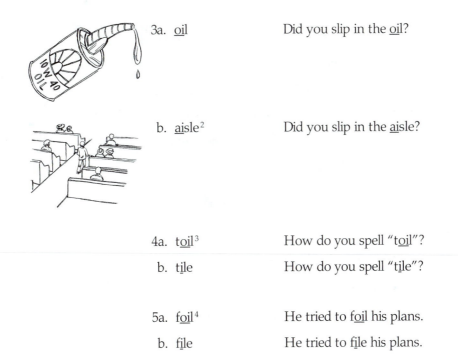

3a. <u>oi</u>l   Did you slip in the <u>oi</u>l?

b. <u>ai</u>sle[2]   Did you slip in the <u>ai</u>sle?

4a. t<u>oi</u>l[3]   How do you spell "t<u>oi</u>l"?

b. t<u>i</u>le   How do you spell "t<u>i</u>le"?

5a. f<u>oi</u>l[4]   He tried to f<u>oi</u>l his plans.

b. f<u>i</u>le   He tried to f<u>i</u>le his plans.

5. Stress and Intonation

1. Before you listen to the tape, underline the letters that represent the sound /ɔy/.

2. As you listen to the tape and repeat the sentences, mark the stressed words you hear with a stress mark (➚).

3. Pay attention to the falling or rising intonation at the end of the sentences, which are marked. (Remember to listen for function words and phrasing.)

EXAMPLE: The p<u>oi</u>nt is not to sp<u>oi</u>l the <u>oi</u>l.

1. I need an **oint**ment[5] for my boil.[6]

2. His voice was full of joy when he spoke of his boy.

3. The child **point**ed to the coin in the soil.

---

[2] Note that the "s" in "aisle" is not pronounced.

[3] _toil:_ work hard

[4] _foil:_ prevent someone from being successful

[5] _ointment:_ medicine in cream form

[6] _boil:_ a painful inflammation of the skin

4. We were **giv**en a choice to a**void** the **boy**cott.[7]

5. Do you think the **cor**duroy[8] pants were a good buy?

6. Who were the **sail**ors that were in the ship **con**voy?[9]

7. The **nois**y crowd was **loy**al to the **roy**al **coup**le.

8. Please point me to the em**ploy**ment **off**ice.

9. Do you like **oys**ters boiled or broiled?

10. I **can**celed my **voy**age when the bank **void**ed my check.

6. Further Practice

In the rhyme below, listen for the vowel sound /ɔy/, which is underlined.

1. Record yourself saying this old rhyme. Pay attention to the linking of words and the rhythm created.

2. Work with a partner. Help each other with the correct sounds, stress, and intonation.

1.   A little b<u>oy</u>

2.   Whose name was R<u>oy</u>

3.   Once had a t<u>oy</u>.

4.   There was a c<u>oi</u>l[10]

5.   Which **need**ed <u>oi</u>l.

6.   He **hat**ed t<u>oi</u>l

7.   And left it dry.

8.   The **en**gine b<u>oi</u>led,

9.   The toy was sp<u>oi</u>led,

10.   Its works were c<u>oi</u>led.

11.   He laid it by.

---

[7] *boycott:* refusal to buy a certain product or do business with a particular store or company

[8] *corduroy:* a strong, thick cloth with soft, raised lines, used to make pants, jackets, and suits

[9] *convoy:* an organized group of formation, especially of ships and trucks

[10] *coil:* something wrapped in a circle or spiral

Unit 18

/ɔ/ **as in _all_**

1. Producing /ɔ/[1]

EXAMPLES: **al**so, h**a**lt, **or**gan, **aw**ful, c**o**st, wr**o**ng, p**au**se, th**ou**ght, l**aw**

- This is the first part of the sound /ɔy/ as in "b**oy**."
- Hold the front part of your tongue low in your mouth, with the tip lightly touching the lower front teeth.
- Raise the _back_ of your tongue towards the roof (soft palate) of your mouth (but do not touch it).
- Drop your jaw, round your lips a little, protruding them (pushing them out) slightly.

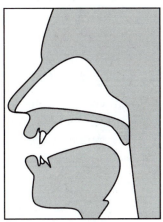

2. Contrast: /ɔ/, /ə/, /ɑ/, **and** /ɔy/

Students sometimes confuse the sound /ɔ/ as in "**all**" with other sounds. These sounds include /ə/ as in "**up**," /ɑ/ as in "n**o**t," and /ɔy/ as in "b**oy**."

A.   Practice these sounds, first normally, then with exaggeration, then normally. Listen and repeat.

    1. /ɔ/   /ɔ . . ./   /ɔ/
    2. /ə/   /ə . . ./   /ə/
    3. /ɑ/   /ɑ . . ./   /ɑ/
    4. /ɔy/   /ɔy . . ./   /ɔy/

---

[1]/ɔ/ as in "**all**" may be replaced by /ɑ/ as in "n**o**t" in some words, depending on which dialect of American English you hear. For example: "cost" (/kɑst/ for /kɔst/) and "wrong" (/rɑŋ/ for /rɔŋ/).

147

B. Now practice these sounds in words. Notice the phonetic spelling. Listen and repeat each word twice.

1.	<u>ough</u>t	/ɔt/	<u>ough</u>t
2.	l<u>aw</u>	/lɔ/	l<u>aw</u>
3.	b<u>oy</u>	/bɔy/	b<u>oy</u>
4.	v<u>oi</u>ce	/vɔys/	v<u>oi</u>ce
5.	f<u>u</u>n	/fən/	f<u>u</u>n
6.	n<u>o</u>ne	/nən/	n<u>o</u>ne
7.	f<u>ar</u>	/fɑr/	f<u>ar</u>
8.	n<u>o</u>t	/nɑt/	n<u>o</u>t
9.	<u>or</u>	/ɔr/	<u>or</u>
10.	s<u>aw</u>	/sɔ/	s<u>aw</u>

3. Check Your Listening

You will hear words with the sounds /ɔ/, /ɔy/, /ə/, and /ɑ/. First, cover the words in the following list with a piece of paper. Then listen to each word. Concentrate on the sound, not the spelling. Which vowel sound do you hear? Write a check mark in the correct column.

		/ɔ/ as in "<u>a</u>ll"	/ɔy/ as in "b<u>oy</u>"	/ə/ as in "<u>u</u>p"	/ɑ/ as in "n<u>o</u>t"
b<u>a</u>ll	1.	_____	_____	_____	_____
b<u>oi</u>l	2.	_____	_____	_____	_____
l<u>aw</u>n	3.	_____	_____	_____	_____
c<u>u</u>t	4.	_____	_____	_____	_____
m<u>u</u>st	5.	_____	_____	_____	_____
c<u>a</u>lm	6.	_____	_____	_____	_____
c<u>o</u>me	7.	_____	_____	_____	_____
j<u>aw</u>	8.	_____	_____	_____	_____
t<u>a</u>ll	9.	_____	_____	_____	_____
v<u>oi</u>ce	10.	_____	_____	_____	_____

4. Practice the Contrast: /ɔ/ as in "*a*ll" with /ɔy/ as in "b*oy*"

A. Practice these contrasting sounds. Listen and repeat each word pair.

/ɔ/	/ɔy/		/ɔ/	/ɔy/
1. all	oil	4.	Saul	soil
2. ball	boil	5.	raw	Roy
3. tall	toil	6.	jaw	joy

B. Now practice the contrasting sounds in sentence pairs. The first sentence of each pair has the sound /ɔy/, and the second has the sound /ɔ/. Listen and repeat.

1a. oil	Did you put oil in the pan?
b. all	Did you put all in the pan?

2a. boil	Did you see that he had a boil?
b. ball	Did you see that he had a ball?

3a. toil	What does "toil" mean?
b. tall	What does "tall" mean?

4a. s<u>oi</u>l	Did you see s<u>oi</u>l on his land?
b. S<u>au</u>l	Did you see S<u>au</u>l on his land?
5a. R<u>oy</u>	Eat it, R<u>oy</u>, be**fore** it gets cold.
b. r<u>aw</u>	Eat it r<u>aw</u> be**fore** it gets cold.
6a. j<u>oy</u>	It's a great j<u>oy</u>.
b. j<u>aw</u>	It's a great j<u>aw</u>.

5. Practice the Contrast: /ɔ/ as in "<u>a</u>ll" with /ə/ as in "<u>u</u>p"

A. Practice these contrasting sounds. Listen and repeat each word pair.

/ɔ/	/ə/		/ɔ/	/ə/
1. d<u>aw</u>n	d<u>o</u>ne	6. d<u>o</u>g	d<u>u</u>g
2. b<u>ough</u>t	b<u>u</u>t	7. l<u>o</u>ng	l<u>u</u>ng
3. c<u>augh</u>t	c<u>u</u>t	8. g<u>o</u>ne	g<u>u</u>n
4. c<u>ough</u>	c<u>u</u>ff	9. cr<u>o</u>ssed	cr<u>u</u>st[2]
5. b<u>o</u>ss	b<u>u</u>s	10. **c<u>a</u>ll**er	**c<u>o</u>l**or

B. Now practice the contrasting sounds in sentence pairs. The first sentence of each pair has the sound /ɔ/, and the second has the sound /ə/. Listen and repeat.

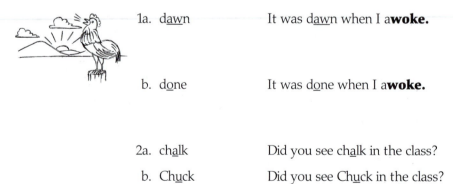

1a. d<u>aw</u>n	It was d<u>aw</u>n when I a**woke.**
b. d<u>o</u>ne	It was d<u>o</u>ne when I a**woke.**
2a. ch<u>a</u>lk	Did you see ch<u>a</u>lk in the class?
b. Ch<u>u</u>ck	Did you see Ch<u>u</u>ck in the class?

---

[2] *crust:* a hard covering

3a.	c<u>augh</u>t	It was c<u>augh</u>t just in time.	
b.	c<u>u</u>t	It was c<u>u</u>t just in time.	

4a.	b<u>o</u>ss	My b<u>o</u>ss **al**ways a**rrives** late.	
b.	b<u>u</u>s	My b<u>u</u>s **al**ways a**rrives** late.	

5a.	c<u>ou</u>gh	He has a c<u>ou</u>gh.	
b.	c<u>u</u>ff	He has a c<u>u</u>ff.	

6a.	**call**er	We can see the **call**er through the door.
b.	**col**or	We can see the **col**or through the door.

6. Practice the Contrast: /ɔ/ as in "<u>a</u>ll" with /ɑ/ as in "n<u>o</u>t"

A. Practice these contrasting sounds. Listen and repeat each word pair.

/ɔ/	/ɑ/		/ɔ/	/ɑ/
1. p<u>aw</u>	P<u>a</u>	6. p<u>or</u>t	p<u>ar</u>t
2. t<u>augh</u>t	t<u>o</u>t	7. p<u>or</u>k	p<u>ar</u>k
3. c<u>augh</u>t	c<u>o</u>t	8. c<u>our</u>t	c<u>ar</u>t
4. f<u>or</u>	f<u>ar</u>	9. c<u>or</u>d	c<u>ar</u>d
5. b<u>or</u>n	b<u>ar</u>n	10. **for**mer[3]	**far**mer

---

[3] *former:* previous; past

B. Now practice the contrasting sounds in sentence pairs. The first sentence of each pair has the sound /ɔ/, and the second has the sound /ɑ/. Listen and repeat.

1a. p<u>aw</u>

His p<u>aw</u> was hurt in the **ac**cident.

b. P<u>a</u>

His P<u>a</u> was hurt in the **ac**cident.

2a. st<u>o</u>re

I see the st<u>o</u>re **ev**ery night.

b. st<u>a</u>r

I see the st<u>a</u>r **ev**ery night.

3a. p<u>o</u>rt [4]

That p<u>o</u>rt was not **ver**y good.

b. p<u>a</u>rt

That p<u>a</u>rt was not **ver**y good.

4a. c<u>ou</u>rt

All the **peo**ple were in the c<u>ou</u>rt.

b. c<u>a</u>rt

All the **peo**ple were in the c<u>a</u>rt.

---

[4] *port:* a type of sweet wine

5a.	c̲ord	He still has the c̲ord we gave him.
b.	c̲ard	He still has the c̲ard we gave him.

6a.	**fo̲r**mer	The **fo̲r**mer is from the state of **Tex**as.
b.	**fa̲r**mer	The **fa̲r**mer is from the state of **Tex**as.

7. Stress and Intonation

A. The following dialog contains the sounds /ɔ/ as in "a̲ll" and /ɑ/ as in "no̲t."

   1. Before you listen to and repeat the following sentences, place a <u>single</u> line under the letter(s) representing the sound /ɔ/ and a <u>double</u> line under the letter(s) representing the sound /ɑ/.

   2. As you listen to the tape, mark the rising or falling intonation patterns with an arrow (⌐⌐ ⌐⌐).

EXAMPLE: **Shopp**ing at a W̲atch **Coun**ter in a De**p̲art**ment St̲ore

   1. Sales Clerk: Good **mor**ning. May I help you?

   2. **Cus**tomer: Yes, I'd like to see a watch, please.

   3. Sales Clerk: **An**ything in par**tic**ular?

   4. **Cus**tomer: I'm **look**ing for a **pres**ent for my **boy**friend.

   5. Sales Clerk: What price range did you have in mind?

   6. **Cus**tomer: **Some**thing a**round** $100.00 (a **hun**dred **doll**ars).

7. Sales Clerk: This is a **Lon**gines. The price is right. It's only $99.99 (**nine**ty-nine, **nine**ty-nine).

8. **Cus**tomer: Is it a quartz? I **on**ly want a quartz.

9. Sales Clerk: Yes, of course it's a quartz.

10. **Cus**tomer: How about that watch, the one in the **cor**ner?

11. Sales Clerk: Oh, the Mo**va**do? That costs $440.99 (four-**hun**dred and **for**ty, **nine**ty-nine).

12. **Cus**tomer: May I see it?

13. Sales Clerk: Of course. But **is**n't it out of your price range?

14. **Cus**tomer: Do you have a Mo**va**do that's **cheap**er—I mean, uh, less ex**pen**sive?

15. Sales Clerk: This is the **cheap**est Mo**va**do we have. They don't come any **cheap**er. What a**bout** the **Lon**gines?

16. **Cus**tomer: But I don't like the **Lon**gines. I like the Mo**va**do.

17. Sales Clerk: Well, you know it's a good buy and it's on sale.

18. **Cus**tomer: Well, I'll think a**bout** it. No, I'll take it! Please gift wrap it.

19. Sales Clerk: I think you've made a good choice. Your **boy**friend will love it.

20. **Cus**tomer: Thank you.

21. Sales Clerk: Have a nice day!

B. Work with a partner. Compare your copy with your partner. Do you have the same markings? Now decide which words you would like to stress and place a stress mark (✔) over them. Take turns reading the dialog to each other. Check each other for "correct" stressing of words, and use of function words, phrasing, and intonation.

C. Did you or someone you know ever pay more than planned for something? Did a sales clerk ever talk you or someone you know into buying something that was not really wanted? Discuss your experience in class.

8. Further Practice

A. Unscramble the letters to make words with the sound /ɔ/ as in "a̱ll." Write the words in the spaces provided. Then say the words aloud.

EXAMPLES: a.   remo   *more*

                     b.   fgthou   *fought*

1. wnad   _____   6. gnlo   _____

2. ngroimn   _____   7. rood   _____

3. lalh   _____   8. alwl   _____

4. lalm   _____   9. kalt   _____

5. eostr   _____   10. drebor   _____

B. Each of the following sentences is missing a word that rhymes with another word in the sentence. Both words have the sound /ɔ/ as in "a̱ll." Choose a word from the list above to complete the sentence. The first letter of the word is given.

EXAMPLE: a.   He to̱re it m*ore*_____.

                     b.   He tho̱ught he fo̱ught.

1. There's **o̱r**der on the b_____.

2. It's on the flo̱or near the d_____.

3. It's a̱ll on the w_____.

4. The fo̱ur went to the s_____.

5. His ba̱ll is in the h_____.

6. See the la̱wn at d_____.

7. Pa̱ul shopped at the m_____.

8. Let's wa̱lk and t_____.

9. The so̱ng is l_____.

10. He was ya̱wning in the m_____.

Unit 19

/ow/ **as in _no_**

1. Producing /ow/

EXAMPLES: <u>o</u>h, **o**pen, h<u>o</u>me,[1] b<u>oa</u>t, s<u>ou</u>l, s<u>ew</u>, **car**g<u>o</u>

- Hold the front part of your tongue low in your mouth, with the tip lightly touching the lower front teeth.
- As you begin to say the sound, raise the _back_ of your tongue towards the roof (soft palate) of your mouth (but do not touch it).
- Round your lips and push them forward a little.
- The opening of your mouth is smaller than for the sound /ɔ/ as in "<u>a</u>ll."

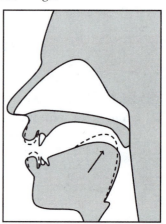

2. Contrast: /ow/, /ɔ/, /ɑ/, **and** /ə/

Sometimes students confuse the sound /ow/ as in "n<u>o</u>" with other sounds. These sounds include /ɔ/ as in "<u>a</u>ll," /ɑ/ as in "n<u>o</u>t," and /ə/ as in "<u>u</u>p."

A. Practice these sounds, first normally, then with exaggeration, then normally. Listen and repeat.

1. /ow/   /ow . . . /   /ow/
2. /ɔ/   /ɔ . . . /   /ɔ/
3. /ɑ/   /ɑ . . . /   /ɑ/
4. /ə/   /ə . . . /   /ə/

---

[1] The final "e" in words such as "home" and "note" signals the /ow/ pronunciation for the letter "o." Compare "not" /nɑt/ with "note" /nowt/.

B. Now practice these sounds in words. Notice the phonetic spelling. Listen and repeat each word twice.

1. <u>o</u>h	/ow/	<u>o</u>h
2. s<u>ew</u>	/sow/	s<u>ew</u>
3. l<u>aw</u>	/lɔ/	l<u>aw</u>
4. t<u>a</u>lk	/tɔk/	t<u>a</u>lk
5. c<u>a</u>lm	/kɑm/	c<u>a</u>lm
6. n<u>o</u>t	/nɑt/	n<u>o</u>t
7. c<u>u</u>t	/kət/	c<u>u</u>t
8. n<u>u</u>t	/nət/	n<u>u</u>t
9. b<u>oa</u>t	/bowt/	b<u>oa</u>t
10. b<u>o</u>ne	/bown/	b<u>o</u>ne

3. Check Your Listening

You will hear words with the sounds /ow/, /ɔ/, /ɑ/, and /ə/. First, cover the words in the following list with a piece of paper. Then listen to each word. Concentrate on the sound, not the spelling. Which vowel sound do you hear? Write a check mark in the correct column.

		/ow/ as in "n<u>o</u>"	/ɔ/ as in "<u>a</u>ll"	/ɑ/ as in "n<u>o</u>t"	/ə/ as in "<u>u</u>p"
b<u>ow</u>l	1.	_____	_____	_____	_____
b<u>a</u>ll	2.	_____	_____	_____	_____
c<u>oa</u>t	3.	_____	_____	_____	_____
c<u>u</u>t	4.	_____	_____	_____	_____
l<u>aw</u>n	5.	_____	_____	_____	_____
p<u>o</u>t	6.	_____	_____	_____	_____
b<u>u</u>t	7.	_____	_____	_____	_____
c<u>o</u>me	8.	_____	_____	_____	_____
c<u>a</u>lm	9.	_____	_____	_____	_____
b<u>oa</u>t	10.	_____	_____	_____	_____

4. Practice the Contrast: /ow/ as in "n<u>o</u>" with /ɔ/ as in "<u>a</u>ll"

A. Practice these contrasting sounds. Listen and repeat each word pair.

	/ow/	/ɔ/			/ow/	/ɔ/
1.	b<u>ow</u>l²	b<u>a</u>ll	6.		b<u>oa</u>t	b<u>ough</u>t
2.	p<u>o</u>le	P<u>au</u>l	7.		w<u>o</u>ke	w<u>a</u>lk
3.	c<u>oa</u>l	c<u>a</u>ll	8.		ch<u>o</u>ke	ch<u>a</u>lk
4.	c<u>oa</u>st	c<u>o</u>st	9.		s<u>ew</u>	s<u>aw</u>
5.	c<u>oa</u>t	c<u>augh</u>t	10.		cl<u>o</u>se	cl<u>au</u>se

B. Now practice the contrasting sounds in sentence pairs. The first sentence of each pair has the sound /ow/, and the second has the sound /ɔ/. Listen and repeat.

1a. b<u>ow</u>l   A b<u>ow</u>l is on the **ta**ble.

b. b<u>a</u>ll   A b<u>a</u>ll is on the **ta**ble.

2a. h<u>o</u>le   Put it in the h<u>o</u>le while we're here.

b. h<u>a</u>ll   Put it in the h<u>a</u>ll while we're here.

3a. l<u>oa</u>n   I'm **in**terested in the l<u>oa</u>n.

b. l<u>aw</u>n   I'm **in**terested in the l<u>aw</u>n.

_____

² When /ow/ is followed by /l/, it usually helps to add the vowel /ə/ as in "<u>u</u>p" before /l/: /bowᵊl/, /powᵊl/.

4a. c<u>oa</u>l   He took the c<u>oa</u>l in the **base**ment.

b. c<u>a</u>ll   He took the c<u>a</u>ll in the **base**ment.

5a. l<u>ow</u>   We all know his voice is l<u>ow</u>.

b. l<u>aw</u>   We all know his voice is l<u>aw</u>.

6a. p<u>o</u>se   Can you p<u>o</u>se by the desk?

b. p<u>au</u>se   Can you p<u>au</u>se by the desk?

5. Practice the Contrast: /ow/ as in "n<u>o</u>," /ɑ/ as in "n<u>o</u>t," and /ə/ as in "<u>up</u>"

A. Practice these contrasting sounds. Listen and repeat each group of three words.

/ow/	/ɑ/	/ə/		/ow/	/ɑ/	/ə/
1. n<u>o</u>te	n<u>o</u>t	n<u>u</u>t	4. c<u>oa</u>t	c<u>o</u>t	c<u>u</u>t
2. c<u>o</u>mb	c<u>a</u>lm	c<u>o</u>me	5. r<u>o</u>be	r<u>o</u>b	r<u>u</u>b
3. c<u>o</u>pe[3]	c<u>o</u>p	c<u>u</u>p	6. ph<u>o</u>ned	f<u>o</u>nd	f<u>u</u>nd

B. Now practice the contrasting sounds in sentences. The first sentence of each group has the sound /ow/, the second has the sound /ɑ/, and the third has the sound /ə/. Listen and repeat.

1a. n<u>o</u>te   Did you see the n<u>o</u>te?

b. kn<u>o</u>t   Did you see the kn<u>o</u>t?

c. n<u>u</u>t   Did you see the n<u>u</u>t?

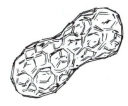

---

[3] *cope:* face difficulties and try to overcome them

2a. c<u>o</u>mb   How do you pro**nounce** "c<u>o</u>mb"?

b. c<u>a</u>lm   How do you pro**nounce** "c<u>a</u>lm"?

c. c<u>o</u>me   How do you pro**nounce** "c<u>o</u>me"?

3a. c<u>oa</u>t   She has a new c<u>oa</u>t.

b. c<u>o</u>t   She has a new c<u>o</u>t.

c. c<u>u</u>t   She has a new c<u>u</u>t.

4a. r<u>o</u>be   He heard him say "r<u>o</u>be."

b. r<u>o</u>b   He heard him say "r<u>o</u>b."

c. r<u>u</u>b   He heard him say "r<u>u</u>b."

5a. c<u>o</u>pe   The word was "c<u>o</u>pe."

b. c<u>o</u>p   The word was "c<u>o</u>p."

c. c<u>u</u>p   The word was "c<u>u</u>p."

6a. ph<u>o</u>ned   Who said it was "ph<u>o</u>ned"?

  b. f<u>o</u>nd   Who said it was "f<u>o</u>nd"?

  c. f<u>u</u>nd   Who said it was "f<u>u</u>nd"?

6. Stress and Intonation

1. Before you listen to the tape, underline the letters that represent the vowel sound /ow/ as in "n<u>o</u>."

2. Now listen to the tape and repeat the sentences. Mark the stressed words you hear with a stress mark (ˊ). Pay attention to function words, phrasing, and intonation.

EXAMPLES: a. J<u>oa</u>n lost her **ov**erc<u>oa</u>t.

    b. Did she lose it in the m<u>oa</u>t?[4]

1a. The **toast**er is **brok**en.

  b. I can't buy one for a **tok**en.

2a. He told me a joke.

  b. I gave him a poke.[5]

3a. I know I'm a**lone.**

  b. I want to go home.

4a. He's a home **ow**ner.

  b. He's **al**so a **lon**er.[6]

5a. Do you know your zip code?

  b. I do, but you won't be told.

---

[4] *moat:* a deep hole filled with water, usually built for defense around a castle
[5] *poke:* a sharp push, usually with one's finger
[6] *loner:* a person who avoids the company of others

7. Further Practice

The following is an Arabic proverb.

1. Draw a single line under all words that have the /ow/ sound as in "n<u>o</u>."

2. The stressed words are marked.

3. Tape-record your reading. Pay attention to the stressed words, especially the phrasing. The first line is marked for you.

1.   He who <u>knows,</u> and <u>knows</u> he <u>knows,</u>

2.   He is wise—**foll**ow him.

3.   He who knows, and knows not he knows,

4.   He is a**sleep**—wake him.

5.   He who knows not, and knows not he knows not,

6.   He is a fool—shun[7] him.

7.   He who knows not, and knows he knows not,

8.   He is a child—teach him.

---

[7] *shun:* turn away from

Unit 20

/uw/ **as in *do***
/ʊ/ **as in *book***

1. Producing /uw/[1]

EXAMPLES: thr<u>ough</u>, wh<u>o</u>se, j<u>ui</u>ce, t<u>oo</u>, sh<u>oe</u>, tr<u>ue</u>, bl<u>ew</u>

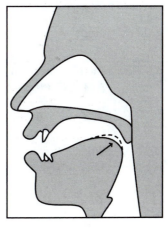

- Hold the front part of your tongue low in your mouth, with the tip lightly touching the lower front teeth.
- As you begin to say the sounds, raise the *back* of your tongue toward the roof (soft palate) of your mouth (but don't touch it).
- Round your lips and push them out. The opening is smaller than for the sound /ow/ as in "n<u>o</u>."
- Place your thumb underneath your chin to feel the *tense* muscles.

---

[1] The combination /**yuw**/ is very common and occurs in words such as "union," "cute," "beauty," and "few." See Unit 32 for other examples and practice.

2. Producing /ʊ/

EXAMPLES: p<u>u</u>t, **b<u>u</u>tch**er, c<u>oo</u>k, **s<u>u</u>g**ar, w<u>o</u>lf, w<u>ou</u>ld

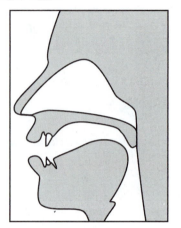

- Hold the front part of your tongue low in your mouth, with the tip lightly touching the lower front teeth.
- As you begin to say the sound, raise the *back* of your tongue toward the roof (soft palate) of the mouth but lower than for the sound /uw/ as in "d<u>o</u>."
- Your lips should be close together and may be slightly rounded (but not pushed out). The jaw is lowered slightly. /ʊ/ is a *short* vowel sound.
- Place your thumb underneath your chin. The muscles are relaxed.

3. Contrast: /uw/, /ʊ/, and /ə/

Students sometimes confuse the sounds /uw/ as in "d<u>o</u>," /ʊ/ as in "b<u>oo</u>k," and /ə/ as in "<u>u</u>p."

A. Practice these sounds, first normally, then with exaggeration, then normally. Listen and repeat.

1. /uw/   /uw . . . /   /uw/

2. /ʊ/   /ʊ . . . /   /ʊ/

3. /ə/   /ə . . . /   /ə/

B. Now practice these sounds in words. Notice the phonetic spelling. Listen and repeat each word twice.

1. tw<u>o</u>   /tuw/   tw<u>o</u>

2. wh<u>o</u>   /huw/   wh<u>o</u>

3. b<u>oo</u>k   /bʊk/   b<u>oo</u>k

4. t<u>oo</u>k   /tʊk/   t<u>oo</u>k

5. s<u>u</u>n   /sən/   s<u>u</u>n

6. m<u>u</u>st   /məst/   m<u>u</u>st

7. f<u>oo</u>d   /fuwd/   f<u>oo</u>d

8. w<u>ou</u>ld   /wʊd/   w<u>ou</u>ld

4. Check Your Listening

You will hear words with the sounds /uw/, /ʊ/, and /ə/. First, cover the words in the following list with a piece of paper. Then listen to each word. Concentrate on the sound, not the spelling. Which vowel sound do you hear? Write a check mark in the correct column.

		/uw/ as in "d**o**"	/ʊ/ as in "b**oo**k"	/ə/ as in "**u**p"
d**o**	1.	_____	_____	_____
b**oo**k	2.	_____	_____	_____
up	3.	_____	_____	_____
f**u**n	4.	_____	_____	_____
c**u**t	5.	_____	_____	_____
t**oo**k	6.	_____	_____	_____
sch**oo**l	7.	_____	_____	_____
st**oo**d	8.	_____	_____	_____
tr**u**e	9.	_____	_____	_____
c**ou**ld	10.	_____	_____	_____

5. Practice the Contrast: /uw/ as in "d**o**" with /ʊ/ as in "b**oo**k"

A. Practice these contrasting sounds. Listen and repeat each word pair.

/uw/	/ʊ/		/uw/	/ʊ/
1. p**oo**l	p**u**ll		4. c**oo**ed[2]	c**ou**ld
2. f**oo**l	f**u**ll		5. wh**o**'d	h**oo**d
3. L**u**ke	l**oo**k		6. st**ew**ed[3]	st**oo**d

[2] *cooed:* past tense of the verb "to coo" (to make a soft murmuring sound)
[3] *stewed:* past tense of the verb "to stew" (to cook)

B. Now practice the contrasting sounds in sentence pairs. The first sentence of each pair has the sound /uw/ and the second has the sound /ʊ/. Listen and repeat.

1a. p<u>oo</u>l[4]   Don't p<u>oo</u>l them right now.

  b. p<u>u</u>ll   Don't p<u>u</u>ll them right now.

2a. f<u>oo</u>l   He **whis**pered "f<u>oo</u>l."

  b. f<u>u</u>ll   He **whis**pered "f<u>u</u>ll."

3a. L<u>u</u>ke   We all cried, "L<u>u</u>ke!"

  b. l<u>oo</u>k   We all cried, "L<u>oo</u>k!"

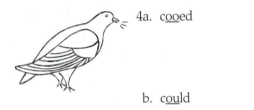

4a. c<u>oo</u>ed   He said they c<u>oo</u>ed.

  b. c<u>ou</u>ld   He said they c<u>ou</u>ld.

5a. wh<u>o</u>'d   Did you say "wh<u>o</u>'d"?

  b. h<u>oo</u>d   Did you say "h<u>oo</u>d"?

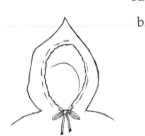

---

[4] *pool:* combine funds for some purpose

6a. st<u>ew</u>ed   It st<u>ew</u>ed on the gas range.

b. st<u>oo</u>d   It st<u>oo</u>d on the gas range.

6. Practice the Contrast: /ʊ/ as in "b<u>oo</u>k" with /ə/ as in "<u>u</u>p"

A. Practice these contrasting sounds. Listen and repeat each word pair.

/ʊ/	/ə/		/ʊ/	/ə/
1. l<u>oo</u>k	l<u>u</u>ck		4. p<u>u</u>t	p<u>u</u>tt[7]
2. t<u>oo</u>k	t<u>u</u>ck[5]		5. st<u>oo</u>d	st<u>u</u>d
3. b<u>oo</u>k	b<u>u</u>ck[6]		6. h<u>oo</u>ks	H<u>u</u>ck's

B. Now practice the contrasting sounds in sentence pairs. The first sentence of each pair has the sound /ʊ/, and the second has the sound /ə/. Listen and repeat.

1a. l<u>oo</u>k   Her l<u>oo</u>k changed **sudd**enly.

b. l<u>u</u>ck   Her l<u>u</u>ck changed **sudd**enly.

2a. t<u>oo</u>k   They **al**ways t<u>oo</u>k the sheet in.

b. t<u>u</u>ck   They **al**ways t<u>u</u>ck the sheet in.

3a. b<u>oo</u>k   I don't need a b<u>oo</u>k.

b. b<u>u</u>ck   I don't need a b<u>u</u>ck.

---

[5] *tuck:* push or put into a desired position
[6] *buck:* a U.S. dollar
[7] *putt:* hit a golf ball a short distance

4a. p<u>u</u>t   Will he p<u>u</u>t the ball there?

 b. p<u>u</u>tt   Will he p<u>u</u>tt the ball there?

5a. st<u>oo</u>d   Why did he say "st<u>oo</u>d"?

 b. st<u>u</u>d[8]   Why did he say "st<u>u</u>d"?

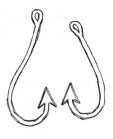

6a. h<u>oo</u>ks   H<u>oo</u>ks are much **bett**er.

 b. H<u>u</u>ck's   H<u>u</u>ck's are much **bett**er.

---

[8] *stud:* a decorative button

7. Stress and Intonation

1. Before you listen to the tape recording, place a <u>single</u> line under the letters for the vowel sound /uw/ as in "do," a <u>double</u> line for /ʊ/ as in book," and a <u>triple</u> line for /ə/ as in "up."

2. As you listen to the tape and repeat the sentences, check your markings.

3. The stressed words and falling and rising intonations are marked.

4. Pay attention to function words and phrasing. Remember that words like "was," "you," "for," and "of," when not stressed, are said in their reduced forms in conversational speech. (See Unit 5.) Listen and repeat.

EXAMPLE: My tooth was pulled by the **den**tist who lives up**stairs.**

1. The fool was pushed.
2. I choose the wool.
3. It's a new book, **is**n't it?
4. Could we go for lunch?
5. Who is that **wom**an?

6. He should make a lot of **mon**ey.
7. Look on the **oth**er page.
8. Would you go with my **un**cle?
9. The soup is full of salt.
10. That **wom**an has **musc**les.

8. Dialog

A. Before you listen to the tape recording, place a <u>single</u> line under the words that contain the sound /uw/ as in "do" and a <u>double</u> line under the words that contain /ʊ/ as in "book."

1. As you listen to the recording and repeat the sentences, mark the falling or rising intonation with an arrow (⌐ ⌐).

2. Pay attention to stressed words, function words, and phrasing.

1. **Mi**chiko: Do you know **any**thing a**bout** Luke—the **fell**ow who was in the **res**taurant?

2. To**mas**:   Luke? You mean the cook?

3. **Mi**chiko: Luke's the cook? But he's so young, and he's such a good cook!

4. To**mas**: That's true. Why do you think I took you there?

5. **Mi**chiko: I had a **won**derful time. Thank you.

6. To**mas**: It was my **pleas**ure. Can we do it a**gain** soon?

7. **Mi**chiko: I'd love it. I had lots of fun. I'm **go**ing out of town to**morr**ow, but I'll be back on **Tues**day.

8. To**mas**: Great! I'll call you **Tues**day, **af**ter school.

9. **Mi**chiko: Cool.[9] Good night.

10. To**mas**: Good night.

B. Work with a partner. Take turns reading the dialog. Check each other for correct pronunciation, stress, and intonation.

9. Further Practice

A. Some common English expressions are listed below. The underlined letters represent either /uw/ as in "d<u>o</u>" or /ʊ/ as in "b<u>oo</u>k." A definition for each expression appears in parentheses.

1. Read each expression and sentence aloud to yourself. Use a dictionary to help you with the pronunciation of any new words.

2. Mark the stressed words you think are important.

EXAMPLE: p<u>u</u>ll thr<u>ough</u> (get better after an illness)

The **ac**cident was so **ser**ious that **ev**en the **doc**tor **did**n't think he would p<u>u</u>ll thr<u>ough</u>.

1. once in a bl<u>ue</u> m<u>oo</u>n (very seldom)

He sees his **un**cle once in a bl<u>ue</u> m<u>oo</u>n.

2. c<u>oo</u>k up (think up something)

Don't **worr**y, we'll c<u>oo</u>k up a **stor**y, **an**y **stor**y.

3. **foo**ling a**round** (doing useless things)

Stop **foo**ling a**round** and get back to work.

---

[9] *cool:* a slang expression meaning "excellent"

4. **could**n't care less (don't mind at all)

   I **could**n't care less if I **nev**er see him a**gain.**

5. do a good turn (do something that benefits someone else)

   You'll do me a good turn if you reco**mmend** me for the job.

6. be on **du**ty; be off **du**ty (working at one's job; not working)

   The nurse went on **du**ty at ten and off **du**ty at four.

7. look down on (regard as inferior)

   He looks down on **an**yone **mak**ing less **mon**ey than he does.

8. foot the bill (pay the cost or expense)

   My **fath**er will foot the bill for my va**ca**tion.

9. in the mood (want something)

   I'm in the mood for a hot fudge **sun**dae.

10. pull some strings (use influence)

    My **fath**er pulled some strings to get me that a**part**ment.

In the columns below, list all words in the sentences that contain the sounds /uw/ or /ʊ/. (Hint: There are six _different_ words that contain the vowel /uw/ and six _different_ words that contain the vowel /ʊ/.

	/uw/ as in "do"	/ʊ/ as in "book"
EXAMPLE:	_through_	_pull_
1.	_____	_____
2.	_____	_____
3.	_____	_____
4.	_____	_____
5.	_____	_____
6.	_____	_____

B. Think of five expressions in your native language that may be similar to those above. Discuss them with the class.

Part 4

Consonant Sounds

The consonant sounds of American English are shown in the chart on pages 176–177. There are three major things to consider when producing consonant sounds:

1. Place of Articulation

Which articulators (lips, teeth, tongue, etc.) help us shape the sound? Say /m/ as in "me." Your lips are closed. Say /f/ as in "food." Your upper teeth touch the inner part of your lower lip. Say /d/ as in "day." Your tongue touches your upper gum ridge.

2. Manner of Production

How does the air flow out of the mouth or nose?

a. For some sounds the flow of air is stopped and then continued. Say /t/ as in "toy." Your tongue stops the flow of air for a moment. As you complete the sound, a puff of air escapes from your mouth. This type of sound is called *stop-plosive*.[1]

b. For some sounds a little noise (friction) is created when the air flows out. Say /f/ as in "food." Do you hear the noise? This type of sound is called *fricative*.[1]

c. For some sounds the air flows out of the nose. Say /m/ as in "me." Your lips are closed. Place your finger underneath your nose and feel the air flowing out. This type of sound is called *nasal*. All sounds that are not stop-plosives (with two exceptions) are called *continuants*[1] because they can be held as long as your breath allows.

---

[1] These terms are for your reference. See the chart on pages 176–177.

d. For some sounds the air flows out of the mouth, in the same way it does for vowel sounds, as the lips and tongue move smoothly (or glide) from one position to another. Say /w/ as in "<u>w</u>alk." Do you feel the air flowing out evenly? This type of sound is called *glide* or *semi-vowel*.[2]

3. Voiced or Voiceless Sounds

In Unit 2 you practiced placing two fingers on your throat while saying /z/ as in "<u>z</u>oo" and /s/ as in "<u>s</u>ee." When you say /z/, your vocal cords vibrate. Sounds made with vocal cords vibrating are *voiced*. When you say /s/, your vocal cords do not vibrate. Sounds made with no vibration of the vocal cords are *voiceless*.

---

[2] These terms are for your reference. See the chart on pages 176–177.

Consonant Chart

Place of Articulation	Manner of Production				
	Stop-plosives		Fricatives		
	VL	VD	VL	VD	
			Continuants		
Two lips	/p/ (pen) /b/ (boy) Lips are closed; air builds up and is released when lips part.				
Teeth and lip			/f/ (food) /v/ (voice) Upper teeth contact inside of lower lip; air is forced through.		
Tongue tip and teeth			/θ/ (thin) /ð/ (the) Tip of tongue is between teeth; air is forced through.		
Tongue tip and upper gum ridge	/t/ (ten) /d/ (day) Tongue tip is on upper gum ridge; air builds up and is released when tongue tip is removed.		/s/ (see) /z/ (zoo) Tongue tip is close to upper gum ridge; air is forced through narrow opening formed by tongue.		
Tongue and roof of mouth (hard palate)			/ʃ/ (she) /ʒ/ (pleasure) Front part of tongue is raised toward roof of mouth; air passes over tongue; lips are rounded.		
Back of tongue and back of roof of mouth (soft palate)	/k/ (cat) /g/ (go) Back of tongue touches soft palate; air builds up and is released when back of tongue is lowered.				
Glottis			/h/ - (house) Formed at the vocal cords as air passes through small opening between them.		

	Nasals VD	Glides/Semi-Vowels VD	Affricates VL VD
	/m/ (<u>m</u>e) Lips are closed; air passes out through nose.	/w/ (<u>w</u>alk) Back of tongue is high in mouth; lips are rounded.	
	/n/ (<u>n</u>o) Tip of tongue is on upper gum ridge; air passes out through nose.	/l/ (<u>l</u>ike) Tongue tip is on upper gum ridge; air passes out over sides of tongue. /r/ (<u>r</u>ed) Tongue tip points to upper gum ridge but does not touch it; air passes over tongue.	
		/y/ (<u>y</u>es) Center part of tongue is raised toward roof of mouth; air passes over tongue.	/tʃ/ /dʒ/ (<u>ch</u>ild) (<u>j</u>ob) Combination of /t/ and /ʃ/; combination of /d/ and /ʒ/. Both are said quickly.
	/ŋ/ (ki<u>ng</u>) Back of tongue touches soft palate; air passes out through nose.		

Unit 21

/l/ as in *like*

1. Producing /l/

EXAMPLES: love, land, luck, be**low**, **col**or, **yell**ow, a**lone**, **fi**nal, fa**ll**,
little [1]

- Place the tip of your tongue against your upper gum
  ridge.
- As you make the sound, air flows out over the sides
  of your tongue.
- Your vocal cords vibrate.

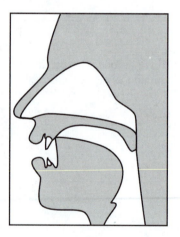

2. Practice the Sound

A. Practice the sound /l/ as in "like," first normally, then with exaggeration,[2] then
normally. Listen and repeat.

/l/   /l . . . /   /l/

------

[1] The last sound of "little" is an example of a "syllabic /l/" (it forms a syllable by itself). See page 209.
[2] Whenever you exaggerate, remember to s-t-r-e-t-c-h out the sound to get the "feel" of it.

> Reminder: Vowel sounds are held longer before _voiced_ consonants than before _voiceless_ consonants. (See Unit 4.)

B. Now practice the sound in words. Notice the phonetic spelling. Listen and repeat each word twice.

1. leave	/liyv/	leave
2. leg	/lɛg/	leg
3. **bal**ance	/bæləns/	**bal**ance
4. **tel**ephone	/tɛləfown/	**tel**ephone
5. school	/skuwl/	school
6. kill	/kɪl/	kill

3. Check Your Listening

In the following pairs of words, one word ends with the sound /l/. Circle the word in which you hear the sound /l/.

1. me	meal		5. so	soul
2. my	mile		6. say	sale
3. boy	boil		7. pay	pail
4. too	tool		8. why	while

4. Different Positions of /l/

Practice the sound /l/ as in "like" in several different positions. Listen and repeat these words.

/l/ IN INITIAL POSITION		
1. look	5. **la**bor	9. **li**cense
2. lunch	6. **le**gal	10. **law**yer
3. laugh	7. **lec**ture	11. **lead**er
4. loud	8. **lov**er	12. **lit**erature

/l/ IN MEDIAL POSITION		
1. a**live**	5. **coll**ege	9. **re**alize
2. a**larm**	6. **fam**ily	10. **is**land[3]
3. be**lieve**	7. po**lite**	11. **pop**ular
4. **doll**ar	8. **toi**let	12. in**tell**igent

/l/ IN FINAL POSITION[4]		
1. a**ll**	5. hee**l**	9. **ann**ual
2. poo**l**	6. **di**al	10. in**stall**
3. sma**ll**	7. **fe**male	11. con**trol**
4. we**ll**	8. **A**pril	12. **sched**ule

5. No Sound for "l"

A. In some words, the letter "l" is not pronounced. Listen and repeat the following words and sentences.

1. pa~~l~~m   There's a pa~~l~~m tree in front of my house.

2. ca~~l~~m   The **wa**ter was ca~~l~~m **af**ter the storm.

3. ta~~l~~k   Don't ta~~l~~k to your **en**emies.

4. wa~~l~~k   Don't wa~~l~~k on that path.

5. cha~~l~~k   Use the cha~~l~~k when you write on the **cha~~l~~k**board.

6. cou~~l~~d   I said you cou~~l~~d go, but not with**out** me.

---

[3] The "s" in "island" is not pronounced.

[4] Adding the sound /ə/ as in "<u>up</u>" before some sounds may help you produce the sound better. For example: "heel" /hiy°l/; "I'll" /ay°l/.

7. wou/d | He said he wou/d go, but not with me.

8. shou/d | We said they shou/d go, all to**geth**er.

9. **Lin**co/n | **A**braham **Lin**co/n was our six**teenth Pres**ident.

10. **sa/m**on | I'd like to eat **sa/m**on for lunch.

B. Think of five sentences with the following words in which "l" is silent. You can use a dictionary to help you with the pronunciation. Be prepared to discuss them in class.

1. so/der   2. sta/king   3. psa/m   4. sa/ve   5. qua/m

6. Stress and Intonation

1. Listen for the sound /l/.

2. Mark the stressed words you hear with a stress mark (ˊ).

3. Mark falling or rising intonation with an arrow (⌢ ⌣).

4. Pay attention to function words and phrasing. Listen and repeat.

The first sentence is marked for you.

1. Bi̱ll and **Lill**ian are a **coup**le; so are Phi̱l and **Lu**cy.

2. Phi̱l to̱ld **Lill**ian she lo̱oked **beau**tifu̱l.

3. **Lill**ian to̱ld Phi̱l, "You lo̱ok **pret**ty good your**self**."

4. **Lu**cy lo̱oked at Phi̱l and asked, "How come you don't **com**pliment me li̱ke that?"

5. "Be**cause** you know you're **beau**tifu̱l," he re**plied**. "And, to the **bar**gain,[5] you're a spoi̱led chi̱ld."

6. They a̱ll sat down to **or**der lu̱nch.

7. **Lill**ian had a **salm**on **sal**ad and lemon**ade** for lu̱nch.

---

[5] *to the bargain:* in addition

8. Phil and Bill had **fill**et of sole and **mel**on for lunch.

9. **Lu**cy had leg of lamb and **yell**ow **Jell**-o for lunch.

10. **Lu**cy acci**den**tally spilled the **Jell**-o on Bill's lap.

11. Bill and **Lill**ian and Phil and **Lu**cy no **long**er have lunch to**geth**er.

7. Further Practice

The following proverbs contain words with the sound /l/ as in "like." Read each proverb aloud. Then explain, in class, the proverb in different words.

1. Live and learn.

2. Live and let live.

3. Like **fa**ther, like son.

4. The love of **mon**ey is the root of all **e**vil.

5. Lend your **mon**ey and lose your friend.

Unit 22

/r/ **as in** _r_ed

1. Producing /r/

EXAMPLES: _r_an, _r_ed, _wr_ite,[1] a**r**ound, to**morr**ow, a_r_e[2]

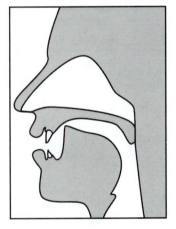

- Raise the *tip* of your tongue towards the upper gum ridge, but do *not* touch it. The tip of your tongue should not touch anything.
- Press the sides of your tongue against your upper back teeth. (Your tongue should be tense.)
- Lips are slightly open. (They may be slightly rounded or pushed out.)
- As you make the sound, air flows out over the tip of your tongue.
- Your vocal cords vibrate.

2. Practice the Sound

A. Practice the sound /r/ as in "_r_ed," first normally, then with exaggeration, then normally. Listen and repeat.

   /r/   /r . . ./   /r/

---

[1] The "w" in "write" is not pronounced. See page 299 for other words like "write."

[2] Depending on which dialect of English you hear, final /r/ may be omitted as in "are" (/ɑ:/ for /ɑr/); "far," (/fɑ:/ for /fɑr/). (":" after a vowel indicates that the sound is lengthened.) However, /r/ is usually pronounced when it is followed by a word that begins with a vowel sound and it is linked to that sound. For example: for a while, are awake.

Reminder: Vowel sounds are held longer before *voiced* consonants than before *voiceless* consonants. (See Unit 4.)

B.

Now practice the sound in words. Notice the phonetic spelling. Listen and re-peat each word twice.

1.	red	/rɛd/	red
2.	write	/rayt/	write
3.	a**rr**ive	/ərayv/	a**rr**ive
4.	**borr**ow	/bɑrow/	**borr**ow
5.	car	/kɑr/	car
6.	far	/fɑr/	far

3. Check Your Listening

A.

The following words contain the sounds /r/ as in "red," /w/ as in "walk," and /l/ as in "like." You will hear one word from each group. Circle the word that you hear.

1.	raid ✓	weighed	laid
2.	rate	wait	late ✓
3.	ray	way ✓	lay
4.	red	wed ✓	led
5.	rot	what³	lot ✓
6.	rye ✓	why³	lie
7.	ride ✓	wide	lied
8.	right	white³ ✓	light

B.

The following words contain the sounds /r/ as in "red" and /l/ as in "like." You will hear one word from each pair. Circle the word you hear.

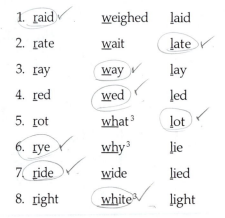

1.	**bur**y	**bell**y ✓		5.	crime	climb ✓
2.	a**rr**ive	a**l**ive ✓		6.	free	flee ✓
3.	e**r**ect ✓	e**l**ect		7.	crown ✓	clown
4.	grass ✓	glass		8.	crowd ✓	cloud

---

³ Some speakers pronounce "what," "why," and "white" with an initial /h/ sound: /hwɑt/, /hway/, /hwayt/. See Unit 33.

4. Practice the Contrast: /r/ as in "<u>r</u>ed" with /l/ as in "<u>l</u>ike"

Some students confuse /r/ with /l/. Remember that /l/ is made by placing your tongue tip on the upper gum ridge. You make /r/ with the tongue tip pointing toward the gum ridge but *not* touching it.

A. Practice these contrasting sounds. Listen and repeat each word pair.

/r/	/l/		/r/	/l/
1. <u>r</u>ock	<u>l</u>ock	6. <u>wr</u>ong	<u>l</u>ong
2. <u>r</u>ace	<u>l</u>ace	7. co<u>rr</u>ect	co<u>ll</u>ect
3. <u>r</u>ed	<u>l</u>ead	8. **pi**<u>r</u>ate	**pi**<u>l</u>ot
4. <u>r</u>oad	<u>l</u>oad	9. f<u>r</u>y	f<u>l</u>y
5. <u>r</u>ight	<u>l</u>ight	10. c<u>r</u>own	c<u>l</u>own

B. Now practice the contrasting sounds in sentence pairs. The first sentence of each pair has the sound /r/, and the second has the sound /l/. Listen and repeat.

1a. <u>r</u>ock   He has a <u>r</u>ock on his desk.

  b. <u>l</u>ock   He has a <u>l</u>ock on his desk.

2a. <u>r</u>ace   Did you see the <u>r</u>ace?

  b. <u>l</u>ace[4]   Did you see the <u>l</u>ace?

---

[4] *lace:* material such as silk woven into fine decorative patterns

3a. <u>r</u>ed   Is that a <u>r</u>ed **pen**cil?

b. <u>l</u>ead   Is that a <u>l</u>ead **pen**cil?

4a. <u>r</u>oad   Which <u>r</u>oad should I take?

b. <u>l</u>oad   Which <u>l</u>oad should I take?

5a. <u>r</u>ight   Give me the <u>r</u>ight one now.

b. <u>l</u>ight   Give me the <u>l</u>ight one now.

6a. <u>wr</u>ong   She said it was the <u>wr</u>ong one.

b. <u>l</u>ong   She said it was the <u>l</u>ong one.

7a. co<u>**rrect**</u>   Can you co<u>**rrect**</u> them?

b. co**<u>ll</u>ect**   Can you co**<u>ll</u>ect** them?

8a. **pi**<u>r</u>ate   The **stor**y's a**bout** a **pi**<u>r</u>ate.

b. **pi**<u>l</u>ot   The **stor**y's a**bout** a **pi**<u>l</u>ot.

9a. f<u>r</u>y   He **want**ed to f<u>r</u>y them.

b. f<u>l</u>y   He **want**ed to f<u>l</u>y them.

10a. c<u>r</u>own   Where did you find the c<u>r</u>own?

b. c<u>l</u>own   Where did you find the c<u>l</u>own?

5. Practice the Contrast: /r/ as in "<u>r</u>ed" with /w/ as in "<u>w</u>alk"

Some students confuse /r/ with /w/. Remember that /r/ is made with the tongue tip pointing toward the gum ridge but *not* touching it. Make /w/ by resting your tongue tip against your bottom teeth and rounding your lips.

A. Practice these contrasting sounds. Listen and repeat each word pair.

/r/	/w/		/r/	/w/
1. <u>r</u>ay	<u>w</u>ay		6. <u>r</u>ed	<u>w</u>ed
2. <u>r</u>age	<u>w</u>age		7. <u>r</u>ent	<u>w</u>ent
3. <u>r</u>aced	<u>w</u>aste		8. <u>r</u>est	<u>w</u>est
4. <u>r</u>ate	<u>w</u>eight		9. <u>r</u>ipe	<u>w</u>ipe
5. <u>r</u>ip	<u>wh</u>ip		10. <u>r</u>ight	<u>wh</u>ite

B. Now practice the contrasting sounds in sentence pairs. The first sentence of each pair has the sound /r/, and the second has the sound /w/. Listen and repeat.

1a. <u>r</u>ay   Is it the long <u>r</u>ay?

b. <u>w</u>ay   Is it the long <u>w</u>ay?

2a. <u>r</u>age   I saw his <u>r</u>age, **did**n't you?

  b. <u>w</u>age   I saw his <u>w</u>age, **did**n't you?

3a. <u>r</u>aced   Do you think they <u>r</u>aced much?

  b. <u>w</u>aste   Do you think they <u>w</u>aste much?

4a. <u>r</u>ate   He's **anx**ious about the <u>r</u>ate, **is**n't he?

  b. <u>w</u>eight   He's **anx**ious about the <u>w</u>eight, **is**n't he?

5a. <u>r</u>ip   It's a big <u>r</u>ip.

  b. <u>w</u>hip   It's a big <u>w</u>hip.

6a. <u>r</u>ed   Did the sign say "<u>r</u>ed"?

  b. <u>w</u>ed   Did the sign say "<u>w</u>ed"?

7a. <u>r</u>ent   Did you say "<u>r</u>ent"?

  b. <u>w</u>ent   Did you say "<u>w</u>ent"?

8a. <u>r</u>est   Let's go to the <u>r</u>est of the **coun**try.

  b. <u>w</u>est   Let's go to the <u>w</u>est of the **coun**try.

9a. <u>r</u>un   They <u>r</u>un all the time.

 b. <u>w</u>on   They <u>w</u>on all the time.

10a. <u>r</u>ight   Is that the <u>r</u>ight one?

  b. <u>wh</u>ite   Is that the <u>wh</u>ite one?

6. Different Positions of /r/

Practice the sound /r/ in several different positions. Listen and repeat.

/r/ IN INITIAL POSITION		
1. <u>r</u>ug	5. <u>r</u>ound	9. **re**alize
2. <u>r</u>oad	6. **riv**er	10. re**ceive**
3. <u>r</u>ich	7. **read**y	11. **re**cent
4. <u>r</u>ight	8. **rea**son	12. **rec**ognize

/r/ IN MEDIAL POSITION		
1. **car<u>r</u>**y	5. pa**rade**	9. **ter<u>r</u>**ible
2. **cho<u>r</u>**us	6. **stor**y	10. **per**iod
3. **fo<u>r</u>**eign	7. di**rec**tion	11. **var**ious
4. **or**ange	8. **sal**a<u>r</u>y	12. **in**vento<u>r</u>y

/r/ IN FINAL POSITION		
1. ca<u>r</u>e	5. you<u>r</u>	9. **em**pi<u>r</u>e
2. doo<u>r</u>	6. sha<u>r</u>e	10. gui**tar**
3. fou<u>r</u>	7. hou<u>r</u>	11. ig**nore**
4. sta<u>r</u>	8. be**fore**	12. in**sure**

Reminder: Depending on which dialect of English you hear, /r/ may not be pronounced in medial and in final positions. For example, the word "farm" might be pronounced /faːm/, and the word "more" might be pronounced /mɔː/. In both cases the vowel sounds are lengthened. However, the majority of Americans pronounce /r/ in all positions.

7. Stress and Intonation

A. Work with a partner.

1. Underline the /l/ sounds in words with a <u>single</u> line and /r/ sounds with a <u>double</u> line. Use a dictionary to help you with meaning and pronunciation of new words.

2. As you take turns reading the passage below, decide which words you would like to stress and mark them with a stress mark (´).

3. Mark the pauses, paying attention to function words and phrasing.

4. Mark the falling or rising intonation with an arrow (⌐ _⌐).

5. Read the passage again. Help each other with the correct sounds, stress, and intonation.

The first sentence is marked for you.

1.   What makes **Ran**dell's **read**y-made mine**stro**ne soup / the

2. best mine**stro**ne soup? / All those sun-**rip**ened, de**lic**ious, as-

3. **sort**ed **veg**etables . . . green and **yell**ow peas, **bar**ley, and

4. vermi**cell**i. They get **simm**ered **slow**ly in a **tast**y, de**lec**table

5. broth. **Ran**dell's does all the work. All you do is **o**pen a can, and

6. in four **min**utes you have a hot soup. When you take your first

7. **spoon**ful, you'll a**gree** it's the best-**sell**ing mine**stro**ne soup.

8. Don't you de**serve** the best? **Ran**dell's mine**stro**ne soup.

B. Do you think people will want to buy the soup? Discuss your reasons in class.

8. Further Practice

A. Read the following riddle aloud. You can use a dictionary to help you with pronunciation of new words.

1. Mark the passage for stress and intonation.

2. Be prepared to read the passage aloud in class.

3. Can you answer the riddle?

Round and round the **rugg**ed[5] rock

The **ragg**ed[6] **ras**cal[7] ran.

How **man**y r's are there in that?

Now tell me if you can.

B. Brain Teaser: What can be found in the center of America and Australia?

---

[5] _rugged:_ large, rough, strong
[6] _ragged:_ old and torn
[7] _rascal:_ a badly behaved person

Unit 23

/p/ **as in _pen_**
/b/ **as in _boy_**

1. Producing /p/

EXAMPLES: pay, put, play, price, speak, spring, slept, maps, jump, help

- First press your lips together, firmly, to stop the flow of air.
- Then open your lips and produce the sound with a strong puff of air.
- Your vocal cords do not vibrate.
- Hold a piece of paper in front of your lips. It should move when you produce the sound. Or hold your hand in front of your lips to feel the puff of air. This sound has an aspirate quality[1] (you can hear the strong puff of air as a whisper).

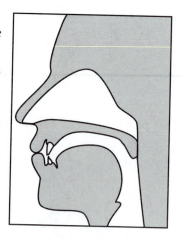

---

[1] _aspirate quality:_ breathiness heard when producing sound(s)

2. Producing /b/

EXAMPLES: b̲e, b̲est, b̲rain, b̲lack, a**bout,** o**b̲ey, a**b̲le, jo̲b̲, trib̲e

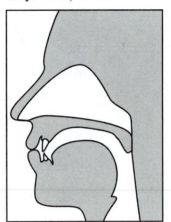

- This sound is produced the same way as /p/, except that /b/ is voiced, and the puff of air is not as strong.
- First, press your lips together, firmly, to stop the flow of air.
- Then open your lips and produce the sound with a puff of air. This sound does _not_ have an aspirate quality.
- Your vocal cords should vibrate.
- Hold a piece of paper or your hand in front of your lips to make sure air is released.

3. Contrast: /p/ **and** /b/

Some students confuse the sound /p/ as in "p̲en" with the sound /b/ as in "b̲oy."

A. Practice these two sounds, first normally, then with exaggeration, then normally. Place your hand in front of your lips to feel a puff of air: aspiration on /p/, none on /b/. Listen and repeat.

    1. /p/   /p . . ./[2]   /p/

    2. /b/   /b . . ./[3]   /b/

Reminder: Vowel sounds are held longer before _voiced_ consonants than before _voiceless_ consonants. (See Unit 4.)

---

[2] Try to prolong the puff of air, being careful _not_ to add a vowel.

[3] A voiced stop-plosive cannot really be prolonged. It's very difficult, if not impossible, to produce /b/ by itself, without adding a vowel, because the release of air takes place at the same time the sound is voiced. However, you can exaggerate /b/ by saying it with force.

B. Now practice the sounds in words. Notice the phonetic spelling. Listen and repeat each word twice.

1.	pan	/pæn/	pan
2.	piece	/piys/	piece
3.	re**pair**	/rɪpɛr/	re**pair**
4.	type	/tayp/	type
5.	bake	/beyk/	bake
6.	ban	/bæn/	ban
7.	**may**be	/meybiy/	**may**be
8.	robe	/rowb/	robe

4. Check Your Listening

A. The following pairs of words contain the sounds /p/ as in "pen" and /b/ as in "boy". You will hear one word from each pair. Circle the word you hear.

1.	pie	buy	5.	**sim**ple	**sym**bol
2.	pack	back	6.	**sta**ple	**sta**ble
3.	peach	beach	7.	lap	lab
4.	pest	best	8.	rip	rib

B. In the following pairs of words, one word ends with the sound /p/ or /b/. You will hear one word from each pair. Circle the word that you hear.

1.	so	soap	6.	Ma	mob
2.	key	keep	7.	too	tube
3.	row	rope	8.	cue	cube
4.	why	wipe	9.	row	robe
5.	bum	bump	10.	try	tribe

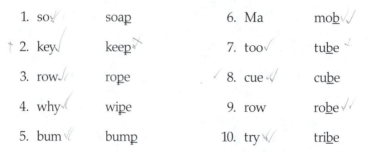

5. Practice the Contrast: /p/ as in "pen" with /b/ as in "boy"

A. Practice these contrasting sounds. When /p/ or /b/ appears at the end of a word, the sound is produced with a weak puff of air. Listen and repeat each word pair.

/p/	/b/		/p/	/b/
1. pig	big	6.	cap	cab
2. pill	bill	7.	tap	tab
3. pat	bat	8.	mop	mob
4. pet	bet	9.	rope	robe
5. **pal**ate	**ball**ot	10.	lap	lab

B. Now practice the contrasting sounds in sentence pairs. The first sentence of each pair has the sound /p/, and the second has the sound /b/. Listen and repeat.

1a.	pat	Give him a pat for me.
b.	bat	Give him a bat for me.
2a.	pet	My pet is a year old.
b.	bet	My bet is a year old.
3a.	pill	Did you take the pill?
b.	bill	Did you take the bill?
4a.	**pal**ate	I'd like to see your **pal**ate.
b.	**ball**ot	I'd like to see your **ball**ot.

would.

5a.	pig	**Is**n't that a **litt**le pig?
b.	big	**Is**n't that a **litt**le big?

6a. ca<u>p</u>   She has the ca<u>p</u> on her list.

b. ca<u>b</u>   She has the ca<u>b</u> on her list.

7a. ro<u>p</u>e   John has the rope a**round** him.

b. ro<u>b</u>e   John has the robe a**round** him.

8a. ta<u>p</u>   Did you find the ta<u>p</u>?

b. ta<u>b</u>   Did you find the ta<u>b</u>?

9a. mo<u>p</u>   Did you see the mo<u>p</u> in there?

b. mo<u>b</u>   Did you see the mo<u>b</u> in there?

10a. la<u>p</u>   I can see it in his la<u>p</u>.

b. la<u>b</u>   I can see it in his la<u>b</u>.

6. Consonant clusters With /p/ as in "pen" and /b/ as in "boy"

When one consonant sound is combined with one or more other consonants, it is called a *cluster*.

A. When /p/ occurs in a cluster, the puff of air is *weak*. However, make sure your lips close to stop the flow of air. Listen and repeat.

Initial /pl/	Medial /pl/	Final /pl/
1. **pl**an	1. a**ppl**y	1. **appl**e
2. **pl**ane	2. su**ppl**y	2. **coupl**e
3. **pl**us	3. re**pl**y	3. **peopl**e
4. **pl**ate	4. em**pl**oy	4. **par**tici**pl**e

Initial /pr/	Medial /pr/	Medial /rp/
1. **pr**ay	1. **a**pron	1. **air**plane
2. **pri**son	2. a**pproach**	2. **car**pet
3. **prom**ise	3. a**pprove**	3. **pur**ple
4. **pr**e**fer**	4. im**prove**	4. **sur**plus

B. When /b/ occurs in a cluster, there is no puff of air. However, make sure your lips close tightly and your vocal cords vibrate. Listen and repeat.

Initial /bl/	Medial /bl/	Final /bl/
1. **bl**ack	1. o**bliv**ious[4]	1. **ta**ble
2. **bl**ank	2. **sib**ling	2. **wash**able
3. **bl**ame	3. **sub**lease[5]	3. **trou**ble
4. **bl**ood	4. **gam**bling	4. **terri**ble

Initial /br/	Medial /br/	Medial /rb/	Final /rb/
1. **br**ain	1. a**broad**	1. **ur**ban	1. **cur**b
2. **br**eak	2. a**bbre**viate	2. **or**bit	2. **ver**b

---

[4] *oblivious:* not noticing; unaware

[5] *sublease:* rent from someone who is the original renter

INITIAL /br/	MEDIAL /br/	MEDIAL /rb/	FINAL /rb/
3. <u>br</u>own	3. **al**ge<u>br</u>a	3. **gar**bage	3. dis**turb**
4. <u>br</u>idge	4. **li**<u>br</u>ary	4. **har**bor	4. **ad**verb

7. Doubled Consonants

A. When a stop-plosive is the final sound in a word and is followed by another word that begins with the same stop-plosive, as in "help paint" and "mob boss," they are linked together and said as one sound. Do not release the air on the first stop-plosive; release it on the second. The air will take longer to release. Listen and repeat.

1.	top part	Would you like the top part of the **chick**en?
2.	hip **pock**et	My **wall**et is in my hip **pock**et.
3.	deep part	He swims in the deep part of the pool.
4.	keep **push**ing	Why do you keep **push**ing me a**way?**
5.	grape **prod**uct	Wine is a grape **prod**uct.
6.	lab book	I'm **us**ing my lab book to**day.**
7.	rob Bill	Did you see them rob Bill?
8.	tube broke	The tube broke as I was **us**ing it.
9.	dis**turb** Bob	Did you dis**turb** Bob in his **off**ice?
10.	cab breaks	His cab breaks down all the time.

B. When a stop-plosive ends one word and a different stop-plosive begins the next word as in "stop Bill" and "rob Paul," do not release the air on the first stop-plosive; release it on the second one. The air will take longer to release. Listen and repeat.

1.	stop **bak**ing	I wish you would stop **bak**ing **cook**ies.
2.	cheap book	When you buy a cheap book, it falls a**part.**
3.	club pass	To use the pool, I need a club pass.
4.	step back	He took a step back and fell down.
5.	**check**up by	He got a **check**up by his **doc**tor.

8. No Sound for "b" and "p"

A. The letter "b" is usually not pronounced when it follows the letter "m." It is also not pronounced before the letter "t" in the same syllable. Listen and repeat.

1. climb   Don't climb up the tree.

2. comb   May I use your comb?

3. dumb   That's a dumb thing I did.

4. lamb   A lamb is a young sheep.

5. limb   A limb is an arm or a leg.

6. numb   To be numb is to feel no pain.

7. thumb   Your thumb is a short, thick **fin**ger.

8. tomb   A tomb is a place where **some**one is **bur**ied.

9. bomb   A bomb went off in the **mar**ket.

10. **plumb**er   A **plumb**er re**pairs wa**ter pipes.

11. doubt   When in doubt, don't use it.

12. debt   A debt is **some**thing owed to **some**one else.

B. When the letters "ps" begin a word, the "p" is not pronounced. "P" is also not pronounced in a few other words. Listen and repeat.

1. psalm[6]   A psalm is a re**lig**ious song or **po**em.

2. psy**chi**atrist   A psy**chi**atrist is a **med**ical **doc**tor who treats **men**tal **ill**ness.

3. psy**chol**ogist   A psy**chol**ogist **al**so treats **men**tal **ill**ness but has no **med**ical de**gree.**

4. corps[7]   The Ma**rine** Corps is part of the Armed **Forc**es.

5. re**ceipt**   You should get a re**ceipt** when you pay the rent.

---

[6] The "l" in "psalm" is also silent.

[7] The "s" in "corps" is also silent.

9. Stress and Intonation

Each of these sentences contains the sound /p/ as in "pen," the sound /b/ as in "boy," or both.

1. Listen for the sounds /p/ and /b/, which are underlined. Clusters with /p/ and /b/ are also underlined.

2. As you listen to the tape and repeat the sentences, mark the stressed words you hear with a stress mark (ˊ).

3. Pay attention to function words, phrasing, and intonation.

The first sentence is marked for you.

1. Let's take the **sub**way to the **pub**lic **li**brary.

2. Can you **par**allel park[8] that car?

3. We **al**ways take the ex**press** bus to the **air**port.

4. Is the bi**ol**ogy lab on **cam**pus?

5. **Brook**lyn and the Bronx are part of New York **Cit**y.

6. The park bench is **paint**ed black.

7. **Pe**ter has a pass for a **Broad**way show.

8. In**spect** the a**part**ment be**fore** you move in.

9. My boss speaks **Span**ish and **Por**tuguese.

10. Please pass the plate of spa**ghett**i and **meat**balls.

10. Further Practice

A. The following is a well-known rhyme. Work with a partner.

1. The /p/ and /b/ consonants are underlined.

2. Mark the words you decide to stress with a stress mark (ˊ).

3. Pay attention to function words and phrasing.

The first line is marked for you.

---

[8] *parallel park:* park alongside a curb

1.   Sing a song of **six**pence,

2.   A **pock**et full of rye,

3.   Four and **twen**ty **black**birds

4.   Baked in a pie.

5.   When the pie was **o**pened

6.   The birds be**gan** to sing

7.   Now **was**n't that a **dain**ty dish

8.   To set be**fore** a king?

B.   Record yourself, monitoring your articulation, stress, and intonation.

understand.

Unit 24

/t/ as in _ten_
/d/ as in _day_

1. Producing /t/

EXAMPLES: _t_o, _t_ime, s_t_op, **litt**le, **au**_t_o, a_t_e, walk_ed_

- First press the _tip_ of your tongue against your _upper gum ridge_ (at the teeth ridge) to stop the flow of air.
- Then quickly drop the tongue tip. As the air is released, the sound is produced with a strong puff of air.
- Your vocal cords do not vibrate.
- Hold a piece of paper in front of your lips. It should move when you produce the sound. Or hold your hand in front of your lips to feel the puff of air. This sound has an aspirate quality[1] (you can hear the strong puff of air as a whisper).

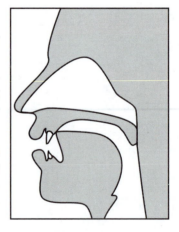

_____
[1] _aspirate quality:_ breathiness heard when producing sound(s)

2. Producing /d/

EXAMPLES: <u>d</u>o, <u>d</u>ark, **can**<u>d</u>y, **lou**<u>d</u>er, **pow**<u>d</u>er, nee<u>d</u>, si<u>d</u>e, calle<u>d</u>

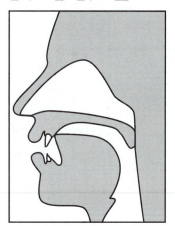

- This sound is produced the same way as /t/ except that /d/ is voiced and the puff of air is not as strong.
- First press the _tip_ of your tongue against your _upper gum ridge_ (at the teeth ridge) to stop the flow of air.
- Then quickly drop the tongue tip. As the air is released, the sound is produced with a puff of air that is not as strong as that for /t/. This sound does _not_ have an aspirate quality.
- Your vocal cords vibrate.
- Hold a piece of paper or your hand in front of your lips to make sure air is released.

3. Contrast: /t/ and /d/

Some students confuse the sound /t/ as in "<u>t</u>en" with the sound /d/ as in "<u>d</u>ay."

A. Practice these two sounds, first normally, then with exaggeration, then normally. Place your hand in front of your lips to feel a puff of air: aspiration on /t/, none on /d/. Listen and repeat.

1. /t/   /t . . ./[2]   /t/

2. /d/   /d . . ./[3]   /d/

---

[2] Try to prolong the puff of air, being careful _not_ to add a vowel.

[3] A voiced stop-plosive cannot really be prolonged. It's very difficult, if not impossible, to produce /d/ by itself without adding a vowel, because the release of air takes place at the same time the sound is voiced. However, you can exaggerate /d/ by saying it with force.

> Reminder: Vowel sounds are held longer before *voiced* consonants than before *voiceless* consonants. (See Unit 4.)

B. Now practice the sounds in words. Notice the phonetic spelling. Listen and repeat each word twice.

1. tea	/tiy/	tea
2. tell	/tɛll/	tell
3. a**ttack**	/ətæk/	a**ttack**
4. coat	/kowt/	coat
5. deep	/diyp/	deep
6. dig	/dɪg/	dig
7. a**dult**	/ədəlt/	a**dult**
8. need	/niyd/	need

4. Check Your Listening

A. The following pairs of words contain the sounds /t/ as in "ten" and /d/ as in "day." You will hear one word from each pair. Circle the word that you hear.

1. tear ✓	dear		6. bat ✓	bad	
2. tie	die ✓		7. neat	need	
3. time ✓	dime		8. hat	had	
4. to	✓ do		9. coat ✓	code	
✓ 5. town	down		10. hit ✓	hid	

B. In the following pairs of words, one word ends with the sound /t/ or /d/. You will hear one word from each pair. Circle the word that you hear.

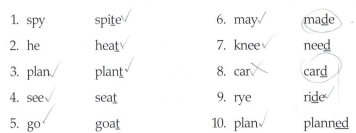

1. spy	spite ✓		6. may ✓	(made)	
2. he	heat ✓		7. knee ✓	need	
3. plan ✓	plant ✓		8. car ✗	card	
4. see ✓	seat		9. rye	ride ✓	
5. go ✓	goat		10. plan ✓	planned	

5. Practice the Contrast: /t/ as in "_ten_" with /d/ as in "_day_"

A. Practice these contrasting sounds. When /t/ or /d/ appears at the end of a word, the sound is produced with a weak puff of air. Listen and repeat each word pair.

/t/	/d/		/t/	/d/
1. tear	dear	6.	at	add
2. tie	dye	7.	neat	need
3. time	dime	8.	coat	code
4. tile	**di**al	9.	debt	dead
5. town	down	10.	bright	bride

B. Now practice the contrasting sounds in sentence pairs. The first sentence of each pair has the sound /t/, and the second has the sound /d/. Listen and repeat.

1a. time   Do you have the time?

  b. dime   Do you have the dime?

2a. tile   Can you tile it in the **kitch**en?

  b. **di**al   Can you **di**al it in the **kitch**en?

3a. tore[4]   John said "tore."

  b. door   John said "door."

---

[4] _tore:_ past tense of the verb "to tear"

4a. tie   **Does**n't the tie look nice?

b. dye[5]   **Does**n't the dye look nice?

5a. write   She likes to write **ev**ery day.

b. ride   She likes to ride **ev**ery day.

6a. seat   The seat is in the **gar**den.

b. seed   The seed is in the **gar**den.

7a. cart   I gave him my cart.

b. card   I gave him my card.

8a. bet   He likes the bet.

b. bed   He likes the bed.

9a. debt   I saw the debt.

b. dead   I saw the dead.

10a. pat   Give her a pat.

b. pad[6]   Give her a pad.

---

[5] *dye:* a solution used to color cloth or hair
[6] *pad:* a stack of paper glued together at one end

6. Consonant Clusters With /t/ as in "<u>t</u>en" and /d/ as in "<u>d</u>ay"

When one consonant sound is combined with one or more other consonants, it is called a *cluster*. When /t/ and /d/ occur in a cluster, the puff of air is *weak*. However, make sure that your tongue tip is pressed lightly against your upper gum ridge so that the flow of air is stopped before it is released.

A. Listen to and repeat the following words.

INITIAL /tr/	MEDIAL /tr/	INITIAL /dr/	MEDIAL /dr/
1. <u>tr</u>ack	1. **en**<u>tr</u>ance	1. <u>dr</u>eam	1. a<u>**dd**</u>ress
2. <u>tr</u>ade	2. **ma**<u>tt</u>ress	2. <u>dr</u>ill	2. **laun**<u>dr</u>y
3. <u>tr</u>ain	3. **me**<u>tr</u>ic	3. <u>dr</u>aw	3. un<u>**dr**</u>ess
4. <u>tr</u>y	4. pa<u>**tr**</u>ol	4. <u>dr</u>y	4. de**hy**<u>dr</u>ate[7]

B. Work with a partner or with a small group. Make up four sentences each with one word from each of the above columns. As you read them aloud, check each other for the correct articulation.

7. When /t/ Sounds Like /d/

When the sound /t/ occurs between two vowel sounds, in an unstressed syllable or at the end of a stressed syllable, it is pronounced quickly, without a puff of air. Many educated Americans pronounce this sound like /d/ (sometimes called a "soft /t/").

A. You will hear two pronunciations for each word. The first will have the /t/ sound and the second the /d/ sound. Listen and repeat.

1. **ci**<u>t</u>y	5. **wri**<u>t</u>er	9. **be**<u>tt</u>er
2. **si**<u>tt</u>ing	6. **wri**<u>t</u>ing	10. **bu**<u>tt</u>er
3. **wa**<u>t</u>er	7. **for**<u>t</u>y	11. **ma**<u>tt</u>er
4. **daugh**<u>t</u>er	8. **dir**<u>t</u>y	12. **li**<u>tt</u>le

B. Work with a partner. Think of twelve sentences (six each) for each sound using the above words. Be prepared to share them with the class.

---

[7] *dehydrate:* make dry by removing all the water

8. Consonant Clusters /lt/ and /ld/

A. Practice these clusters. Listen to the contrast between the single sound and the cluster; then repeat each word pair.

/l/	/lt/		/l/	/ld/
1. fell	felt	6. coal	cold
2. haul	halt	7. goal	gold
3. fall	fault	8. bill	build
4. bell	belt	9. hole	hold
5. mall	malt[8]	10. sole	sold

B. Now practice the sounds in sentence pairs. The first sentence of each pair has a word that ends in /l/. The second has a word that ends in /lt/ or /ld/. Listen and repeat.

1a. fell — He fell as if he were sick.

 b. felt — He felt as if he were sick.

2a. haul[9] — Who can haul a car?

 b. halt — Who can halt a car?

3a. fall — I'm re**spon**sible for my fall.

 b. fault[10] — I'm re**spon**sible for my fault.

4a. bell — She gave him a bell as a **pres**ent.

 b. belt — She gave him a belt as a **pres**ent.

5a. mall — We a**pprove** of the mall.

 b. malt — We a**pprove** of the malt.

---

[8] *malt:* a grain used for making drinks
[9] *haul:* carry a load
[10] *fault:* a flaw; a defect

6a.	coa<u>l</u>[11]	The coa<u>l</u> may stay for a week.
b.	co<u>ld</u>	The co<u>ld</u> may stay for a week.
7a.	goa<u>l</u>	Was it your goa<u>l</u>?
b.	go<u>ld</u>	Was it your go<u>ld</u>?
8a.	bi<u>ll</u>	Will you bi<u>ll</u> for it?
b.	bui<u>ld</u>	Will you bui<u>ld</u> for it?
9a.	ho<u>l</u>e	Put it in the ho<u>l</u>e.
b.	ho<u>ld</u>[12]	Put it in the ho<u>ld</u>.
10a.	so<u>l</u>e	The fish is so<u>l</u>e.
b.	so<u>ld</u>	The fish is so<u>ld</u>.

9. Syllabic /l/ After /t/ and /d/

A. When /l/ is in an unstressed syllable following /t/ or /d/, no vowel sound is produced. This occurs even when a vowel letter appears between /tl/ and /dl/. For example,

1. **litt**le   /lɪtl̩/
2. **midd**le   /mɪdl̩/
3. **to**tal   /towtl̩/
4. **med**al   /mɛdl̩/

This /l/ sound is called *syllabic* because it forms a syllable without a vowel sound. (The dot underneath /l̩/ indicates a syllable.)

---

[11] *coal:* a mineral that is burned for heat
[12] *hold:* the container area of a ship

Reminder: /t/, /d/, and /l/ are all made with the tongue tip pressed against the upper gum ridge.

- To produce /t/ or /d/, press your tongue tip against the upper gum ridge. This action stops the flow of air.
- Instead of releasing the tongue tip, keep it in place and then make the "l." The air will escape over the sides of your tongue as you make the sound /l/.

B. Listen and repeat these words and sentences. Note that some educated speakers may use a "soft /t/" in words spelled with "t" or "tt." (See page 207.)

1.	**bott**le	/batl̩/	Did you give the **ba**by the **bott**le?
2.	**batt**le	/bætl̩/	The **sol**diers fought in a big **batt**le.
3.	**kett**le	/kɛtl̩/	**Wa**ter is boiled in a **kett**le.
4.	**sett**le	/sɛtl̩/	Don't **sett**le for less than it's worth.
5.	**hos**pital	/haspɪtl̩/	We took him to the **hos**pital.
6.	**can**dle	/kændl̩/	Light a **can**dle when it gets dark.
7.	**ridd**le	/rɪdl̩/	What's the **an**swer to the **ridd**le?
8.	**nee**dle	/niydl̩/	Do you have a **nee**dle and thread?
9.	**sadd**le	/sædl̩/	Put a **sadd**le on the horse.
10.	**san**dals	/sændl̩z/	I like to wear **san**dals, not closed shoes.

10. Stress and Intonation

A. Listen for the sounds /t/ and /d/.

1. Mark the stressed words you hear with a stress mark (ˊ).

2. Mark the falling or rising intonation with an arrow (⌐ ⌐).

3. Pay attention to function words and phrasing. Listen and repeat.

The first sentence is marked for you.

1. **Dur**ing the **win**ter the days are short.

2. Does your **teach**er get paid on **Fri**days?

3. I ate all the tomatoes **yes**terday.

4. She told us a ro**man**tic **stor**y.

5. <u>T</u>om bough<u>t</u> a lo<u>t</u> of **dough**nu<u>t</u>s.

6. The **door**man <u>t</u>ol<u>d</u> us to go <u>d</u>own.

7. The **Pil**grims came here in six**teen twen**ty.

8. **Sat**urday nigh<u>t</u> is the **lone**lies<u>t</u> nigh<u>t</u> of the week.

9. <u>D</u>o you **u**sually **vis**i<u>t</u> your aun<u>t</u> on **Mon**days?

10. <u>D</u>i<u>d</u> you make an a**ppoint**men<u>t</u> with your **doc**tor?

B. After you've listened to the tape, work with a partner. Compare your markings. Take turns reading the sentences aloud and check each other for sounds, stress, and intonation.

11. Pronunciation of the "-ed" Ending

Form the past tense of regular verbs by adding the ending "-ed" to the base form. The ending has three different pronunciations. The pronunciation of "-ed" depends on whether a voiced or voiceless sound comes before it.

A. Verbs Ending in Voiceless Consonants

When a verb ends in a *voiceless* consonant (except for /t/), pronounce "-ed" as /t/. Voiceless consonants include /p/, /k/, /f/, /θ/, /s/, /ʃ/, and /tʃ/. Listen and repeat.

1a.	ki<u>ss</u>	/kɪs/	Did you kiss me?
b.	ki<u>ssed</u>	/kɪst/	I ki<u>ss</u>ed you be**fore.**
2a.	wal<u>k</u>	/wɔk/	I'll wal<u>k</u> a**lone.**
b.	wal<u>ked</u>	/wɔkt/	I wal<u>ked</u> a**lone.**

B. Verbs Ending in Voiced Consonants

When a verb ends in a *voiced* consonant (except for /d/), pronounce "-ed" as /d/. Voiced consonants are those not listed above. Listen and repeat.

1a.	ca<u>ll</u>	/kɔl/	Did you ca<u>ll</u> me?
b.	ca<u>lled</u>	/kɔld/	Yes, I ca<u>ll</u>ed you.
2a.	be**lieve**	/bəliyv/	I be**lieve** in him.
b.	be**lieved**	/bəliyvd/	I be**lieved** in him.

C. **Verbs Ending in Vowels**

Remember that all vowels are *voiced*. Thus, when a verb ends in a vowel sound, "-ed" is pronounced /d/. Listen and repeat.

1a. pl<u>ay</u> /pley/ Did you pl<u>ay</u> drums?

b. pl<u>ayed</u> /pleyd/ No, I pl<u>ayed</u> pi**an**o.

2a. sh<u>ow</u> /ʃow/ I'll sh<u>ow</u> it to you.

b. sh<u>owed</u> /ʃowd/ I sh<u>owed</u> it to you.

D. **Verbs Ending in** /t/ **or** /d/

When a verb ends in /t/ or /d/, pronounce "-ed" as /ɪd/. In this case, "-ed" is a separate syllable. Listen and repeat.

1a. pain<u>t</u> /peynt/ Pain<u>t</u> one wall.

b. **pain<u>t</u>ed** /peyntɪd/ I **pain<u>t</u>ed** one wall.

2a. wan<u>t</u> /wɑnt/ I wan<u>t</u> a piece.

b. **wan<u>t</u>ed** /wɑntɪd/ I **wan<u>t</u>ed** a piece.

3a. nee<u>d</u> /niyd/ I nee<u>d</u> it now.

b. **nee<u>d</u>ed** /niydɪd/ I **nee<u>d</u>ed** it **yes**terday.

4a. de**ci<u>d</u>e** /dɪsayd/ Don't de**ci<u>d</u>e** to**day.**

b. de**ci<u>d</u>ed** /dɪsaydɪd/ I de**ci<u>d</u>ed** to**day.**

12. **Practice** /t/, /d/, **and** /ɪd/ **Endings**

Work with a partner. Take turns reading the sentences. Check each other for correct pronunciation of the "-ed" endings. Then start the tape.

A. /t/ **Ending**

In the sentences below, pronounce "-ed" as /t/. Listen and repeat.

1. I bak<u>ed</u> a cake for my **boy**friend.

2. I wrapp<u>ed</u> the **pack**age for the **cus**tomer.

3. They reach<u>ed</u> the top of the **moun**tain.

4. I help_ed_ him with his **home**work.

5. He miss_ed_ **hav**ing his **break**fast this **mor**ning.

B. /d/ **Ending**

In the sentences below, pronounce "-ed" as /d/. Listen and repeat.

1. The **ba**by scream_ed_ all night for her **moth**er.

2. He liv_ed_ a long time **af**ter his **ill**ness.

3. I re**ceiv**_ed_ the **tel**ephone bill last night.

4. He con**tin**_ued_ to win at cards.

5. They **ad**vertis_ed_ for an a**part**ment in the **pa**per.

C. /ɪd/ **Ending**

In the sentences below, pronounce "-ed" as /ɪd/. Listen and repeat.

1. He reco**mmend**_ed_ me for the **com**puter job.

2. We **board**_ed_ the plane on time.

3. She was ad**mitt**_ed_ to the **hos**pital.

4. I re**quest**_ed_ a room with a view.

5. They de**cid**_ed_ to go by train in**stead** of by plane.

13. Further Practice

A. Form the past tense of the following verbs.

1. Pronounce the base form of the verb. You can use a dictionary to help you with the pronunciation.

2. Write the past tense form in the space provided. Then write the phonetic symbol for the "-ed" ending (/t/, /d/, or /ɪd/).

3. Pronounce the past tense form.

EXAMPLES:

a. add	*added*	/ɪd/
b. e**lect**	*elected*	/ɪd/
c. laugh	*laughed*	/t/
d. de**lay**	*delayed*	/d/

1. **trav**el _____ /_____/

2. dream _____ /_____/

3. wash _____ /_____/

4. re**ceive** _____ /_____/

5. **stud**y _____ /_____/

6. re**port** _____ /_____/

7. type _____ /_____/

8. stop _____ /_____/

9. vote _____ /_____/

10. ex**pect** _____ /_____/

B. Think of at least five verbs you may have had difficulty pronouncing in the past tense. Write sentences with these verbs in the present tense and then in the past tense. Read them aloud as you write. Be prepared to discuss them in class.

C. Tongue twisters are phrases that are difficult to say quickly. Say the following selection aloud, slowly, and mark the phrases. Record the selection, and when you play it back, check your articulation and marking.

A **tu**tor who **toot**ed[13] the flute

Tried to **tu**tor two **toot**ers to toot.

Said the two to the **tu**tor:

"Is it **hard**er to toot, or

To **tu**tor two **toot**ers to toot?"

_____

[13] *toot:* blow a horn, whistle, etc. in short loud sounds

Unit 25

/k/ as in <u>c</u>at
/g/ as in *go*

1. Producing /k/

EXAMPLES: <u>k</u>iss, <u>c</u>ame, <u>k</u>ey, **char**a<u>c</u>ter, **qui**et, **liq**uid, **pic**ture, **chick**en, **ac**cident, si<u>ck</u>, boo<u>k</u>, bra<u>k</u>e

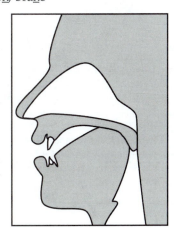

- First press the *back* part of your tongue to the *back* of the roof of your mouth (soft palate) to stop the flow of air.
- Then quickly lower the back of your tongue. As the air is released, the sound is produced with a strong puff of air.
- Your vocal cords do not vibrate.
- Hold a piece of paper in front of your lips. It should move when you produce the sound. Or hold your hand in front of your lips to feel the puff of air. This sound has an aspirate quality[1] (you can hear the puff of air as a whisper).

---

[1] *aspirate quality:* breathiness heard when producing sound(s)

2. Producing /g/

EXAMPLES: get, g̲host, g̲uest, for**get**, be**gan,** bag̲, eg̲g̲, leag̲ue

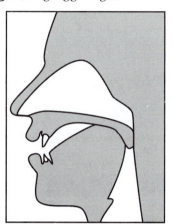

- This sound is produced the same way as /k/, except that /g/ is voiced and the puff of air is not as strong.
- First press the *back* part of your tongue to the *back* of the roof of your mouth (soft palate) to stop the flow of air.
- Then quickly lower the back of your tongue. As the air is released, the sound is produced with a puff of air that is not as strong as that for /k/. This sound does *not* have an aspirate quality.
- Your vocal cords should vibrate.
- Hold a piece of paper or your hand in front of your lips to make sure air is released.

3. Contrast: /k/ and /g/

Some students confuse the sound /k/ as in "c̲at" with the sound /g/ as in "g̲o."

A. Practice these two sounds, first normally, then with exaggeration, then normally. Place your hand in front of your lips to feel a puff of air: aspiration on /k/, none on /g/. Listen and repeat.

1. /k/   /k . . ./[2]   /k/

2. /g/   /g . . ./[3]   /g/

> Reminder: Vowel sounds are held longer before *voiced* consonants than before *voiceless* consonants. (See Unit 4.)

---

[2] Try to prolong the puff of air, being careful *not* to add a vowel.

[3] A voiced stop-plosive cannot really be prolonged. It's very difficult, if not impossible, to produce /g/ by itself without adding a vowel, because the release of air takes place at the same time the sound is voiced. However, you can exaggerate /g/ by saying it with force.

B. Now practice the sounds in words. Notice the phonetic spelling. Listen and repeat each word twice.

1. c̲an	/kæn/	c̲an
2. k̲ey	/kiy/	k̲ey
3. bec̲**ame**	/bɪkeym/	bec̲**ame**
4. mak̲e	/meyk/	mak̲e
5. g̲o	/gow/	g̲o
6. g̲ive	/gɪv/	g̲ive
7. a**g̲ain**	/əgɛn/	a**g̲ain**
8. bag̲	/bæg/	bag̲

4. Check Your Listening

A. The following pairs of words contain the sounds /k/ as in "c̲at" and /g/ as in "g̲o." You will hear one word from each pair. Circle the word that you hear.

1. c̲ame	game		6. snac̲k	snag
2. c̲ome	gum		7. lac̲k	lag
3. c̲ane	gain		8. duc̲k	dug
4. c̲oal	goal		9. pic̲k	pig
5. c̲lass	glass		10. froc̲k	frog

B. In the following pairs of words, one word ends with the sound /k/ or /g/. You will hear one word from each pair. Circle the word that you hear.

1. see	seek̲		6. Lee	leag̲ue
2. stay	steak̲		7. play	plag̲ue
3. way	wak̲e		8. more	morg̲ue
4. we	week̲		9. row	rog̲ue
5. lay	lak̲e		10. few	fug̲ue

5. Practice the Contrast: /k/ as in "c̲at" with /g/ as in "g̲o"

A. Practice these contrasting sounds. Listen and repeat each word pair.

/k/	/g/		/k/	/g/
1. c̲url	girl	6. pic̲k	pig
2. c̲ard	g̲uard	7. loc̲k	log[4]
3. c̲ould	good	8. rac̲k	rag
4. c̲oast	g̲host	9. leac̲k	leag̲ue
5. c̲old	gold	10. bac̲k	bag

B. Now practice the contrasting sounds in sentence pairs. The first sentence of each pair has the sound /k/, and the second has the sound /g/. Listen and repeat.

1a. c̲url		That's a nice **litt**le c̲url you have.
b. girl		That's a nice **litt**le girl you have.

2a. c̲ard		Did you see my c̲ard?
b. g̲uard		Did you see my g̲uard?

---

[4] Some Americans say /lɔg/ rather than /lɑg/.

3a. c̲ould   We all said "c̲ould."

  b. good   We all said "good."

4a. c̲oast   We can see the c̲oast from here.

  b. g̲host   We can see the g̲host from here.

5a. c̲old   It was c̲old in there.

  b. gold   It was gold in there.

6a. pic̲k[5]   You can have your pic̲k.

  b. pig   You can have your pig.

7a. loc̲k   Where is the loc̲k we had?

  b. log   Where is the log we had?

8a. rac̲k   A rac̲k is on the wall.

  b. rag   A rag is on the wall.

---

[5] *pick:* choice

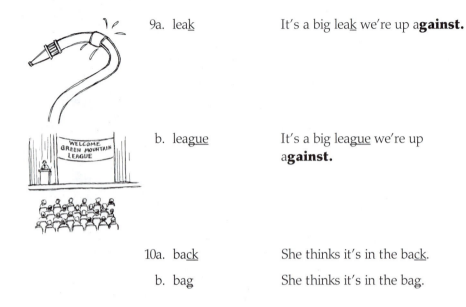

9a. lea<u>k</u>   It's a big lea<u>k</u> we're up a**gainst.**

b. lea<u>gue</u>   It's a big lea<u>gue</u> we're up a**gainst.**

10a. ba<u>ck</u>   She thinks it's in the ba<u>ck</u>.

b. ba<u>g</u>   She thinks it's in the ba<u>g</u>.

6. Consonant Clusters With /k/ as in "c̲at" and /g/ as in "g̲o"

When one consonant sound is combined with one or more other consonants, it is called a *cluster*.

A. When /k/ occurs in a cluster, the puff of air is *weak*. However, make sure the back of your tongue is pressed lightly against your soft palate so that the flow of air is stopped before it is released. Listen and repeat.

Initial /kl/	Medial /kl/	Final /kl/
1. <u>cl</u>aim	1. de**cl**ine	1. **cir**<u>cl</u>e
2. <u>cl</u>ause	2. **Frank**lin	2. **un**<u>cl</u>e
3. <u>cl</u>ap	3. un**like**ly	3. **lo**<u>cal</u>
4. <u>cl</u>ear	4. ex**clu**sive	4. **wrin**<u>kl</u>e

Initial /kr/	Medial /kr/
1. <u>cr</u>y	1. **se**<u>cr</u>et
2. <u>cr</u>owd	2. a**cross**
3. <u>cr</u>eam	3. **air**<u>cr</u>aft
4. <u>cr</u>oss	4. **mi**<u>cr</u>obe

B. When /g/ occurs in a cluster, there is no puff of air. However, make sure the back of your tongue is pressed lightly against your soft palate so that the flow of air is stopped before it is released. Listen and repeat.

Initial /gl/	Medial /gl/	Final /gl/
1. g̲love	1. **eye**g̲lass	1. **ea**g̲le
2. g̲lad	2. ne**g̲lect**	2. ille**g̲al**
3. g̲lue	3. **En**g̲land	3. **strug**g̲le
4. **g̲lam**our	4. un**g̲lued**	4. **jun**g̲le

Initial /gr/	Medial /gr/
1. g̲rade	1. **hun**g̲ry
2. g̲rass	2. **con**g̲ress
3. g̲reat	3. dis**g̲race**
4. g̲raph	4. **an**g̲ry

7. Sounds for the Letters "cc"

A. The letters "cc" sometimes represent the sound /k/ as in "c̲at." Listen and repeat.

1. a**cc**ount	**O**pen an a**cc**ount with the bank.
2. a**cc**use	Don't a**cc**use me of **an**ything.
3. o**cc**ur	When did that e**vent** o**cc**ur?
4. **socc**er	Do you play **socc**er with him?
5. a**cc**omplish	I'll a**cc**omplish that in due time.[6]
6. a**cc**ordion	My **broth**er plays the a**cc**ordion.
7. o**cc**asion	What's the o**cc**asion for the **par**ty?
8. a**cc**ountant	That man is my a**cc**ountant.

---

[6] *in due time:* at the right or proper time

B. Sometimes the letters "cc" represent the sounds /ks/. Notice the syllable break in this form of "cc." Listen and repeat.

1. ac**cel**erate   To ac**cel**erate means to move **fast**er.

2. **vac**cine   A **vac**cine pro**tects** us a**gainst** di**sease.**

3. **ac**cent   He speaks with an **ac**cent.

4. ac**cede**   To ac**cede** means to a**gree.**

5. ac**cept**   Are you **will**ing to ac**cept** the grade?

6. **ac**cident   It was an **ac**cident **wait**ing to **happ**en.[7]

7. suc**ceed**   She'll suc**ceed** in **ev**erything she does.

8. suc**cess**   The **par**ty was a huge suc**cess.**

8. Sounds for the Letter "x"

A. In the middle of a word, the letter "x" usually represents the sound /ks/. Listen and repeat.

1. **ex**ercise   Do you **al**ways **ex**ercise in the **mor**ning?

2. ex**plain**   Please ex**plain** the **less**on to me.

3. **ex**tra   We **al**ways get an **ex**tra plate.

4. ex**pect**   Did you ex**pect** that child to be**have?**

5. ex**pense**   I'll spare no ex**pense** for the gift.

B. At the end of a word, "x" always represents /ks/. Listen and repeat.

1. a**x**   We chop wood with an a**x**.

2. fi**x**   When will we fi**x** the pipe?

3. ta**x**   We all pay our **in**come ta**x**.

4. mi**x**   Did you mi**x** the paint?

5. re**lax**   When we come home, we try to re**lax**.

---

[7] *an accident waiting to happen:* an accident that is expected

C. Sometimes "x" represents /gz/. Listen and repeat.

1. ex**am**ple   Please read the ex**am**ple first.

2. ex**ist**   How do we know that we ex**ist?**

3. ex**hib**it   Did you see the art ex**hib**it?

4. ex**act**   We need the ex**act** change for the bus.

5. ex**agg**erate   That dress tends to ex**agg**erate her size.

9. Sounds for the Letters "qu"

A. In the initial (beginning) position, the letters "qu" usually represent the sound /kw/. Listen and repeat.

1. <u>qu</u>iz   My **teach**er gave us a <u>qu</u>iz.

2. <u>qu</u>ick   I'll take a <u>qu</u>ick **show**er now.

3. <u>qu</u>een   She'd like to be <u>qu</u>een for a day.

4. **qui**et   My house is very **qui**et at night.

5. <u>qu</u>ite   The food was **reall**y <u>qu</u>ite good.

B. In the medial (middle) position as well, the letters "qu" usually represent /kw/. Listen and repeat.

1. **e**qual   All of us have **e**qual qualifi**ca**tions.

2. e**qua**tion   It's a math e**qua**tion.

3. **liq**uid   Pour the **liq**uid from the **bott**le.

4. s<u>qu</u>eeze   We all tried to s<u>qu</u>eeze **in**to the car.

5. re**quest**   They re**quest** an **an**swer to the invi**ta**tion.

10. No Sound for "k" and "g"

A. When the letters "kn" begin a word, the "k" is not pronounced. Listen and repeat.

1. ǩnee   The ǩnee is a joint in the leg.

2. ǩneel   To ǩneel means to get down on your knees.

3. ǩnow   Do you ǩnow that to**day's** a **hol**iday?

4. ǩnew   Of course, I ǩnew that!

5. ǩnife   He used the ǩnife to cut the bread.

B. When the letter "g" comes before the letter "n" or "m" in the same syllable, it is not pronounced. Listen and repeat.

1. siǧn   Did you see the siǧn in the **win**dow?

2. re**siǧn**   I'll re**siǧn** from my job soon.

3. reiǧn   The reiǧn of the king is a long one.

4. **for**eiǧn   The ship docks at **for**eiǧn ports.

5. de**siǧn**er   She **al**ways buys de**siǧn**er clothes.

6. **di**aphraǧm The **di**aphraǧm is a **musc**le that **sep**arates the lungs from the **stom**ach.

11. Stress and Intonation

Before you listen to and repeat the sentences on the tape:

1. Read the following sentences aloud to yourself and underline the letter or letters that represent the sound /k/ with a single line and the sound /g/ with a double line. Then circle the clusters.

2. Mark the falling or rising intonation with an arrow (⌐ ⌐).

3. As you listen to the tape, mark the stressed words you hear with a stress mark (´). Pay attention to function words, phrasing, and intonation.

EXAMPLE: They were **ver**y (qu)iet when they gót their (gr)ades.

1. The me**chan**ic said the car was **read**y.

2. I need a **gall**on of a good grade of gas.

3. If you come **quick**ly, we'll carve the **tur**key.

4. Did he **grad**uate in **Au**gust?

5. We don't have e**nough** to pay for the **pack**age.

6. When she's in **En**gland, she goes **jogg**ing **ev**ery day.

7. The bank a**cross** from school was **crowd**ed.

8. We're co**llec**tors of good archi**tec**tural **pic**tures.

9. That was a great game we saw.

10. I'm **giv**ing you a good **rea**son for not **go**ing.

12. Further Practice

Here's another tongue twister. How well can you do this one?

1. Say this selection aloud to yourself and mark the stressed words and pauses.

2. Record the selection. When you play it back, check your articulation and markings.

How **man**y **cuck**oos[8] should a good cook cook

If a good cook could cook **cuck**oos?

As **man**y **cuck**oos as a good cook could cook,

If a good cook could cook **cuck**oos.

---

[8] *cuckoo* /kuwkuw/: a gray bird whose call sounds like "cuckoo." (This word is also a slang expression for a crazy person.)

Unit 26

/f/ as in _food_
/v/ as in _voice_

1. Producing /f/

EXAMPLES: <u>f</u>un, <u>ph</u>one, re**<u>f</u>er**, **co<u>ff</u>**ee, **lau<u>gh</u>**ing, gra<u>ph</u>, stu<u>ff</u>, rou<u>gh</u>

- Lightly but firmly, touch the upper teeth with the inner part of the lower lip.
- Produce the sound by forcing air out through the opening. Do not stop the flow of air.
- Your vocal cords do not vibrate.
- Hold your hand in front of your lips to feel the flow of air as you hear it.

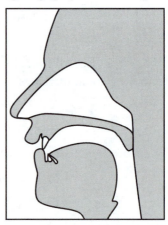

2. Producing /v/

EXAMPLES: <u>v</u>erb, **<u>v</u>ill**age, **o<u>v</u>**er, **cle<u>v</u>**er, bra<u>v</u>e, gi<u>v</u>e

- This sound is produced the same way as /f/, except that /v/ is voiced.
- Lightly but firmly, touch the upper teeth with the inner part of the lower lip.
- Produce the sound by forcing air out through the opening. Do not stop the flow of air.
- Your vocal cords should vibrate.
- Hold your hand in front of your lips to feel the flow of air as you hear it.

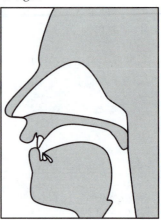

3. Contrast: /f/ and /v/

Some students confuse the sound /f/ as in "food" with the sound /v/ as in "voice."

A. Practice these two sounds, first normally, then with exaggeration, then normally. Place your hand in front of your lips to feel the flow of air. Listen and repeat.

    1. /f/   /f . . ./   /f/

    2. /v/   /v . . ./   /v/

> Reminder:
> - Vowel sounds are held longer before _voiced_ consonants than before _voiceless_ consonants.
> - _Final voiceless_ consonants are held longer than _final voiced_ consonant sounds, with the exception of stop-plosives. (See Unit 4.)

B. Now practice the sounds in words. Notice the phonetic spelling. Listen and repeat each word twice.

    1. **f**ood   /fuwd/   **f**ood

    2. a**ff**ord   /əfɔrd/   a**ff**ord

    3. bee**f**   /biyf/   bee**f**

    4. tou**gh**   /təf/   tou**gh**

    5. **v**oice   /vɔys/   **v**oice

    6. dri**v**er   /drayvər/   dri**v**er

    7. a**bov**e   /əbəv/   a**bov**e

    8. ca**v**e   /keyv/   ca**v**e

4. Check Your Listening

A. The following pairs of words contain the sounds /f/ as in "food" and /v/ as in "voice." You will hear one word from each pair. Circle the word that you hear.

1. **f**ast	**v**ast		5. **sur**f**ace**	**ser**v**ice**
2. **f**an	**v**an		6. re**f**use	re**views**
3. **ferry**	**ver**y		7. sa**f**e	sa**v**e
4. **f**ew	**v**iew		8. hal**f**	ha**v**e

B. In the following pairs of words, one word ends with the sound /f/ or /v/. You will hear one word from each pair. Circle the word that you hear.

1. say	sa<u>fe</u>		6. say	sa<u>ve</u>
2. bee	bee<u>f</u>		7. dry	dri<u>ve</u>
3. lie	li<u>fe</u>		8. lie	li<u>ve</u>
4. why	wi<u>fe</u>		9. we	we'<u>ve</u>
5. low	loa<u>f</u>		10. way	wa<u>ve</u>

5. Practice the Contrast: /f/ as in "<u>f</u>ood" with /v/ as in "<u>v</u>oice"

A. Practice these contrasting sounds. Listen and repeat each word pair.

/f/	/v/		/f/	/v/
1. <u>f</u>an	<u>v</u>an		6. **saf**er	**sav**er
2. **ferr**y	**ver**y		7. hal<u>f</u>	ha<u>ve</u>
3. <u>f</u>ault	<u>v</u>ault [1]		8. sa<u>f</u>e	sa<u>ve</u>
4. <u>f</u>ew	<u>v</u>iew		9. lea<u>f</u>	lea<u>ve</u>
5. **ri**<u>f</u>le	**ri**<u>v</u>al		10. li<u>f</u>e	li<u>ve</u>

B. Now practice the contrasting sounds in sentence pairs. The first sentence of each pair has the sound /f/, and the second has the sound /v/. Listen and repeat.

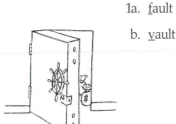

1a. <u>f</u>ault   Don't tell me it's my <u>f</u>ault.

 b. <u>v</u>ault   Don't tell me it's my <u>v</u>ault.

2a. <u>f</u>an   I bought a large <u>f</u>an **yes**terday.

 b. <u>v</u>an   I bought a large <u>v</u>an **yes**terday.

---

[1] *vault:* a safe (usually in a bank) in which money is kept

3a. <u>f</u>ew — We thought we had a <u>f</u>ew of them.

 b. <u>v</u>iew — We thought we had a <u>v</u>iew of them.

4a. **ri**<u>f</u>le — Do you want a **ri**<u>f</u>le?

 b. **ri**<u>v</u>al[2] — Do you want a **ri**<u>v</u>al?

5a. a li<u>f</u>e — A li<u>f</u>e like that is no **bar**gain.

 b. ali<u>v</u>e — Ali<u>v</u>e like that is no **bar**gain.

6a. **<u>f</u>en**der — We saw that the **<u>f</u>en**der was old.

 b. **<u>v</u>en**der[3] — We saw that the **<u>v</u>en**der was old.

7a. **<u>fi</u>**nal — He walked out and said, "That's **<u>fi</u>**nal!"

 b. **<u>vi</u>**nyl — He walked out and said, "That's **<u>vi</u>**nyl!"

8a. sa<u>f</u>e — We thought he said "sa<u>f</u>e."

 b. sa<u>v</u>e — We thought he said "sa<u>v</u>e."

9a. **<u>f</u>err**y — Did you say "**<u>f</u>err**y"?

 b. **<u>v</u>er**y — Did you say "**<u>v</u>er**y"?

10a. hal<u>f</u> — How does one spell "hal<u>f</u>"?

 b. ha<u>v</u>e — How does one spell "ha<u>v</u>e"?

---

[2] _rival:_ a person who tries to win something away from someone
[3] _vender:_ a person who sells something

6. Practice the Contrast: /f/ as in "food" with /p/ as in "pen"

Some speakers confuse /f/ as in "food" with /p/ as in "pen." Remember that when you pronounce /f/, the air flows out without stopping. When you say /p/, you stop the air flow and then let it escape with a puff. Both of these sounds are voiceless.

A. Practice these contrasting sounds. Listen and repeat each word pair.

/f/	/p/		/f/	/p/
1. fade	paid	6.	cliff	clip
2. fool	pool	7.	chief	cheap
3. fork	pork	8.	laugh	lap
4. fast	past	9.	cuff	cup
5. **suff**er	**supp**er	10.	wife	wipe

B. Now practice the contrasting sounds in sentence pairs. The first sentence of each pair has the sound /f/, and the second has the sound /p/. Listen and repeat.

1a.	fade	Is the word "fade"?
b.	paid	Is the word "paid"?
2a.	fool	The fool is out in the back.
b.	pool	The pool is out in the back.
3a.	fork	Would you like the fork now?
b.	pork	Would you like the pork now?
4a.	fast	I'm **worr**ied that it's fast.
b.	past	I'm **worr**ied that it's past.

5a. **suff**er   He's **go**ing to **suff**er late at night.

 b. **supp**er   He's **go**ing to **supp**er late at night.

6a. cli**ff**   It's hard to find a cli**ff**.

 b. cli**p**   It's hard to find a cli**p**.

7a. chie**f**   It was the chie**f** one.

 b. chea**p**   It was the chea**p** one.

8a. lau**gh**   It's in her lau**gh**.

 b. la**p**   It's in her la**p**.

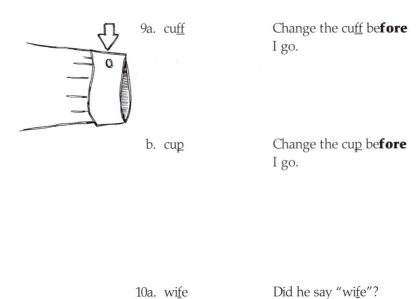

9a. cu<u>ff</u> Change the cu<u>ff</u> be**fore** I go.

b. cu<u>p</u> Change the cu<u>p</u> be**fore** I go.

10a. wi<u>fe</u> Did he say "wi<u>fe</u>"?

b. wi<u>pe</u> Did he say "wi<u>pe</u>"?

7. Practice the Contrast: /v/ as in "<u>v</u>oice" with /b/ as in "<u>b</u>oy"

Some students confuse /v/ as in "<u>v</u>oice" with /b/ as in "<u>b</u>oy." Remember that when you pronounce /v/, the air flows out without stopping. When you say /b/, you stop the air flow and then let it escape with a puff. Both of these sounds are voiced.

 A. Practice these contrasting sounds. Listen and repeat each word pair.

/v/	/b/		/v/	/b/
1. "<u>v</u>"	<u>b</u>e	6.	<u>v</u>ent	<u>b</u>ent
2. <u>v</u>eil	<u>b</u>ail	7.	<u>v</u>an	<u>b</u>an
3. **<u>ver</u>**y	**<u>bur</u>**y	8.	<u>v</u>ote	<u>b</u>oat
4. <u>v</u>et	<u>b</u>et	9.	<u>v</u>ow	<u>b</u>ow
5. <u>v</u>est	<u>b</u>est	10.	cur<u>v</u>e	cur<u>b</u>

B. Now practice the contrasting sounds in sentence pairs. The first sentence of each pair has the sound /v/, and the second has the sound /b/. Listen and repeat.

1a.	<u>v</u>est	She's got the <u>v</u>est.
b.	<u>b</u>est	She's got the <u>b</u>est.

2a.	<u>v</u>eil	I've the <u>v</u>eil we want.
b.	<u>b</u>ail [4]	I've the <u>b</u>ail we want.

3a.	**ver**y	Is it "**ver**y" that you've said?
b.	**bur**y	Is it "**bur**y" that you've said?

4a.	<u>v</u>et [5]	I like the <u>v</u>et you've **chos**en.
b.	<u>b</u>et	I like the <u>b</u>et you've **chos**en.

5a.	"v"	Have you seen the **lett**er "v"?
b.	"b"	Have you seen the **lett**er "b"?

---

[4] _bail:_ money left with a court of law when a person awaiting trial is released from jail

[5] _vet:_ short for veterinarian (an animal doctor); short for veteran (any person formerly in the military)

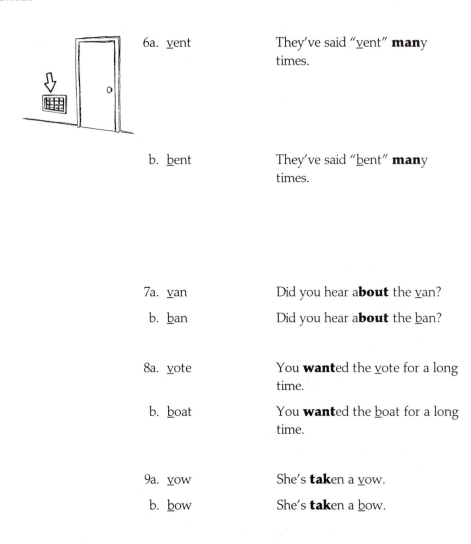

6a. <u>v</u>ent

They've said "<u>v</u>ent" **man**y times.

b. <u>b</u>ent

They've said "<u>b</u>ent" **man**y times.

7a. <u>v</u>an

Did you hear a**bout** the <u>v</u>an?

b. <u>b</u>an

Did you hear a**bout** the <u>b</u>an?

8a. <u>v</u>ote

You **want**ed the <u>v</u>ote for a long time.

b. <u>b</u>oat

You **want**ed the <u>b</u>oat for a long time.

9a. <u>v</u>ow

She's **tak**en a <u>v</u>ow.

b. <u>b</u>ow

She's **tak**en a <u>b</u>ow.

10a. cur<u>v</u>e

He parked the car on the cur<u>v</u>e.

b. cur<u>b</u>

He parked the car on the cur<u>b</u>.

 ## 8. Consonant Clusters With /fl/ and /fr/

When one consonant is combined with one or more other consonants, it is called a *cluster*. When /f/ occurs in a cluster, the force of air is *weak*. However, make sure that your upper teeth touch your lower inner lip and that the air is forced out before you make the following sound. Listen and repeat.

Initial /fl/	Medial /fl/	Final /fl/
1. **fl**ag	1. **con**fl**ict	1. **rif**fle
2. **flu**ent	2. **pam**phlet	2. **tri**fle[6]
3. **flo**resc**ent	3. in**fla**tion	3. **raff**le
4. **fla**vor	4. **muff**ler	4. **sniff**le[7]

Initial /fr/	Medial /fr/
1. **fr**ee	1. re**fresh**
2. ph**r**ase	2. de**frost**
3. **fr**ied	3. in**fre**quent
4. **Fri**day	4. re**frig**erator

Note: Some speakers find it easier, when making the /fl/ and /fr/ clusters, to get placement first for /l/ or /r/ and then produce /f/ followed by /l/ or /r/.

9. Stress and Intonation

A. Before you listen to and repeat the following dialog, place a <u>single</u> line under the letter(s) representing the sound /f/ as in "<u>f</u>ood" and a <u>double</u> line under the letter(s) representing /v/ as in "<u>v</u>oice."

    1. As you listen to the tape, mark the stressed words you hear with a stress mark (ˊ) and the rising or falling intonation with an arrow (⌐ ⌐).

    2. Pay attention to function words and phrasing.

The first sentence is marked for you.

    1. Phil: What's new, Vic?

    2. Vic: I'm **mak**ing a list of food and su**pplies.**

    3. Phil: What for?

    4. Vic: What for? For the **par**ty, of course!

    5. Phil: **Par**ty? What **par**ty?

---

[6] _trifle:_ an unimportant thing
[7] _sniffle:_ breathe in noisily when nose is running, especially when you have a cold

6. Vic: You for**got** we're **hav**ing a **Val**entine's[8] **par**ty?

7. Phil: Oh, yeah, I for**got.** Who are you in**vit**ing?

8. Vic: Some guys from our **fresh**man class.

9. Phil: Great! I'll help you buy the stuff we need.

10. Vic: Well, here's a list of some of the food you could get.

11. Phil: Mmm. Roast beef, franks, French fries, po**ta**to **sal**ad, and **pret**zels. How much should I get?

12. Vic: We'll **fig**ure it out **af**ter we de**cide** how **man**y we're in**vit**ing.

13. Phil: We'll **al**so have to **fig**ure out how **man**y forks, knives, plates, cups, and **nap**kins we'll need.

14. Vic: Oh, gee. I for**got** a**bout** that.

15. Phil: Leave it to me; I'll take care of it.

16. Vic: O**kay**. See you at the frat[9] house at five. Don't for**get.**

17. Phil: Don't **worr**y, I won't for**get!** See you at five.

---

[8] *Valentine:* usually a card or letter sent to a sweetheart or friend. A party is sometimes celebrated on Valentine's Day, February. 14.

[9] *frat:* an abbreviated expression for *fraternity,* a college social organization for male students usually sharing the same housing

B. Suppose you were planning a party. Whom would you invite? What type of food would you get? Discuss your ideas in class.

10. Further Practice

A. Make up a sentence for each of the following phrases. Mark the sentences for stress and intonation. Bring them to class and exchange them with your partner. Monitor each other for correct articulation, stress, and intonation. Your instructor may ask you to read your sentences to the class.

1. French fries
2. flew to **free**dom
3. in**fre**quent **vis**itor
4. de**frost** the re**frig**erator
5. **flu**ent in French

6. **cov**er the **tel**evision
7. save the **veg**etables
8. knives on the stove
9. vote for **sev**en
10. twelve vans

B. Make up a list of words with /f/ and /v/ that you may have difficulty pronouncing. Bring them to class. (Most likely, others in the class will have the same difficulty.)

Unit 27

/θ/ as in *thin*
/ð/ as in *the*

1. Producing /θ/

EXAMPLES: <u>th</u>ank, **thir**ty, **noth**ing, **heal**thy, **sym**pathy, fif<u>th</u>, tru<u>th</u>

- Lightly place your tongue tip between your upper and lower front teeth (not between your lips).
- Your upper teeth rest on your tongue, lightly.
- Produce the sound by forcing air out through the narrow opening between your teeth and tongue.
- Your vocal cords do not vibrate.
- Hold your hand in front of your lips to feel the flow of air as you hear it.

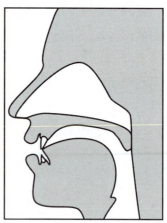

Note: The tongue tip may also be placed just behind the cutting edge of the upper teeth. Make sure that air is forced out through the narrow opening between the tongue tip and the upper teeth in a steady stream over the tongue tip.

2. Producing /ð/

EXAMPLES: this, they, **both**er, **fath**er, **south**ern, clo**the**

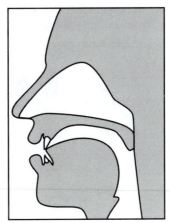

- This sound is produced the same way as /θ/, except that /ð/ is voiced.
- Lightly place your tongue tip between your upper and lower front teeth (not between your lips).
- Your upper teeth rest on your tongue, lightly.
- Produce the sound by forcing air out through the narrow opening between your teeth and tongue. Say /ð/ with less force than you use for /θ/.
- Your vocal cords should vibrate.
- Hold your hand in front of your lips to feel the flow of air as you hear it.

3. Contrast: /θ/ and /ð/

Students sometimes confuse the sound /θ/ as in "<u>th</u>in" with the sound /ð/ as in "<u>th</u>e."

A. Practice these two sounds, first normally, then with exaggeration, then normally. Place your hand in front of your lips to feel the stream of air. Listen and repeat.

   1. /θ/   /θ . . . /   /θ/
   2. /ð/   /ð . . . /   /ð/

B. Now practice these sounds in words. Notice the phonetic spelling. Listen and repeat each word twice.

   1. <u>th</u>umb   /θəm/   <u>th</u>umb
   2. **au**<u>th</u>or   /ɔθər/   **au**<u>th</u>or
   3. pa<u>th</u>   /pæθ/   pa<u>th</u>
   4. ma<u>th</u>   /mæθ/   ma<u>th</u>
   5. a**noth**er   /ənəðər/   a**noth**er
   6. smoo<u>th</u>   /smuwð/   smoo<u>th</u>
   7. ba<u>the</u>   /beyð/   ba<u>the</u>
   8. clo<u>the</u>   /klowð/   clo<u>the</u>

4. Check Your Listening

A. You will hear words with the sounds /θ/ and /ð/. First, cover the words in the following list with a piece of paper. Then listen to each word. Concentrate on the sound, not the spelling. Which consonant sound do you hear? Write a check mark in the correct column.

		/θ/ as in "<u>th</u>in"	/ð/ as in "<u>th</u>e"
<u>th</u>is	1.		✓
<u>th</u>en	2.		✓
<u>th</u>ink	3.	✓	
ba<u>th</u>	4.	✓	
bo<u>th</u>	5.	✓	
ba<u>the</u>	6.		✓
sou<u>th</u>	7.	✓	
fif<u>th</u>	8.	✓	✗
<u>th</u>ese	9.		✓
brea<u>the</u>	10.		✓

B. In the following pairs of words, one word ends with the sound /θ/. You will hear one word from each pair. Circle the word you hear.

1. true   (truth)
2. (bow)   both
3. (nine)   ninth
4. tea   (teeth)
5. owe   (oath)
6. ten   (tenth)

5. Most Common Words With /ð/

The /ð/ sound is found in the following words, which are very common in the English language. Practice these words; they are the most-used words that contain /ð/. Listen and repeat.

1. the	6. their (there)	11. though
2. then	7. this	12. **fath**er
3. them	8. than	13. **moth**er
4. they	9. that	14. **broth**er
5. these	10. those	15. **oth**er

Reminder:

- Vowel sounds are held longer before _voiced_ consonants than before _voiceless_ consonants.
- _Final voiceless_ consonants are held longer than _final voiced_ consonant sounds, with the exception of stop-plosives. (See Unit 4.)

---

6. Practice the Contrast: /θ/ as in "_th_in" with /t/ as in "_t_en"

Some students confuse /θ/ as in "_th_in" with /t/ as in "_t_en." When you pronounce /θ/, air flows out without stopping. When you pronounce /t/, the air stops, then escapes with a puff.

A. Practice these contrasting sounds. Listen and repeat each word pair.

/t/	/θ/	/t/	/θ/
1. taught	thought	5. tent	tenth
2. team	theme	6. debt	death
3. tin	thin	7. boot	booth
4. tank	thank	8. mat	math

B. Now practice the contrasting sounds in sentence pairs. The first sentence of each pair has the sound /t/, and the second has the sound /θ/. Listen and repeat.

1a. <u>t</u>aught   He <u>t</u>aught a lot last night.

b. <u>th</u>ought   He <u>th</u>ought a lot last night.

2a. <u>t</u>eam   I need a <u>t</u>eam for my school.

b. <u>th</u>eme   I need a <u>th</u>eme for my school.

3a. <u>t</u>in   Do you like it when it's <u>t</u>in?

b. <u>th</u>in   Do you like it when it's <u>th</u>in?

4a. <u>t</u>ank   She said "<u>t</u>ank."

b. <u>th</u>ank   She said "<u>th</u>ank."

5a. ten<u>t</u>   It's my ten<u>t</u>.

b. ten<u>th</u>   It's my ten<u>th</u>.

6a. deb<u>t</u>   It's his deb<u>t</u> I'm **worr**ied a**bout.**

b. dea<u>th</u>   It's his dea<u>th</u> I'm **worr**ied a**bout.**

7a. boo<u>t</u>   She has my boo<u>t</u>.

b. boo<u>th</u>   She has my boo<u>th</u>.

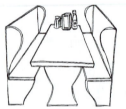

8a. ma<u>t</u>   He said his ma<u>t</u> is hard.

b. ma<u>th</u>   He said his ma<u>th</u> is hard.

7. Practice the Contrast: /ð/ as in "<u>the</u>" with /d/ as in "<u>day</u>"

Some students confuse /ð/ as in "<u>the</u>" with /d/ as in "<u>day</u>." When you pronounce /ð/, the air flows out without stopping. When you pronounce /d/, the air stops, then escapes with a puff.

A. Practice these contrasting sounds. Listen and repeat each word pair.

/d/	/ð/		/d/	/ð/
1. <u>d</u>ay	<u>th</u>ey	5.	la<u>dd</u>er	la<u>th</u>er[1]
2. <u>d</u>oze	<u>th</u>ose	6.	loa<u>d</u>ing	loa<u>th</u>ing[2]
3. <u>d</u>ough	<u>th</u>ough	7.	wor<u>d</u>	wor<u>th</u>
4. <u>d</u>are	<u>th</u>ere	8.	sue<u>d</u>	soo<u>th</u>e[3]

B. Now practice the contrasting sounds in sentence pairs. The first sentence of each pair has the sound /d/, and the second has the sound /ð/. Listen and repeat.

1a. <u>d</u>ay   Will <u>d</u>ay **ev**er come?

b. <u>th</u>ey   Will <u>th</u>ey **ev**er come?

2a. <u>d</u>oze   It's not fair to <u>d</u>oze in class.

b. <u>th</u>ose   It's not fair to <u>th</u>ose in class.

---

[1] *lather:* bubbles formed by soap when mixed with water
[2] *loathing:* hating
[3] *soothe:* ease mental or physical pain

3a.	d̲ough	Can you spell "d̲ough"?
b.	th̲ough	Can you spell "th̲ough"?
4a.	**la̲dd̲er**	Look at the **la̲dd̲er**.
b.	**la̲th̲er**	Look at the **la̲th̲er**.
5a.	**loa̲d̲ing**	He was **loa̲d̲ing** it.
b.	**loa̲th̲ing**	He was **loa̲th̲ing** it.
6a.	wor̲d̲	Who said "wor̲d̲"?
b.	wor̲th̲	Who said "wor̲th̲"?
7a.	sue̲d̲	We sue̲d̲ him.
b.	soo̲th̲e	We soo̲th̲e him.

8. Consonant Clusters With /θ/ as in "th̲in"

When one consonant is combined with one or more other consonants, it is called a cluster. When /θ/ appears in a cluster, the force of air is *weak*. However, make sure the air is forced through the narrow opening in a steady stream. Listen and repeat.

Initial /θr/	Medial /θr/; /rθ/	Final /rθ/
1. th̲rough	1. **ba̲th̲room**	1. ear̲th̲
2. th̲ree	2. **ba̲th̲robe**	2. four̲th̲
3. th̲row	3. **bir̲th̲day**	3. bir̲th̲
4. th̲roat	4. **wor̲th̲less**	4. gir̲th̲[4]

---

[4] *girth:* the measurement around the body of something (luggage or package, etc.)

9. Practice the Contrast: /θ/ as in "thin" with /f/ as in "food"

Some students confuse /θ/ as in "thin" with /f/ as in "food." When you pronounce /θ/, place your tongue tip between your teeth. When you say /f/, touch your upper teeth with the inner part of your lower lip.

A. Practice these contrasting sounds. Listen and repeat each word pair.

/f/	/θ/		/f/	/θ/
1. first	thirst	6. deaf	death
2. fought	thought	7. oaf	oath
3. Fred	thread	8. roof	Ruth
4. frill[5]	thrill[6]	9. miff[7]	myth
5. free	three	10. reef	wreath

B. Now practice the contrasting sounds in sentence pairs. The first sentence of each pair has the sound /f/, and the second has the sound /θ/. When /t/ or /d/ comes before or after the /θ/ sound, /t/ and /d/ are made with the tongue tip against the teeth (one sounds anticipates the other). Listen and repeat.

1a.	first	It's not the first.
b.	thirst	It's not the thirst.
2a.	fought	He fought all the time.
b.	thought	He thought all the time.
3a.	Fred	Was it Fred you **want**ed?
b.	thread	Was it thread you **want**ed?

---

[5] _frill:_ any unnecessary decoration
[6] _thrill:_ a feeling of strong excitement
[7] _miff:_ put in a bad mood

4a. f<u>r</u>ill   She **does**n't need a f<u>r</u>ill.

 b. th<u>r</u>ill   She **does**n't need a th<u>r</u>ill.

5a. f<u>r</u>ee   Is it f<u>r</u>ee for all of us?

 b. th<u>r</u>ee   Is it th<u>r</u>ee for all of us?

6a. oa<u>f</u>[8]   The word "oa<u>f</u>" is in the book.

 b. oa<u>th</u>   The word "oa<u>th</u>" is in the book.

7a. dea<u>f</u>   Did you say "dea<u>f</u>"?

 b. dea<u>th</u>   Did you say "dea<u>th</u>"?

8a. roo<u>f</u>   My roo<u>f</u> does a lot of good.

 b. Ru<u>th</u>   My Ru<u>th</u> does a lot of good.

9a. mi<u>ff</u>   He said it was "mi<u>ff</u>."

 b. my<u>th</u>   He said it was "my<u>th</u>."

10a. ree<u>f</u>   We saw a **love**ly ree<u>f</u>.

 b. wrea<u>th</u>   We saw a **love**ly wrea<u>th</u>.

---
[8] *oaf*: a stupid person

10. Practice the Contrast: /ð/ as in "<u>the</u>" with /v/ as in "<u>v</u>oice"

Some students confuse /ð/ as in "<u>the</u>" with /v/ as in "<u>v</u>oice." When you pronounce /ð/, place your tongue tip between your teeth. When you pronounce /v/, touch your upper teeth with the _inner_ part of your lower lip.

A. Listen and repeat these contrasting sounds.

/v/	/ð/		/v/	/ð/
1. "<u>v</u>"	<u>th</u>ee	4.	<u>v</u>eil	<u>th</u>ey'll
2. <u>v</u>an	<u>th</u>an	5.	<u>v</u>ine	<u>th</u>ine[9]
3. <u>v</u>at	<u>th</u>at	6.	**le<u>v</u>er**[10]	**lea<u>th</u>er**

B. Now practice the contrasting sounds in sentence pairs. The first sentence of each pair has the sound /v/, and the second has the sound /ð/. Listen and repeat.

1a. <u>v</u>at   It's one <u>v</u>at I want.

b. <u>th</u>at   It's one <u>th</u>at I want.

2a. <u>v</u>eil   It's not "<u>v</u>eil."

b. <u>th</u>ey'll   It's not "<u>th</u>ey'll."

---

[9] _thine:_ old English word meaning "yours" (usually found in the Bible and in songs)

[10] _lever:_ a flat piece of metal or wood that you press to move something heavy

3a. <u>v</u>ine   Can you spell "<u>v</u>ine"?

b. <u>th</u>ine   Can you spell "<u>th</u>ine"?

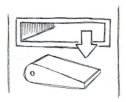

4a. **le<u>v</u>**er   He held the **le<u>v</u>**er for me.

b. **lea<u>th</u>**er   He held the **lea<u>th</u>**er for me.

11. Stress and Intonation

1. Before you listen to and repeat the following sentences, place a <u>single</u> line under the letters representing the voiceless /θ/ sound and a <u>double</u> line under the letters representing the voiced /ð/.

2. As you listen to the tape, mark the stressed words you hear with a stress mark (ˊ).

3. Pay attention to the "th" words, the phrasing, and the intonation that is already marked.

EXAMPLE: Ru<u>th</u> <u>th</u>ought her **bro<u>th</u>**er's <u>th</u>roat hurt.

1. Did your **moth**er give him three **leath**er belts?

2. Thanks for **think**ing of him.

3. She'd like to throw a **birth**day **par**ty for her **fath**er.

4. He wants **ev**erything or **noth**ing; that's a threat!

5. Is this the third house that **Ar**thur's built?

6. Can you breathe in and then breathe out?

7. Both **broth**ers are **health**y, **wealth**y, and wise.

8. We went there and thought **noth**ing of it.

9. I thought I saw my **moth**er go through the door.

10. Al**though** the **weath**er is bad, they'll go through it.

12. Further Practice

A. Read the following poem (author unknown) aloud. Use a dictionary to help you with the pronunciation and meaning of new words.

1. Place /θ/ over the letters representing voiceless "th" and /ð/ over the letters representing voiced "th."

2. Mark the poem for stress and intonation.

3. Record the poem, and when you listen to the playback monitor the articulation, function words, and intonation.

EXAMPLE:

     θ   θ

In **thir**ty-three days

      ð

Will come the **hol**idays.

1.   **Thir**ty **Thou**sand **Thought**less Boys

2.   **Thir**ty **thou**sand **thought**less boys

3.   Thought they'd make a **thun**dering noise;

4.   So with **thir**ty **thou**sand thumbs,

5.   They thumped on **thir**ty **thou**sand drums.

B. Make a list of "th" words you may have difficulty with. Put them in sentences that you usually use. Bring the sentences to class for discussion. It's a good bet[11] that others will have the same difficulty.

C. Brain Teaser: Mr. North says his grand<u>fa</u>ther is only <u>three</u> years older than his <u>fa</u>ther. Is that possible?

---

[11] *it's a good bet:* there's a good chance

Unit 28

/s/ **as in s͟ee**
/z/ **as in z͟oo**

1. Producing /s/

EXAMPLES: s͟o, c͟ent, s͟c͟ene, **miss͟**ing, de**c͟ide**, rac͟e, kis͟s͟, c͟eas͟e

- Raise the front part of your tongue toward the front part of the hard palate, but do not touch it.
- Point the tongue tip toward the upper gum ridge, but do not touch it.
- Press the sides of your tongue against the upper teeth.
- Produce the sound by forcing air out over the tongue and through the narrow opening between your tongue and upper teeth. The air escapes with a hiss.
- Your vocal cords do not vibrate.

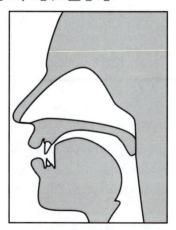

2. Producing /z/

EXAMPLES: **<u>ze</u>ro**, **cra<u>z</u>y**, **di<u>zz</u>y**, **noi<u>s</u>y**, bu<u>zz</u>, the<u>s</u>e, crie<u>s</u>

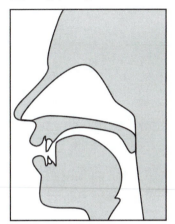

- This sound is produced the same way as /s/ except that /z/ is voiced.
- Raise the front part of your tongue toward the front part of the hard palate, but do not touch it.
- Point the tongue tip toward the upper gum ridge, but do not touch it.
- Press the sides of your tongue against the upper teeth.
- Produce the sound by forcing air out over the tongue and through the narrow opening between your tongue and upper teeth. The air escapes with a buzz-ing sound.
- Your vocal cords should vibrate.

3. Contrast: /s/ and /z/

Some students confuse the sound /s/ as in "<u>s</u>ee" with the sound /z/ as in "<u>z</u>oo."

A.   Practice these two sounds, first normally, then with exaggeration, then nor-mally. Place your hand in front of your lips to feel the stream of air. Listen and repeat.

     1. /s/   /s . . . /   /s/

     2. /z/   /z . . . /   /z/

B.   Now practice the sounds in words. Notice the phonetic spelling. Listen and repeat each word twice.

     1. <u>s</u>ad   /sæd/   <u>s</u>ad

     2. <u>s</u>afe   /seyf/   <u>s</u>afe

     3. **e<u>ss</u>**ay   /ɛsey/   **e<u>ss</u>**ay

     4. i<u>c</u>e   /ays/   i<u>c</u>e

     5. "z"   /ziy/   "z"

     6. **free<u>z</u>**er   /friyzər/   **free<u>z</u>**er

     7. pau<u>s</u>e   /pɔz/   pau<u>s</u>e

     8. <u>z</u>ip   /zɪp/   <u>z</u>ip

4. Check Your Listening

A. The following pairs of words contain the sounds /s/ as in "s̲ee" and /z/ as in "z̲oo." You will hear one word from each pair. Circle the word that you hear.

1. s̲ue	z̲oo	6. ric̲e	ris̲e
2. s̲ip	z̲ip	7. ad**vic̲e**	ad**vis̲e**
3. s̲ink	z̲inc	8. dic̲e	dies̲
4. s̲ewn	z̲one	9. rac̲e	rays̲
5. s̲ing	z̲ing	10. los̲s̲	laws̲

B. In the following pairs of words, one word ends with the sound /s/ or /z/. You will hear one word from each pair. Circle the word that you hear.

1. den	dens̲e	6. who	whos̲e
2. sin	sinc̲e	7. go	goes̲
3. for	forc̲e	8. though	thos̲e
4. saw	sauc̲e	9. no	nos̲e
5. see	ceas̲e	10. pray	prais̲e

> **Reminder:**
> • Vowel sounds are held longer before *voiced* consonants than before *voiceless* consonants.
> • Final *voiceless* consonants are held longer than final *voiced* consonant sounds, with the exception of stop-plosives. (See Unit 4.)

5. Practice the Contrast: /s/ as in "s̲ee" with /z/ as in "z̲oo"

A. Practice these contrasting sounds. Listen and repeat each word pair.

/s/	/z/		/s/	/z/
1. s̲eal	z̲eal	6. niec̲e	knees̲
2. s̲ink	z̲inc	7. ic̲e	eyes̲
3. s̲ip	z̲ip	8. plac̲e	plays̲
4. de**c̲eas̲ed**	di**s̲eas̲ed**	9. pric̲e	priz̲e
5. **rac̲**ing	**rais̲**ing	10. spic̲e	spies̲

B. Now practice the contrasting sounds in sentence pairs. The first sentence of each pair has the sound /s/, and the second has the sound /z/. Listen and repeat.

1a. <u>s</u>eal   He said it was "<u>s</u>eal."

b. <u>z</u>eal[1]   He said it was "<u>z</u>eal."

2a. <u>s</u>ink   Take the <u>s</u>ink back to the store.

b. <u>z</u>inc[2]   Take the <u>z</u>inc back to the store.

3a. <u>s</u>ip   He'll <u>s</u>ip it **slow**ly.

b. <u>z</u>ip[3]   He'll <u>z</u>ip it **slow**ly.

4a. de**<u>c</u>ea<u>s</u>ed**   We all thought he was de**<u>c</u>ea<u>s</u>ed.**

b. di**<u>s</u>ea<u>s</u>ed**   We all thought he was di**<u>s</u>ea<u>s</u>ed.**

---
[1] *zeal:* eagerness
[2] *zinc:* a bluish-white metallic chemical
[3] *zip:* open, close, or fasten with a zipper

5a. **rac**ing   He's **rac**ing his dog.

b. **rais**ing   He's **rais**ing his dog.

6a. nie<u>c</u>e   Did you see her nie<u>c</u>e?

b. knee<u>s</u>   Did you see her knee<u>s</u>?

7a. i<u>c</u>e   I see the i<u>c</u>e from here.

b. eye<u>s</u>   I see the eye<u>s</u> from here.

8a. pla<u>c</u>e   Which pla<u>c</u>e do you like best?

b. play<u>s</u>   Which play<u>s</u> do you like best?

9a. pri<u>c</u>e   What's the pri<u>c</u>e you have in mind?

b. pri<u>z</u>e   What's the pri<u>z</u>e you have in mind?

10a. spi<u>c</u>e   We want the spi<u>c</u>e now.

b. spie<u>s</u>   We want the spie<u>s</u> now.

6. Practice the Contrast: /s/ as in "<u>s</u>ee" with /θ/ as in "<u>th</u>in"

Some speakers may confuse /θ/ as in "<u>th</u>in" with /s/ as in "<u>s</u>ee." When you pronounce /θ/, place your tongue tip between your teeth. When you pronounce /s/, point your tongue tip toward your upper gum ridge (but do not touch it).

A. Practice these contrasting sounds. Listen and repeat each word pair.

/s/	/θ/		/s/	/θ/
1. <u>s</u>ick	<u>th</u>ick	5.	fa<u>c</u>e	fai<u>th</u>
2. <u>s</u>igh	<u>th</u>igh	6.	ten<u>s</u>e	ten<u>th</u>
3. <u>s</u>eam	<u>th</u>eme	7.	mou<u>s</u>e	mou<u>th</u>
4. <u>s</u>ank	<u>th</u>ank	8.	u<u>s</u>e	you<u>th</u>

B. Now practice the contrasting sounds in sentence pairs. The first sentence of each pair has the sound /s/, and the second has the sound /θ/. Listen and repeat.

1a. <u>s</u>ick   I be**lieve** it's <u>s</u>ick.

b. <u>th</u>ick   I be**lieve** it's <u>th</u>ick.

2a. <u>s</u>igh   It's not a <u>s</u>igh.

b. <u>th</u>igh   It's not a <u>th</u>igh.

3a. <u>s</u>eam   We need a <u>s</u>eam.

b. <u>th</u>eme   We need a <u>th</u>eme.

4a. <u>s</u>ank   I said "<u>s</u>ank."

b. <u>th</u>ank   I said "<u>th</u>ank."

5a. fa<u>c</u>e   He has a fa<u>c</u>e I'd like to have.

b. fai<u>th</u>   He has a fai<u>th</u> I'd like to have.

6a. ten<u>s</u>e Were you ten<u>s</u>e **wait**ing in line?

b. ten<u>th</u> Were you ten<u>th</u> **wait**ing in line?

7a. mou<u>s</u>e It's my mou<u>s</u>e I'm **think**ing of.

b. mou<u>th</u> It's my mou<u>th</u> I'm **think**ing of.

8a. u<u>s</u>e It's for your u<u>s</u>e.

b. you<u>th</u> It's for your you<u>th</u>.

7. Practice the Contrast: /z/ as in "<u>z</u>oo" with /ð/ as in "<u>th</u>e"

Some speakers may confuse /ð/ as in "<u>th</u>e" with /z/ as in "<u>z</u>oo." When you pronounce /ð/, place your tongue tip between your teeth. When you pronounce /z/, point your tongue tip toward your upper gum ridge (but do not touch it).

A. Practice these contrasting sounds. Listen and repeat each word pair.

1. "<u>z</u>"   <u>th</u>ee   4. **clo<u>s</u>**ing   **clo<u>th</u>**ing

2. <u>Z</u>en   <u>th</u>en   5. tea<u>s</u>e   tee<u>th</u>e

3. **tea<u>s</u>**ing **tee<u>th</u>**ing[4] 6. clo<u>s</u>e   clo<u>th</u>e

---

[4] *teething:* when babies grow teeth

B. Now practice the contrasting sounds in sentence pairs. The first sentence of each pair has the sound /z/, and the second has the sound /ð/. Listen and repeat.

1a.	"z"	Is it "z"?
b.	<u>th</u>ee	Is it <u>th</u>ee?
2a.	<u>Z</u>en	I be**lieve** it was <u>Z</u>en.
b.	<u>th</u>en	I be**lieve** it was <u>th</u>en.
3a.	**tea<u>s</u>ing**	The **ba**by is **tea<u>s</u>ing.**
b.	**tee<u>th</u>ing**	The **ba**by is **tee<u>th</u>ing.**
4a.	tea<u>s</u>e	**Ba**bies will tea<u>s</u>e.
b.	tee<u>th</u>e	**Ba**bies will tee<u>th</u>e.
5a.	**clo<u>s</u>ing**	It's not **clo<u>s</u>ing.**
b.	**clo<u>th</u>ing**	It's not **clo<u>th</u>ing.**
6a.	clo<u>s</u>e	Can you clo<u>s</u>e it?
b.	clo<u>th</u>e	Can you clo<u>th</u>e it?

8. Consonant Clusters With /s/

When one consonant sound is combined with one or more other consonants, it is called a *cluster*. Many English words begin with the sound /s/ followed by one or more consonants (for example, "<u>s</u>chool," "<u>s</u>top"). Some students have difficulty pronouncing these clusters. They may say the sound /ɛ/ as in "m<u>e</u>t" before /s/. "School" then sounds like /ɛskuwl/. To correct this problem, try to hold the /s/ sound longer than usual.

A. Consonant Clusters /sk/, /sl/, /sm/, **and** /sn/
Listen and repeat.

/sk/	/sl/	/sm/	/sn/
1. <u>sk</u>i	1. <u>sl</u>ow	1. <u>sm</u>ack	1. <u>sn</u>ow
2. <u>sk</u>y	2. <u>sl</u>ap	2. <u>sm</u>all	2. <u>sn</u>ap
3. <u>sk</u>irt	3. <u>sl</u>eep	3. <u>sm</u>art	3. <u>sn</u>ob
4. <u>sk</u>in	4. <u>sl</u>ip	4. <u>sm</u>oke	4. <u>sn</u>eeze

B. Consonant Clusters /sp/, /st/, /sw/, **and** /str/
Listen and repeat.

/sp/	/st/	/sw/	/str/
1. <u>sp</u>eak	1. <u>st</u>op	1. <u>sw</u>im	1. <u>str</u>eet
2. <u>sp</u>oon	2. <u>st</u>ay	2. <u>sw</u>ell	2. <u>str</u>ing
3. <u>sp</u>ell	3. **stud**y	3. <u>sw</u>eet	3. <u>str</u>ike
4. **spe**cial	4. **stu**dent	4. <u>sw</u>ear	4. <u>str</u>ess

9. Consonant Clusters /sks/, /sps/, and /sts/

Students may have difficulty with the consonant clusters /sks/, /sps/, and /sts/.

A. Consonant Clusters /sks/
Practice the following words and sentences with /sks/. Listen and repeat.

1. a<u>sks</u>   She **al**ways a<u>sks</u> **stu**dents to **vis**it her home.
2. ma<u>sks</u>   The **chil**dren wear ma<u>sks</u> for the **cos**tume **par**ty.
3. ba<u>sks</u>[5]   The cat ba<u>sks</u> in the sun for hours.
4. ta<u>sks</u>   A **moth**er has **man**y ta<u>sks</u> to do at home.
5. de<u>sks</u>   How **man**y de<u>sks</u> are there?

B. Consonant Clusters /sps/
Practice the following words and sentences with /sps/. Listen and repeat.

1. li<u>sps</u>   A **per**son who li<u>sps</u> says "thit" for "sit."

---

[5] *bask:* sit and enjoy heat, sun, or something pleasurable

2. ga<u>sps</u>   A man with a heart a**ttack** ga<u>sps</u> for air.

3. wa<u>sps</u>   Wa<u>sps</u> are **fly**ing **in**sects that sting.

4. cla<u>sps</u>   When **some**one cla<u>sps</u> your hand, it is held **tight**ly.

5. gra<u>sps</u>   When a **per**son under**stands** what you're **say**ing, he/she gra<u>sps</u> your **mean**ing.

C.   Consonant Clusters /sts/
Practice the following words and sentences with /sts/. Listen and repeat.

1. co<u>sts</u>   That car co<u>sts</u> a lot of **mon**ey.

2. te<u>sts</u>   That in**struc**tor gives **man**y te<u>sts</u>.

3. ta<u>stes</u>   He ta<u>stes</u> all the food on the **ta**ble.

4. li<u>sts</u>   All the li<u>sts</u> are on the board.

Note: In the above /sts/ clusters, /t/ can be omitted. Say "s-s" with a slight hesitation: "cos–s," "tes–s," etc.

10. Pronunciation of the "-s" Ending

You can form many plurals, possessives, and contractions by adding "-s" to a noun. Form the "s form" of a verb by adding "-s" to the base form. This ending has three different pronunciations. The pronunciation of "-s" depends on which sound, voiced or voiceless, comes before it.

A.   Nouns Ending in Voiceless Consonants
When a noun ends in the voiceless consonant /p/, /t/, /f/, /k/, or /θ/, pronounce "-s" as /s/, as in "<u>s</u>ee." Listen and repeat.

	Singular	Plural	Possessive	Contraction
1.	one sho<u>p</u>	two sho<u>ps</u>	the sho<u>p's</u> **win**dow	The sho<u>p's</u> closed.
2.	one boa<u>t</u>	two boa<u>ts</u>	the boa<u>t's</u> **cap**tain	The boa<u>t's</u> in the **wa**ter.
3.	one chie<u>f</u>	two chie<u>fs</u>	the chie<u>f's</u> son	The chie<u>f's</u> in his **off**ice.
4.	one bi<u>ke</u>	two bi<u>kes</u>	the bi<u>ke's</u> tire	The bi<u>ke's</u> in the house.
5.	one mon<u>th</u>	two mon<u>ths</u>	in a mon<u>th's</u> time	The mon<u>th's</u> June.

B. **Nouns Ending in Voiced Consonants**

When a noun ends in the voiced consonants /b/, /d/, /g/, /v/, /m/, /n/, /ŋ/, /l/, or /r/, pronounce "-s" as /z/, as in "<u>z</u>oo." Listen and repeat.

	Singular	Plural	Possessive	Contraction
1.	one ca<u>b</u>	two ca<u>bs</u>	the ca<u>b</u>'s lights	The ca<u>b</u>'s late.
2.	one be<u>d</u>	two be<u>ds</u>	the be<u>d</u>'s frame	The be<u>d</u>'s **bro**ken.
3.	one ba<u>g</u>	two ba<u>gs</u>	the ba<u>g</u>'s **col**or	The ba<u>g</u>'s torn.
4.	one glo<u>v</u>e	two glo<u>ves</u>	the glo<u>v</u>e's **col**or	The glo<u>v</u>e's torn.
5.	one far<u>m</u>	two far<u>ms</u>	the far<u>m</u>'s crop	The far<u>m</u>'s in New York.

C. **Nouns Ending in Vowels**

Remember that all vowels are voiced. Thus, when a noun ends in a vowel sound, "-s" is pronounced /z/. Listen and repeat.

	Singular	Plural	Possessive	Contraction
1.	one da<u>y</u>	two da<u>ys</u>	a da<u>y</u>'s **jour**ney	The da<u>y</u>'s **o**ver.
2.	one b<u>ee</u>	two b<u>ees</u>	the b<u>ee</u>'s hive[6]	The b<u>ee</u>'s on the **flow**er.
3.	one b<u>oy</u>	two b<u>oys</u>	the b<u>oy</u>'s toy	The b<u>oy</u>'s **com**ing.
4.	one **cit**y	two **cit**ies	the **cit**y's stores	The **cit**y's near.
5.	one fl<u>y</u>	two fl<u>ies</u>	the fl<u>y</u>'s wings	The fl<u>y</u>'s here.

Note: Possessives and contractions have the same pronunciation.

---

[6] *hive:* a place where bees live

D. "-s" or "-es" Pronounced as /ɪz/

When a noun ends in /s/, /z/, /ʃ/ as in "bru<u>sh</u>," /ʒ/ as in "garage,"[7] /tʃ/ as in "bea<u>ch</u>," or /dʒ/ as in "bri<u>dge</u>," pronounce "-s" or "-es" as /ɪz/. Pronounce /ɪz/ as a separate syllable. Listen and repeat.

	Singular	Plural	Singular POSSESSIVE	Plural POSSESSIVE
1.	one bo<u>ss</u>	two **boss**es	the **boss'**s store	the **boss**es' **meet**ing
2.	one chee<u>se</u>	**man**y **chees**es	the **cheese'**s **o**dor	the **chees**es' **o**dor
3.	one bru<u>sh</u>	two **brush**es	the bru<u>sh'</u>s **hand**le	the **brush**es' **hand**les
4.	one ga**rage**	two ga**rag**es	the ga**rage'**s door	the ga**rag**es' doors
5.	one ben<u>ch</u>	two **bench**es	the **bench'**s paint	the **bench**es' paint
6.	one bri<u>dge</u>	two **bridg**es	the **bridge'**s ropes	the **bridg**es' ropes

Note: Singular possessives and plural possessives have the same pronunciation.

Reminder: Noun Endings

- When a noun ends with /s/, /z/, /ʃ/, /ʒ/, /tʃ/, or /dʒ/, the plural ending is pronounced as an *extra syllable*.
- When a noun ends in a *voiceless consonant* sound (except for /s/, /ʃ/, and /tʃ/), the plural is pronounced as *voiceless* /s/.
- When a noun ends in a *voiced consonant* or *vowel* sound (except for /z/, /ʒ/, and /dʒ/), the plural is pronounced as *voiced* /z/.

---

[7] American speakers may pronounce this word /ɡərɑʒ/ or /ɡərɑdʒ/.

E. Verbs Ending in Voiceless Consonants

When a verb ends in the voiceless consonant /p/, /t/, /k/, or /f/, pronounce "-s" as /s/, as in "<u>s</u>ee." Listen and repeat.

1. I jum<u>p</u>. He jum<u>ps</u>. 3. I spea<u>k</u>. She spea<u>ks</u>.
2. I si<u>t</u>. She si<u>ts</u>. 4. I lau<u>gh</u>. He lau<u>ghs</u>.

F. Verbs Ending in Voiced Consonants

When a verb ends in the voiced consonant /b/, /d/, /g/, /v/, /ð/, /m/, /n/, /ŋ/, /l/, or /r/, pronounce "-s" as /z/, as in "<u>z</u>oo." Listen and repeat.

1. I ru<u>b</u>. He ru<u>bs</u>. 6. I swi<u>m</u>. He swi<u>ms</u>.
2. I nee<u>d</u>. She nee<u>ds</u>. 7. I wi<u>n</u>. She wi<u>ns</u>.
3. I be<u>g</u>. He be<u>gs</u>. 8. I si<u>ng</u>. He si<u>ngs</u>.
4. I sa<u>ve</u>. She sa<u>ves</u>. 9. I fee<u>l</u>. She fee<u>ls</u>.
5. I brea<u>the</u>. He brea<u>thes</u>. 10. I hea<u>r</u>. He hea<u>rs</u>.

G. Verbs Ending in Vowels

Remember that all vowels are voiced. Thus, when a verb ends in a vowel sound, "-s" or "-es" is pronounced /z/. Listen and repeat.

1. I s<u>ay</u>. He s<u>ays</u>. 3. I w<u>eigh</u>. He w<u>eighs.</u>
2. I s<u>ee</u>. She s<u>ees</u>. 4. I fl<u>y</u>. She fl<u>ies</u>.

H. "-s" or "-es" Pronounced /ɪz/

When a verb ends in /s/, /z/, /ʃ/ as in "wi<u>sh</u>," /ʒ/ as in "massage," /ʧ/ as in "tea<u>ch</u>," or /ʤ/, as in "ple<u>dge</u>," pronounce "-es" /ɪz/. Pronounce /ɪz/ as a separate syllable. Listen and repeat.

1. I mi<u>ss</u>. He **miss**es. 4. I ma**ssage.** She ma**ssag**es.
2. I pau<u>se</u>. She **paus**es. 5. I tea<u>ch</u>. He **teach**es.
3. I wi<u>sh</u>. She **wish**es. 6. I ple<u>dge</u>. She **pledg**es.

Reminder: Verb Endings

- When a verb ends in /s/, /z/, /ʃ/, /ʒ/, /ʧ/, and /ʤ/, add /ɪz/ to the *third person singular*. This forms an *extra syllable*.
- When a verb ends in a *voiceless consonant* sound (except for /s/, /ʃ/, and /ʧ/), add (voiceless) /s/ to the *third person singular*.
- When a verb ends in a *voiced consonant* or *vowel* sound (except for /z/, /ʒ/, and /ʤ/), add (voiced) /z/ to the *third person singular*.

11. Stress and Intonation

Work with a partner.

1. Follow the instructions below for the plural, contraction, possessive, and third person singular endings.

2. Mark the stressed words you think are important.

3. Mark the intonation.

4. Read your sentences to each other. Check each other for meaning, correct "endings," and intonation.

5. Hand your papers in to your instructor.

A. Place /s/, /z/, or /ɪz/ over the appropriate plural endings.

EXAMPLES:
   a. She re**mem**ber<u>s</u> her dream<u>s</u>.

   b. He **pol**ish<u>es</u> his car **ev**ery week.

1. The **ba**by crie<u>s</u> all day long.

2. She **ex**ercis<u>es</u> three time<u>s</u> a week.

3. Did she say the **col**or **match**<u>es</u> her suit<u>s</u>?

4. She be**lieve<u>s</u>** in fate.

5. Do you think it add<u>s</u> up to a lot?

B. Change the following to contractions.

EXAMPLES:
   a. My **mu**sic is in the book.
      My **mu**sic's in the book.

   b. Where is my **hus**band?
      Where's my **hus**band?

1. The sleeve is too short.

2. My **head**ache is gone.

3. The math is **diff**icult.

4. The **ta**ble is in the room.

5. The **wo**man is **cra**zy.

C. Change the following to the possessives.

EXAMPLES: a. The eyes of the doll were **o**pen.

The doll's eyes were **o**pen.

b. We heard the **voic**es of the men.

We heard the men's **voic**es.

1. The de**ci**sion of the **judg**es is final.

2. Did the **fam**ilies of the **dip**lomats come?

3. The tires of the truck were flat.

4. Is the **li**brary of the **coll**ege large?

5. Is it a **ques**tion of the rights of the states?

D. Change the following to the third person singular.

EXAMPLES: a. I work all day.

He works all day.

b. I go to school **ev**ery day.

She goes to school **ev**ery day.

1. I say it's good.

2. I wash **dish**es all the time.

3. I **pur**chase food once a week.

4. I lease my a**part**ment.

5. I grow **flow**ers in my **gar**den.

12. Further Practice

A. Form the plural endings of the following nouns as you say them aloud. Use the phonetic symbol /s/, /z/, or /ɪz/. You may use a dictionary to help you with any new words. Write the answers on a separate sheet of paper and hand it in to your instructor.

EXAMPLES:

a. lamp	*lamps*	/s/
b. **flow**er	*flowers*	/z/
c. prize	*prizes*	/ɪz/

1. bridge _____ /_____/
2. **trav**eler _____ /_____/
3. speed _____ /_____/
4. **bi**cycle _____ /_____/
5. horse _____ /_____/
6. ho**tel** _____ /_____/
7. **suit**case _____ /_____/
8. shop _____ /_____/
9. **mar**ket _____ /_____/
10. **tour**ist _____ /_____/
11. **cabb**age _____ /_____/
12. **ol**ive _____ /_____/
13. meat _____ /_____/
14. spice _____ /_____/
15. ba**nan**a _____ /_____/
16. **co**conut _____ /_____/
17. **man**go _____ /_____/
18. **cer**eal _____ /_____/
19. **carr**ot _____ /_____/
20. **or**ange _____ /_____/

B. Brain Teaser: There are ten black and ten white socks in a drawer. In the dark, what is the minimum number of socks you must take out before you are sure of having a pair that matches?

Unit 29

/ʃ/ as in _she_
/ʒ/ as in _pleasure_

1. Producing /ʃ/

EXAMPLES: <u>sh</u>oe, <u>s</u>ure, ma**chine**, o<u>c</u>ean, **na**<u>t</u>ion, **ten**<u>s</u>ion, **preci**ous, ru<u>sh</u>

- First raise the front part of your tongue toward the front part of the hard palate, but do not touch it.
- Then press the sides of your tongue against the sides of your upper back teeth.
- Produce the sound by forcing air out over the tongue and through your teeth.
- Your lips are rounded and protruded (pushed out) slightly.
- Your vocal cords do not vibrate.
- This is the sound you make when you want someone to be quiet (Sh!).

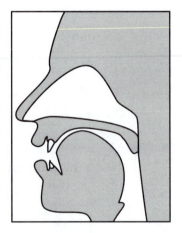

2. Producing /ʒ/

EXAMPLES: **treas**ure, **visi**on, ex**plo**sion, mir**age**

• This sound is produced the same way as /ʃ/, except that /ʒ/ is voiced.
• First raise the front part of your tongue toward the front part of the hard palate, but do not touch it.
• Then press the sides of your tongue against the sides of the your upper back teeth.
• Produce the sound by forcing air out over the tongue and through your teeth.
• Your lips are rounded and protruded (pushed out) slightly.
• Your vocal cords should vibrate.

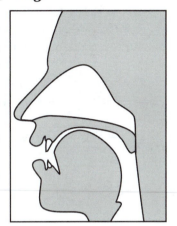

3. Contrast: /ʃ/ and /ʒ/

Some students confuse the sound /ʃ/ as in "<u>sh</u>e" with the sound /ʒ/ as in "plea<u>s</u>ure."

A. Practice these two sounds, first normally, then with exaggeration, then normally. Listen and repeat.

1. /ʃ/   /ʃ . . . /   /ʃ/
2. /ʒ/   /ʒ . . . /   /ʒ/

B. Now practice the sound in words. Notice the phonetic spelling. Listen and repeat each word twice.

1. <u>sh</u>ip	/ʃɪp/	<u>sh</u>ip
2. ma**chine**	/məʃiyn/	ma**chine**
3. wi<u>sh</u>	/wɪʃ/	wi<u>sh</u>
4. **vis**ual	/vɪʒuwəl/	**vis**ual
5. con**fus**ion	/kənfyuwʒən/	con**fus**ion
6. **es**pionage	/ɛspiyənɑʒ/	**es**pionage
7. wa<u>sh</u>	/wɑʃ/	wa<u>sh</u>
8. **treas**ure	/trɛʒər/	**treas**ure

4. Check Your Listening

You will hear words with the sounds /θ/, /s/, /z/, /ʃ/, and /ʒ/. First, cover the words in the following list with a piece of paper. Then listen to each word. Concentrate on the sound, not the spelling. Which consonant do you hear? Write a check mark in the correct column.

		/θ/ as in "thin"	/s/ as in "see"	/z/ as in "zoo"	/ʃ/ as in "sure"	/ʒ/ as in "pleasure"
through	1.	_____	_____	_____	_____	_____
sue	2.	_____	_____	_____	_____	_____
crazy	3.	_____	_____	_____	_____	_____
shoe	4.	_____	_____	_____	_____	_____
truce	5.	_____	_____	_____	_____	_____
truth	6.	_____	_____	_____	_____	_____
days	7.	_____	_____	_____	_____	_____
mi**rage**	8.	_____	_____	_____	_____	_____
brush	9.	_____	_____	_____	_____	_____
youthful	10.	_____	_____	_____	_____	_____
occu**pa**tion	11.	_____	_____	_____	_____	_____
useful	12.	_____	_____	_____	_____	_____
user	13.	_____	_____	_____	_____	_____
usual	14.	_____	_____	_____	_____	_____

5. Practice the Contrast: /ʃ/ as in "she" with /s/ as in "see"

A. Practice these contrasting sounds. Listen and repeat each word pair.

/s/	/ʃ/		/s/	/ʃ/
1. sip	ship	4. **class**es	**clash**es
2. sew	show	5. class	clash
3. leased	leashed	6. bass	bash

B. Now practice the contrasting sounds in sentence pairs. The first sentence of each pair has the sound /s/, and the second has the sound /ʃ/. Listen and repeat.

1a. sip   Did you see him take a sip?

 b. ship   Did you see him take a ship?

2a. sew   Don't sew it un**til** I re**turn.**

 b. show   Don't show it un**til** I re**turn.**

3a. leased   It was leased for a week.

 b. leashed[1]   It was leashed for a week.

4a. **class**es   They had **class**es for a long time.

 b. **clash**es[2]   They had **clash**es for a long time.

5a. class   Was it a big class?

 b. clash   Was it a big clash?

----

[1] _leash:_ hold by a cord (usually refers to an animal)
[2] _clash:_ violent disagreement

6a. ba<u>ss</u>[3]   They had a big ba<u>ss</u>.

b. ba<u>sh</u>[4]   They had a big ba<u>sh</u>.

6. Stress and Intonation

1. Before you listen to and repeat the following sentences, place a <u>single</u> line under the letter(s) representing the sound /ʃ/ as in "<u>she</u>" and a <u>double</u> line under the letter(s) representing the sound /ʒ/ as in "plea<u>s</u>ure."

2. As you listen to the tape, mark the stressed words you hear with a stress mark (ˊ), and the falling or rising intonation with an arrow (⌐\ ⌐ˊ).

3. Pay attention to function words and phrasing.

EXAMPLE: The <u>ch</u>ef **mea<u>s</u>**ured the **<u>su</u>**gar for one of his **di<u>sh</u>**es.

1. Did you wash the car in the ga**rage?**

2. Some of our **nati**onal **treas**ures are in the White House.

3. We ate the de**lici**ous food, and we **did**n't need a great deal of per**sua**sion.

4. Do you know if the ship has pro**visi**ons for a short cruise?

5. The invi**ta**tion said to dress **for**mally, not **cas**ually.

6. The **pa**tient asked for a ma**ssage.**

7. The day we met was a **speci**al o**cca**sion.

---

[3] *bass:* a freshwater fish
[4] *bash:* a forceful blow

8. Did he hurt his **shoul**der in the co**llisi**on?

9. When you **fin**ish, will you give me your de**cisi**on?

10. **Shake**speare wrote the play *Measure for Measure*.

7. Further Practice

Read the following poem aloud.

Rich the **treas**ure,

Sweet the **pleas**ure,

Sweet is **pleas**ure after pain.

The above was written by John Dryden. He lived in the seventeenth century, wrote poetry and prose, and had an enormous influence on English literature.

Discuss the meaning of the poem in class.

Unit 30

/tʃ/ as in _child_
/dʒ/ as in _job_

1. Producing /tʃ/

EXAMPLES: <u>ch</u>eck, <u>ch</u>ur<u>ch</u>, **tea<u>ch</u>**er, **na<u>t</u>**ural, lun<u>ch</u>, ma<u>tch</u>

- This sound is a combination of /t/ (a stop-plosive) as in "<u>t</u>en" and /ʃ/ (a fricative) as in "<u>sh</u>e."
- First press the tip of your tongue against your upper gum ridge. This stops the flow of air.
- Then lower the tip of the tongue quickly, keeping the sides of your tongue pressed against the upper back teeth and forcing the explosion of air out over the tongue.
- Lips are rounded and protruded (pushed out) slightly.
- Your vocal cords do not vibrate. (This sound is similar to the sound of a sneeze, "achoo," or "choo-choo train.")

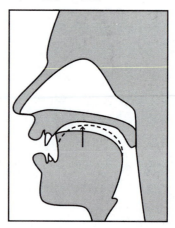

272

2. Producing /ʤ/

EXAMPLES: joy, germ, ju__dge__, en**joy, dan**ger, wage, cage

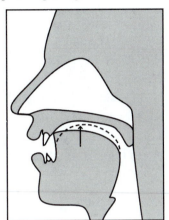

- This sound is a combination of /d/ (a stop-plosive) as in "__d__ay" and /ʒ/ (a fricative) as in "plea__s__ure." It is produced the same way as /ʧ/, except that /ʤ/ is voiced.
- First press the tip of the tongue against your upper gum ridge. This stops the flow of air.
- Then lower the tip of tongue quickly, keeping the sides of your tongue pressed against the upper back teeth and forcing the explosion of air out over the tongue.
- Lips are rounded and protruded (pushed out) slightly.
- Your vocal cords should vibrate.

3. Contrast: /ʧ/ and /ʤ/

Some students confuse the sound /ʧ/ as in "__ch__ild" with the sound /ʤ/ as in "job."

A. Practice these two sounds, first normally, then with exaggeration, then normally. Listen and repeat.

1. /ʧ/   /ʧ . . . /   /ʧ/

2. /ʤ/   /ʤ . . . /   /ʤ/

B. Now practice the sound in words. Notice the phonetic spelling. Listen and repeat each word twice.

1. __ch__eese   /ʧiyz/   __ch__eese

2. **ki__tch__**en   /kɪʧən/   **ki__tch__**en

3. ea__ch__   /iyʧ/   ea__ch__

4. __j__am   /ʤæm/   __j__am

5. **ma__g__**ic   /mæʤɪk/   **ma__g__**ic

6. pa__g__e   /peyʤ/   pa__g__e

7. __ch__oose   /ʧuwz/   __ch__oose

8. __j__oke   /ʤowk/   __j__oke

4. Check Your Listening

A. The following pairs of words contain the sounds /tʃ/ as in "<u>ch</u>ild" and /dʒ/ as in "job." You will hear one word from each pair. Circle the word that you hear.

1.	<u>ch</u>eap	jeep	5.	**rich**es	**ridg**es
2.	<u>ch</u>oke	joke	6.	lun<u>ch</u>	lunge
3.	<u>ch</u>ew	Jew	7.	ma<u>tch</u>	Ma<u>dg</u>e
4.	<u>ch</u>oice	Joyce	8.	e<u>tch</u>	e<u>dg</u>e

B. In the following pairs of words, one word ends with the sound /tʃ/ or /dʒ/. You will hear one word from each pair. Circle the word you hear.

1.	hat	ha<u>tch</u>	5.	bad	ba<u>dg</u>e
2.	hit	hi<u>tch</u>	6.	aid	age
3.	it	i<u>tch</u>	7.	paid	page
4.	beat	bea<u>ch</u>	8.	head	he<u>dg</u>e

5. Practice the Contrast: /tʃ/ as in "<u>ch</u>ild" with /dʒ/ as in "job"

A. Practice these contrasting sounds. Listen and repeat each word pair.

	/tʃ/	/dʒ/		/tʃ/	/dʒ/
1.	<u>ch</u>in	gin	6.	**é<u>tch</u>**ing	**é<u>dg</u>**ing
2.	<u>ch</u>ain	Jane	7.	ba<u>tch</u>	ba<u>dg</u>e
3.	<u>ch</u>est	jest	8.	Mar<u>ch</u>	Marge
4.	<u>ch</u>ills	Jill's	9.	"h"	age
5.	**<u>ch</u>ok**ing	**jok**ing	10.	ri<u>ch</u>	ri<u>dg</u>e

B. Now practice the contrasting sounds in sentence pairs. The first sentence has the sound /tʃ/, and the second has the sound /dʒ/. Listen and repeat.

1a.	<u>ch</u>in	I said I liked his <u>ch</u>in.
b.	gin	I said I liked his gin.

2a. <u>ch</u>ain   That's my <u>ch</u>ain you're **look**ing at.

b. <u>J</u>ane   That's my <u>J</u>ane you're **look**ing at.

3a. <u>ch</u>est[1]   I don't care for that <u>ch</u>est.

b. <u>j</u>est[2]   I don't care for that jest.

4a. <u>ch</u>ills[3]   The **doc**tor asked, "Is it <u>ch</u>ills?"

b. <u>J</u>ill's   The **doc**tor asked, "Is it <u>J</u>ill's?"

5a. **<u>ch</u>ok**ing   He's not **<u>ch</u>ok**ing.

b. **jok**ing   He's not **jok**ing.

6a. **et<u>ch</u>**ing   That's a nice **et<u>ch</u>**ing.

b. **e<u>dg</u>**ing   That's a nice **e<u>dg</u>**ing.

---

[1] *chest:* a small cabinet
[2] *jest:* a funny remark, joke
[3] *chills:* a cold feeling

7a. ba<u>tch</u>   I saw the ba<u>tch</u> be**fore** I left.

  b. ba<u>dge</u>   I saw the ba<u>dge</u> be**fore** I left.   _badche._

8a. Mar<u>ch</u>   Did you say that Mar<u>ch</u> is cold?

  b. Marge   Did you say that Marge is cold?

9a. "h"   Do you think it's an "h?"

  b. age   Do you think it's an age?

10a. ri<u>ch</u>   We **al**ways look at the ri<u>ch</u>.

  b. ri<u>dge</u>[4]   We **al**ways look at the ri<u>dge</u>.

6. Practice the Contrast: Final /ʧ/ with final /ts/

Some students confuse /ʧ/ as in "ca<u>tch</u>" with /ts/ as in "ca<u>ts</u>."

A. Practice these contrasting sounds. Listen and repeat each word pair.

/ts/	/ʧ/		/ts/	/ʧ/
1. ma<u>ts</u>	ma<u>tch</u>	4. ba<u>ts</u>	ba<u>tch</u>
2. ca<u>ts</u>	ca<u>tch</u>	5. coa<u>ts</u>	coa<u>ch</u>
3. bee<u>ts</u>	bea<u>ch</u>	6. pi<u>ts</u>	pi<u>tch</u>

B. Now practice the contrasting sounds in sentence pairs. The first sentence of each pair has the sounds /ts/, and the second has the sound /ʧ/. Listen and repeat.

1a. ma<u>ts</u>   How do you like the ma<u>ts</u>?

  b. ma<u>tch</u>   How do you like the ma<u>tch</u>?

---

[4] *ridge:* a long, narrow, high piece of land

2a. ca<u>ts</u>   He saw the ca<u>ts</u>.

  b. ca<u>tch</u>   He saw the ca<u>tch</u>.

3a. bee<u>ts</u>   She likes the bee<u>ts</u>.

  b. bea<u>ch</u>   She likes the bea<u>ch</u>.

4a. ba<u>ts</u>   Did you put a**way** the ba<u>ts</u>?

  b. ba<u>tch</u>   Did you put a**way** the ba<u>tch</u>?

5a. coa<u>ts</u>   We **want**ed to see the coa<u>ts</u>.

  b. coa<u>ch</u>   We **want**ed to see the coa<u>ch</u>.

6a. pi<u>ts</u>   We threw the pi<u>ts</u> a**way**.

  b. pi<u>tch</u>   We threw the pi<u>tch</u> a**way**.

7. Practice the Contrast: /tʃ/ as in "<u>child</u>" with /ʃ/ as in "<u>she</u>"

Some students confuse /tʃ/ as in "<u>child</u>" with /ʃ/ as in "<u>she</u>." When you pronounce /tʃ/, be sure to press your tongue tip to the upper gum ridge. Then drop the tip quickly and let the air rush out.

A. Practice these contrasting sounds. Listen and repeat each word pair.

/ʃ/	/tʃ/		/ʃ/	/tʃ/
1. <u>sh</u>are	<u>ch</u>air	4. **wa<u>sh</u>**ing	**wa<u>tch</u>**ing
2. <u>sh</u>eet	<u>ch</u>eat	5. wa<u>sh</u>	wa<u>tch</u>
3. **<u>sh</u>opp**ing	**<u>ch</u>opp**ing	6. ca<u>sh</u>	ca<u>tch</u>

B   Now practice the contrasting sounds in sentence pairs. The first sentence of each pair has the sound /ʃ/, and the second has the sound /tʃ/. Listen and repeat.

1a. <u>sh</u>are   I said I want my <u>sh</u>are.

b. <u>ch</u>air   I said I want my <u>ch</u>air.

2a. <u>sh</u>eet   Did you see the <u>sh</u>eet?

b. <u>ch</u>eat   Did you see the <u>ch</u>eat?

3a. **shopp**ing   He did the **shopp**ing **yes**terday.

b. **chopp**ing   He did the **chopp**ing **yes**terday.

4a. **wash**ing   She did the **wash**ing on **Mon**day.

b. **watch**ing   She did the **watch**ing on **Mon**day.

5a. wa<u>sh</u>   Did he take out the wa<u>sh</u>?

b. wa<u>tch</u>   Did he take out the wa<u>tch</u>?

6a. ca<u>sh</u>   I'd like to ca<u>sh</u> it.

b. ca<u>tch</u>   I'd like to ca<u>tch</u> it.

8. Stress and Intonation

1. Before you listen to and repeat the following sentences, place a single line under the letter(s) representing the sounds /tʃ/ as in "child" and a double line under the letter(s) representing the sound /dʒ/ as in "job."

2. As you listen to the tape, mark the falling or rising intonation with an arrow (—↘ ⌣↗).

3. Pay attention to function words, stressing of words, and phrasing.

The first sentence is marked for you.

1. Did you watch them go to jail?

2. The high **tém**perature did a lot of **dam**age.

3. Were you **cho**sen to serve on the **jur**y?

4. Which car can I rent with un**lim**ited **mile**age?

5. The French **lan**guage is **ver**y **mu**sical.

6. The child is **jeal**ous of his **sis**ter.

7. The **fu**ture looks good for a **sol**dier, **does**n't it?

8. Don't you have **ques**tions to ask a**bout** regi**stra**tion?

9. Is speech a re**quired** course at your **coll**ege?

10. **Chow**der is a thick soup that is pre**pared** with fish, **veg**etables, and milk.

9. Further Practice

A. In the following words, the underlined letters represent these sounds.

/ʃ/ as in "<u>sh</u>e"   /tʃ/ as in "<u>ch</u>ild"   /s/ as in "<u>s</u>ee"

/dʒ/ as in "<u>j</u>ob"   /z/ as in "<u>z</u>oo"

Say each word aloud; then write the correct phonetic symbol in the blank. (Your instructor may ask you to hand it in on a separate piece of paper.)

EXAMPLES:

a. <u>Chi</u>ca<u>g</u>o   /ʃ/

b. **<u>chil</u>**dren   /tʃ/

c. <u>j</u>ob   /dʒ/

d. e<u>ras</u>er   /s/

e. noi<u>s</u>e   /z/

1. Ju**ly** /dʒ/

2. sear<u>ch</u> /s/

3. lar<u>g</u>e /___/

4. **<u>sci</u>**ence /z/

5. **rea**<u>s</u>on /ʒ/

6. bru<u>sh</u> /ʃ/

7. ri<u>ch</u> /tʃ/

8. <u>ch</u>art /ʃ/

9. <u>s</u>ee /ʃ/

10. plea<u>s</u>e /ʃ/

11. fi**nan**<u>c</u>ial /ʃ/

12. <u>ch</u>ase /tʃ/

13. **re<u>g</u>**ister /dʒ/

14. rai<u>s</u>e /s/

15. **bi**<u>c</u>ycle /ʃ/

16. **ma**<u>j</u>or /dʒ/

17. <u>ch</u>am**pagne** /ʃ/

18. <u>j</u>ump /dʒ/

19. be**cause** /s/

20. **ba<u>ch</u>**elor /tʃ/

21. mi<u>ss</u> /z/

22. in**fec**<u>ti</u>on /tʃ/

23. **pa<u>ck</u>**age /tʃ/

24. **mer**<u>ch</u>ant /ʃ/

B. Read the following poem aloud as you mark it for pauses and intonation. Pay attention to function words and linking words.

1. **Mon**day's child is fair of face,

2. **Tues**day's child is full of grace,

3. **Wednes**day's child is full of woe,

4. **Thurs**day's child has far to go.

5. **Fri**day's child is **lov**ing and **giv**ing,

6. **Sat**urday's child has to work for its **liv**ing.

7. But a child that's born on the **Sabb**ath day

8. Is fair and wise and good and gay.

Discuss, in class, the meaning of the above poem.

Unit 31

/h/ **as in _house_**

1. Producing /h/

EXAMPLES: <u>h</u>e, <u>h</u>ow, <u>wh</u>o,[1] a**h**ead, per**h**aps

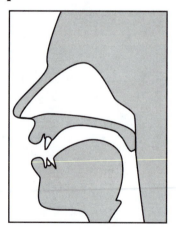

- This sound is always followed by a vowel sound. As you say /h/, you breathe out, and your tongue and lips shape the vowel sound that follows.
- Lower your jaw slightly, and let your tongue rest in a relaxed position.
- Force air out of your throat, through open lips. (It sounds like a whisper of air.)
- Your vocal cords do not vibrate.

2. Practice the Sound

A. Practice the sound /h/, first normally, then with exaggeration, then normally. Listen and repeat.

/h/   /h . . . /   /h/

---

[1] The "w" is not pronounced in some words that begin with "wh." See page 300.

282

B. Now practice the sound in words. Notice the phonetic spelling. Listen and repeat each word twice.

1. w<u>h</u>om	/huwm/	w<u>h</u>om
2. <u>h</u>ome	/howm/	<u>h</u>ome
3. <u>h</u>ole	/howl/	<u>h</u>ole
4. <u>h</u>ave	/hæv/	<u>h</u>ave
5. in**hale**	/ɪnheyl/	in**hale**
6. re**hearse**	/rɪhərs/	re**hearse**

3. Check Your Listening

In the following pairs of words, one word begins with the sound /h/. You will hear one word from each pair. Circle the word that you hear.

1. as	<u>h</u>as	5. ear	<u>h</u>ear
2. old	<u>h</u>old	6. and	<u>h</u>and
3. I'd	<u>h</u>ide	7. am	<u>h</u>am
4. all	<u>h</u>all	8. at	<u>h</u>at

4. Practice the Contrast: Words with initial /h/ as in "<u>h</u>ouse" and words without /h/

Some students leave out the sound /h/ when it appears at the beginning of a word.

A. Listen and repeat each word pair.

Without /h/	With /h/	Without /h/	With /h/
1. art	<u>h</u>eart	5. I	<u>h</u>igh
2. eat	<u>h</u>eat	6. arm	<u>h</u>arm
3. air	<u>h</u>air	7. it	<u>h</u>it
4. ate	<u>h</u>ate	8. owl	<u>h</u>owl[2]

---

[2] *howl:* cry loudly

B.   The second sentence of each pair has the sound /h/. Listen and repeat.

1a. art   It's my art I'm **worr**ied a**bout.**

 b. <u>h</u>eart   It's my <u>h</u>eart I'm **worr**ied a**bout.**

2a. eat   Did you eat it right a**way?**

 b. <u>h</u>eat   Did you <u>h</u>eat it right a**way?**

3a. air   I can tell it's in the air.

 b. <u>h</u>air   I can tell it's in the <u>h</u>air.

4a. I   Who said it was I?

 b. <u>h</u>igh   Who said it was <u>h</u>igh?

5a. arm[3]   Did you arm the man?

 b. <u>h</u>arm   Did you <u>h</u>arm the man?

6a. it   We **did**n't think it was it.

 b. <u>h</u>it   We **did**n't think it was <u>h</u>it.

5. Practice the Contrast: /h/ as in "<u>h</u>ouse" with /f/ as in "<u>f</u>ood"

Some students confuse /h/ as in "<u>h</u>ouse" with /f/ as in "<u>f</u>ood." When you say /f/, touch your upper front teeth with the inner part of your lower lip. When you say /h/, let air flow out of your throat through open lips.

A.   Practice these contrasting words. Listen and repeat each word pair.

1. <u>h</u>all   <u>f</u>all   4. <u>h</u>eight   <u>f</u>ight

2. <u>h</u>at   <u>f</u>at   5. <u>h</u>orse   <u>f</u>orce

3. <u>h</u>ate   <u>f</u>ate   6. <u>h</u>eat   <u>f</u>eet

---

[3] *arm:* provide with a weapon

B. Now practice the contrasting sounds in sentence pairs. The first sentence of each pair has the sound /h/, and the second has the sound /f/. Listen and repeat.

1a.	hall	It **happ**ened in the hall.
b.	fall	It **happ**ened in the fall.
2a.	hat	Take off the hat, will you?
b.	fat	Take off the fat, will you?
3a.	hate	It could be hate, **could**n't it?
b.	fate	It could be fate, **could**n't it?
4a.	height	Was it the height you **want**ed?
b.	fight	Was it the fight you **want**ed?
5a.	horse	Is the horse with you?
b.	force	Is the force with you?
6a.	heat	It was the heat that a**nnoy**ed me.
b.	feet	It was the feet that a**nnoy**ed me.

6. No Sound for "h" and "gh"

A. The letter "h" is not pronounced in the following words. Listen and repeat these words and sentences.

1.	ḥour	An ḥour is **e**qual to **six**ty **min**utes.
2.	**ḥon**or	When you **ḥon**or **some**one, you show your re**spect.**

3. **h**onest   If you're **h**onest, you tell the truth.

4. **h**eir   An **h**eir is a **per**son who is **le**gally in line to re**ceive mon**ey, **prop**erty, or a **ti**tle when **some**one dies.

5. **h**erb[4]   An **h**erb is a plant that's used to give food **fla**vor.

6. **rhy**thm   **Mu**sic beats out a **rhy**thm you can dance to.

7. ex**h**i**biti**on   An ex**h**i**biti**on shows things in **pub**lic.

8. g**h**ost   A g**h**ost is the **spir**it of a dead **per**son who su**ppos**edly a**ppears** a**gain.**

9. Jo**h**n   Jo**h**n is the name of my friend.

10. **Th**omas   **Th**omas is the name of John's friend.

11. **ve**h**icle   A car is re**ferred** to as a **ve**h**icle.

B. The letters "gh" are not pronounced in the following words. Listen and repeat these words and sentences.

1. **neigh**bor   My **neigh**bor lives next door to me.

2. **dough**nut   Did he eat a **dough**nut with his **coff**ee?

3. thou**gh**t   I thou**gh**t I saw him.

4. throu**gh**   Did you go throu**gh** my drawer?

5. **thor**ou**gh**   I made a **thor**ou**gh** search.

6. al**though**   I'll go, al**though** I'm a**fraid.**

7. cau**gh**t   I cau**gh**t a cold last night.

8. fou**gh**t   They fou**gh**t like cats and dogs.

9. tau**gh**t   Were you tau**gh**t to do that?

10. fi**gh**t   They fi**gh**t **ev**ery day.

11. hei**gh**t   His hei**gh**t is six feet.

12. ni**gh**t   The house is **qui**et at ni**gh**t.

---

[4] This word may also be pronounced with /h/.

7. Stress and Intonation

1. Before you listen to and repeat the following sentences, underline the letter(s) representing /h/ as in "house."

2. As you listen to the tape, mark the stressed words you hear with a stress mark (‚) and the falling or rising intonation with an arrow (‿ ‿).

3. Pay attention to function words and phrasing.

The first sentence is marked for you.

1. Whose old hat is that on the hook?

2. Don't **hes**itate to go to the **hos**pital.

3. **Harr**y wants a hot dog, and I want a ham on rye.

4. **Hurr**y up! My **hus**band is **hun**gry and he wants a **ham**burger.

5. When did you hear Hal say he**llo** to **Hel**en?

6. How a**bout tak**ing half of it home?

7. Where did you hurt your head when you fell in the hall?

8. The **heav**y smog in the air is bad for my **hair**do.

9. It's in**hu**man to hold a re**hears**al in such hot **weath**er.

10. Who had a **horr**ible **head**ache **af**ter in**hal**ing the **al**cohol?

8. Further Practice

A. Make up five sentences with the sound /h/ as in "house" in initial position and five with /h/ in medial position. Choose words from the lists below. Underline the word in each sentence. (_Remember:_ The sound /h/ never occurs in final position in English.)

/h/ IN INITIAL POSITION		/h/ IN MEDIAL POSITION	
1. him	5. **hol**iday	1. be**have**	5. **fore**head
2. hold	6. **hurr**y	2. **sweet**heart	6. be**hav**ior
3. who	7. whose	3. be**hind**	7. in**hale**
4. whole	8. **his**tory	4. **some**how	8. re**heat**

B. Work with a partner. Exchange papers and read each other's sentences. Check each other for correct pronunciation.

C. The following are expressions that are of common use in American English. Make up sentences for each one. Be prepared to read and discuss them in class.

1. have one's hands full (be extremely busy with something that requires all your energy)

2. have the **upp**er hand (have the advantage over someone or some-thing)

3. do with a **heav**y hand (behave awkwardly or clumsily)

4. fly off the **han**dle (lose one's temper)

5. have a heart (be sympathetic or merciful)

D. What are some of the common expressions used in your native language? Trans-late them into English and bring them to the class discussion.

Unit 32

/y/ **as in yes**

1. Producing /y/

EXAMPLES: you, young, **yes**terday, **on**ion, **mill**ion

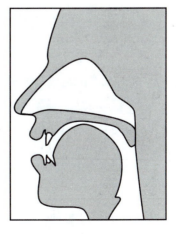

- This sound is always followed by a vowel sound. As you say /y/, your tongue and lips glide from their original position. Then they shape the vowel sound.
- Raise the center part of your tongue toward the roof of your mouth, but do not touch it.
- Press the sides of your tongue against the upper back teeth. Produce the sound by letting air flow out over your tongue. Then pronounce the vowel.
- Your vocal cords should vibrate.

2. Practice the Sound

Remember to combine the sound /y/ with the vowel sound that follows it.

A. Practice these sounds first normally, then with exaggeration, then normally. Listen and repeat.

/you/   /y . . . uw/   /you/

B. Now practice the sound in words. Notice the phonetic spelling. Listen and repeat each word twice.

1. y̱et   /yɛt/   y̱et
2. y̱es   /yɛs/   y̱es
3. y̱outh   /yuwθ/   y̱outh
4. **mill**i̱on   /mɪlyən/   **mill**i̱on
5. **on**i̱on   /ənyən/   **on**i̱on
6. **jun**i̱or   /ʤuwnyər/   **jun**i̱or

3. Check Your Listening

In the following pairs of words, one word begins with the sound /y/. You will hear one word from each pair. Circle the word that you hear.

1. "s"   y̱es   5. oak   y̱olk[1]
2. ear   y̱ear   6. east   y̱east[2]
3. ail   Y̱ale   7. am   y̱am[3]
4. or   y̱our   8. **awn**ing   **y̱awn**ing

4. Practice the Contrast: /y/ as in "y̱es" with /ʤ/ as in "job"

Some students confuse /y/ as in "y̱es" with /ʤ/ as in "job." When you pronounce /y/, no part of your tongue touches the gum ridge. When you pronounce /ʤ/, the tongue tip touches the upper gum ridge, stopping the air flow for a moment.

---

[1] *yolk:* the yellow part of an egg
[2] *yeast:* a preparation that is used for making bread, wine, and cheese
[3] *yam:* a sweet potato

A. Practice these contrasting sounds. Listen and repeat each word pair.

/y/	/ʤ/		/y/	/ʤ/
1. **yell**ow	**Jell**-o		5. year	jeer[4]
2. Yale	jail		6. yolk	joke
3. yet	jet		7. yam	jam
4. yes	Jess			

B. Now practice the contrasting sounds in sentence pairs. The first sentence of each pair has the sound /y/, and the second has the sound /ʤ/. Listen and repeat.

1a. **yell**ow I thought it was **yell**ow.

 b. **Jell**-o I thought it was **Jell**-o.

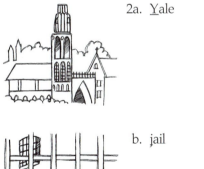

2a. Yale He's **go**ing to Yale.

 b. jail He's **go**ing to jail.

---

[4] *jeer:* a rude remark

3a. yet   Did you say "yet"?

b. jet   Did you say "jet"?

4a. yes   She said "yes," **did**n't she?

b. Jess   She said "Jess," **did**n't she?

5a. year   He was **think**ing of the
             year.

b. jeer   He was **think**ing of the
             jeer.

6a. yolk   We **did**n't like the yolk.

b. joke   We **did**n't like the joke.

7a. yam   Please pass the yam.

b. jam   Please pass the jam.

5. Consonant–Vowel Combination /yuw/

The combined sound /yuw/ is very common. Sometimes it is not represented by a letter but is heard as the first part of the vowel sound. Listen and repeat these words and sentences.

1. **un**ion   He's a **mem**ber of the **un**ion.

2. **u**nit   We are **al**most **fin**ished with this **u**nit.

3. **beau**ty   Do you think **beau**ty is **on**ly skin deep?

4. **beau**tiful   What a **beau**tiful **sun**set!

5. f<u>ew</u>   There are a f<u>ew</u> **sand**wiches left.

6. ref**use**   I ref**use** to be part of this.

7. c<u>u</u>te   **Is**n't that **ba**by's face c<u>u</u>te?

8. conf**use**   Don't conf**use** me.

9. **Jan**<u>u</u>ary   My **birth**day is in **Jan**<u>u</u>ary.

10. **cu**cumbers   Some **peo**ple don't like **cu**cumbers.

6. Stress and Intonation

1. Before you listen to and repeat the following sentences, place a <u>single</u> line under the letter(s) representing the sound /y/ as in "<u>y</u>es" and a <u>double</u> line under the letter(s) representing the consonant–vowel combination /yuw/ as in "<u>u</u>se."

2. As you listen to the tape, mark the stressed words you hear with a stress mark (´).

3. Pay attention to function words, phrasing, and the intonation that is already marked.

The first sentence is marked for you.

1. A <u>y</u>acht [5] is a small ship <u>u</u>sed for **sail**ing.

2. Yale is the name of a large uni**ver**sity.

---

[5] In this word, "ch" is not pronounced. The word is pronounced /yɑt/.

3. The **Yell**ow **pag**es are the **yell**ow-**col**ored **pag**es in the **tel**ephone

   book that list you a**cord**ing to your **bus**iness.

4. Did you know that "Yule" is a**noth**er word you can use for

   Christmas?

5. A mute **per**son is one who does not use his voice to speak.

6. A **brill**iant **per**son is **u**sually called a **gen**ius.

7. Cali**for**nia is **larg**er than New York.

8. New York is **larg**er than Pennsyl**van**ia.

9. Pennsyl**van**ia is **larg**er than Vir**gin**ia.

10. Vir**gin**ia is **larg**er than West Vir**gin**ia.

7. Further Practice

A. Make up a sentence for each of the words listed below. Use a dictionary to look up new words. Say each sentence aloud. Place a <u>single</u> line under the sound for /y/ and place a <u>double</u> line under the sound for /yuw/. Mark the sentences for stress and intonation.

> EXAMPLES: a. mu**se**um
>
>   The man in the mu**se**um called the **am**bulance.
>
>   b. ex**cuse**
>   Do <u>you</u> need an exc**use** to call your **law**yer?

1. **hu**man	6. **u**niform
2. **mu**sic	7. **Jan**uary
3. **se**nior	8. **pop**ular
4. **vol**ume	9. par**tic**ular
5. **fu**neral	10. repu**ta**tion

B. Work with a partner. Read your partner's sentences aloud, using the indicated stress and intonation markings. Check each other for correct pronunciation, stress, and intonation. Do you both agree on the same pronunciation and markings?

C. Record yourself reading the following selection. Pay attention to rhythm and pauses.

1. The New Year

2. A year to be glad in,

3. And not to be sad in,

4. To gain in, to give in,

5. A **happ**y new year.

6. A new year for **try**ing

7. And **nev**er for **sigh**ing;

8. A new year to live in;

9. Oh, hold it most dear!

Unit 33

/w/ **as in _walk_**

1. Producing /w/

EXAMPLES: <u>w</u>ant, <u>w</u>ord, <u>wh</u>ite,[1] a<u>wh</u>ile,[1] a<u>w</u>ake, s<u>w</u>eet, high<u>w</u>ay, quart,[2] <u>o</u>ne,[3] <u>o</u>nce[3]

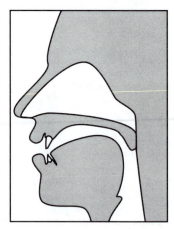

- This sound is always followed by a vowel sound. As you say /w/, your tongue and lips shape the vowel sound that follows.
- Raise the back of your tongue up toward the roof of your mouth (soft palate), but do not touch it.
- Round your lips, push them out, and relax them as you let air flow out through your lips.
- Your vocal cords should vibrate.

---

[1] Some American speakers pronounce "wh" with an initial /h/ sound: "<u>wh</u>ite" /hwayt/, "a<u>wh</u>ile" /əhwayl/. In this text no distinction is made between voiceless /hw/ and voiced /w/ as in "<u>w</u>alk."

[2] See Unit 25, page 223, for words that begin with /kw/.

[3] /w/ is the first sound in "<u>o</u>ne" /wən/ and "<u>o</u>nce" /wəns/.

2. Practice the Sound

A. Practice the sound /w/, first normally, then with exaggeration, then normally. Listen and repeat.

/wiy/   /w . . . iy/ /wiy/

B. Now practice the sound in words. Notice the phonetic spelling. Listen and repeat each word twice.

1. <u>w</u>ife   /wayf/   <u>w</u>ife
2. <u>w</u>ait   /weyt/   <u>w</u>ait
3. <u>w</u>eek   /wiyk/   <u>w</u>eek
4. <u>w</u>ell   /wɛl /   <u>w</u>ell
5. <u>wh</u>en   /wɛn/   <u>wh</u>en
6. a<u>**way**</u>   /əwey/   a<u>**way**</u>
7. **net**<u>w</u>ork /nɛtwərk/ **net**<u>w</u>ork
8. **hard**<u>w</u>are /hɑrdwɛr/ **hard**<u>w</u>are

3. Check Your Listening

Cover the list of words below with a piece of paper. Listen and put a check mark under /w/ or /v/ for the sound that you hear.

		/w/	/v/
<u>v</u>erse	1.	_____	_____
<u>wh</u>ile	2.	_____	_____
<u>w</u>et	3.	_____	_____
<u>v</u>est	4.	_____	_____
<u>wh</u>eel	5.	_____	_____
<u>w</u>ord	6.	_____	_____
<u>v</u>eal	7.	_____	_____
"v"	8.	_____	_____

4. Practice the Contrast: /w/ as in "<u>w</u>alk" with /v/ as in "<u>v</u>oice"

Some students confuse /w/ as in "<u>w</u>alk" with /v/ as in "<u>v</u>oice." When you pronounce /v/, touch your upper teeth with the inner part of your lower lip. Do not touch your teeth with your lip when you say /w/.

 A.   Listen and repeat each word pair.

/w/	/v/		/w/	/v/
1. <u>w</u>est	<u>v</u>est		5. <u>w</u>e	"<u>v</u>"
2. <u>w</u>ine	<u>v</u>ine		6. <u>w</u>et	<u>v</u>et
3. <u>w</u>orse	<u>v</u>erse		7. <u>wh</u>eel	<u>v</u>eal
4. <u>w</u>ail[4]	<u>v</u>eil		8. <u>wh</u>ile	<u>v</u>ile[5]

 B.   The first sentence of each pair has the sound /w/. The second sentence has the sound /v/. Listen and repeat.

1a. <u>w</u>est	I like the <u>W</u>est, don't you?
b. <u>v</u>est	I like the <u>v</u>est, don't you?

2a. <u>w</u>ine	She thinks it's a nice <u>w</u>ine.
b. <u>v</u>ine	She thinks it's a nice <u>v</u>ine.

3a. <u>w</u>orse	Is it <u>w</u>orse?
b. <u>v</u>erse	Is it <u>v</u>erse?

4a. <u>w</u>ail	It was a long <u>w</u>ail.
b. <u>v</u>eil	It was a long <u>v</u>eil.

---

[4] *wail:* sad cry
[5] *vile:* evil, wicked

5a. <u>we</u>   He said "<u>we</u>," **did**n't he?

  b. "v"   He said "v," **did**n't he?

6a. <u>wet</u>   I'm sure she said "<u>wet</u>."

  b. <u>yet</u>   I'm sure she said "<u>yet</u>."

7a. <u>wheel</u>   Take the <u>wheel</u> be**fore**
                        you go.

  b. <u>veal</u>   Take the <u>veal</u> be**fore**
                        you go.

8a. <u>while</u>   Who said it was "<u>while</u>"?

  b. <u>vile</u>   Who said it was "<u>vile</u>"?

5. No Sound for "w"

A. The letter "w" is not pronounced in words that begin with "wr." Listen and repeat these words and sentences.

1. write   Will you write to me?

2. wrote   I wrote a long **lett**er.

3. wrong   You're wrong. You **did**n't.

4. wrap   I'll wrap the **pack**age.

5. wrist   Did you fall and hurt your wrist?

6. wreck   **Af**ter the **ac**cident, the car was a wreck.

7. wreath   At **Christ**mas[6] time we'll hang a wreath
                         on the door.

8. **wrin**kle   Did you **wrin**kle your dress?

---
[6] The "t" in "Christmas" is not pronounced.

B. The letter "w" is not pronounced in the following words that begin with "wh." (Not all words that begin with "wh" have a "w" that represents no sound.) Listen and repeat these words and sentences.

1. who   The man who saw us is here.

2. whom   The man whom I spoke to is here.

3. whose   I don't know whose it is.

4. whole   Did you eat the whole pie?

5. whoever   I don't care, whoever it is.

C. The letter "w" is also not pronounced in the following words. Listen and repeat.

1. two   Did you buy two of them?

2. toward[7]   The car came toward us at a high speed.

3. **ans**wer   Did you **ans**wer the **ques**tion?

4. sword   **Fenc**ing is the art of **fight**ing with a sword.

5. **kno**wledge[8] A **litt**le **kno**wledge is a **dan**gerous thing.

6. Stress and Intonation

1. Before you listen to and repeat the following sentences, underline all the letter(s) representing the sound of /w/ as in "walk."

2. As you listen to the tape, mark the stressed words you hear with a stress mark (ˊ) and the falling and rising intonation with an arrow (⌐ ⌐).

3. Pay attention to function words and phrasing.

The first sentence is marked for you.

1. I **al**ways eat **sand**wiches for lunch.

2. There was **on**ly one **war**ning **sig**nal on the wet road.

3. It was once a good wool **sweat**er, **was**n't it?

4. There were two world wars.

5. **Ev**eryone who is **an**yone was there.

---

[7] This word may also be pronounced with /w/.

[8] The "k" in "knowledge" is not pronounced.

6. Is "Where or When" the name of an old song?

7. The White House is in **Wash**ington, D.C.

8. He takes the **sub**way to work, **does**n't he?

9. I don't know **wheth**er I'll walk in this **weath**er.

10. Do you know if the **wait**er **o**pens the **win**dow when it gets warm?

7. Further Practice

A. Read the following paragraph aloud as you underline all the words that have the sound /w/ as in "_w_alk." (Hint: There are 22 words.) Use a dictionary to help you with any new words.

1. Mark the paragraph for stress and intonation. Pay attention to function words and linking of words.

2. Record yourself on tape.

3. Listen for the correct pronunciation of /w/ and for the stress and intonation as you marked it.

1. My **Dai**ly **Rou**tine

2. **Dur**ing the week I **u**sually wake up at a **quar**ter to **sev**en.

3. **Af**ter I wash up I get dressed **quick**ly. For **break**fast, I have two

4. **slic**es of whole wheat toast and wash it down with a cup of **cof-**

5. **f**ee. I leave for school at eight o'**clock.** I **u**sually walk, but when

6. the **weath**er is bad, I take the **sub**way. **Af**ter school, I go to work

7. as a **wait**er. When I come home from work, I have just e**nough**

8. time to do my **home**work, write some **lett**ers home, and watch

9. TV. I go to sleep at twelve **mid**night. Oh, by the way, I **al**so work

10. on **week**ends.

B. Describe your daily routine to the class.

Unit 34

/m/ **as in _me_**

1. Producing /m/

EXAMPLES: <u>m</u>y, <u>m</u>ake, **da<u>m</u>**age, **fa<u>m</u>**ous, **swi<u>mm</u>**er, ai<u>m</u>, co<u>m</u>e, ha<u>m</u>

- Close your lips, lightly but firmly. This stops the air from flowing out of your mouth.
- Produce the sound by letting air flow out through your nose. As you say the sound, you can feel your lips vibrate.
- Your vocal cords also vibrate.

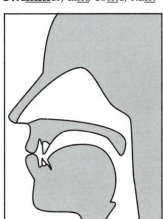

2. Practice the Sound

A. Practice the sound /m/, first normally, then with exaggeration, then normally. Listen and repeat.

/m/   /m . . ./   /m/

B. Now practice the sound in words. Notice the phonetic spelling. Listen and repeat each word twice.

1. <u>m</u>e	/miy/	<u>m</u>e
2. <u>m</u>ad	/mæd/	<u>m</u>ad
3. **ca<u>m</u>**era	/kæmərə/	**ca<u>m</u>**era
4. **co<u>m</u>**ic	/kɑmɪk/	**co<u>m</u>**ic
5. ti<u>m</u>e	/taym/	ti<u>m</u>e
6. ho<u>m</u>e	/howm/	ho<u>m</u>e

3. Check Your Listening

In the following pairs of words, one word ends with the sound /m/. You will hear one word from each pair. Circle the word that you hear.

1. say	same	5. blue	bloo<u>m</u>
2. see	see<u>m</u>	6. nay	na<u>me</u>
3. gay	ga<u>me</u>	7. "a"	ai<u>m</u>
4. cry	cri<u>me</u>	8. glue	gloo<u>m</u>

> Reminder: Vowel sounds are held longer before *voiced* consonants than before *voiceless* consonants. (See Unit 4.)

4. Practice the Contrast: Words with final /m/ as in "co<u>me</u>" and words without final /m/

Some students leave out the sound /m/ when it occurs at the end of a word.

A. Listen and repeat each word pair.

WITHOUT /m/	WITH /m/		WITHOUT /m/	WITH /m/
1. rye[1]	rhy<u>me</u>	6. Ma	Mo<u>m</u>
2. due[2]	doo<u>m</u>[3]	7. tie	ti<u>me</u>
3. dough[4]	do<u>me</u>	8. who	who<u>m</u>
4. dye	di<u>me</u>	9. tea	tea<u>m</u>
5. day	da<u>me</u>[5]	10. row	roa<u>m</u>[6]

---

[1] *rye:* a cereal grain used to make bread
[2] *due:* what someone deserves
[3] *doom:* a terrible fate
[4] *dough:* a mixture of flour with other ingredients that are baked. (Also a slang expression for "money.")
[5] *dame:* In England, a title given to a woman. In American English, a slang expression for a woman.
[6] *roam:* go freely over a large area; wander

B. The second sentence of each pair has the final /m/ sound. Listen and repeat.

1a.	rye	That rye was very good.
b.	rhy<u>me</u>	That rhy<u>me</u> was very good.

2a.	due	I'll give him his due.
b.	doo<u>m</u>	I'll give him his doo<u>m</u>.

3a.	dough	We all like that dough.
b.	do<u>me</u>	We all like that do<u>me</u>.

4a.	dye	Did you see the dye?
b.	di<u>me</u>	Did you see the di<u>me</u>?

5a.	day	What a day!
b.	da<u>me</u>	What a da<u>me</u>!

6a.	Ma	**Should**n't you call Ma?
b.	Mo<u>m</u>	**Should**n't you call Mo<u>m</u>?

7a. tie   It's not the tie, is it?

  b. ti<u>m</u>e   It's not the ti<u>m</u>e, is it?

8a. who   Did you say "who"?

  b. who<u>m</u>   Did you say "who<u>m</u>"?

9a. tea   Let's look at the tea, shall we?

  b. tea<u>m</u>   Let's look at the tea<u>m</u>, shall we?

10a. row   You row there, don't you?

  b. roa<u>m</u>   You roa<u>m</u> there, don't you?

5. Contraction "I'm"

The function word "am" is usually not stressed. In conversation, native speakers use the contraction "I'm."

A. Listen and repeat the following pairs of sentences. The first sentence has the stressed form of "am." The second sentence has the contraction.

STRESSED FORM	CONTRACTION
1. I am **go**ing to school.	I'm **go**ing to school.
2. I am **bus**y right now.	I'm **bus**y right now.
3. I am sure I did it.	I'm sure I did it.
4. I am **sorr**y I did it.	I'm **sorr**y I did it.
5. I am **read**ing the book.	I'm **read**ing the book.

B. Work with a partner or with a small group. Discuss the change in meaning of the stressed form with the contraction.

6. Stress and Intonation

A. Work with a partner or with a group of three or four.

1. Underline <u>once</u> all the letters that represent the sound /m/ as in "<u>m</u>e." Use a dictionary to help you with the pronunciation and meaning of new words.

2. Underline <u>twice</u> the stressed syllable in words of two or more syllables.

3. Take turns reading each line aloud while you mark for phrasing, stress, and intonation.

4. Pay attention to function words.

The first sentence is marked for you.

1.   To <u>e</u>verything there is a <u>sea</u>son, / and a ti<u>me</u> to

2.   every <u>pur</u>pose / <u>un</u>der the <u>hea</u>ven: /

3.   A time to be born, and a time to die;

4.   A time to kill, and a time to heal;

5.   A time to break down, and a time to build up;

6.   A time to weep, and a time to laugh;

7.   A time to get, and a time to lose;

8.   A time to keep, and a time to cast away;

9.   A time to rend, and a time to sew;

10.   A time to keep silence, and a time to speak;

11.   A time to love, and a time to hate;

12.   A time of war, and a time of peace.

(Lines from Ecclesiastics 3:1–8)

B. Record yourself reading the above passage. Check to see if you follow the markings you and your partner or group decided upon.

7. Further Practice

A. Read the "family tree" aloud, and fill in the blanks in the sentences that follow.

    1. Underline all words in the sentences that have the sound /m/.

    2. Read the sentences aloud as you mark them for stress and intonation.

    3. Read the sentences aloud once more.

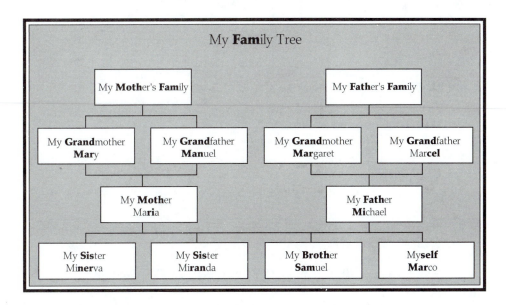

    1. My **grand**mothers' names are _____ and

        _____.

    2. My **grand**fathers' names are _____ and

        _____.

    3. My **moth**er's name is _____.

    4. My **fath**er's name is _____.

    5. My **sis**ters' names are _____ and

        _____.

    6. My **broth**er's name is _____.

    7. My name is _____.

B. Make a diagram of your own family tree. Bring it to class for discussion.

Unit 35

/n/ **as in _no_**

1. Producing /n/

EXAMPLES: <u>n</u>ice, <u>n</u>ose, in**vite,** a**nnounce,** ca<u>n</u>, <u>n</u>i<u>n</u>e, ma<u>n</u>

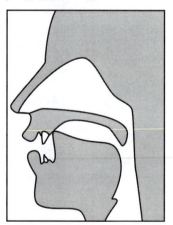

- Place the tip of your tongue on your upper gum ridge, lightly but firmly. The back part of the tongue closes off the passage of air through the mouth.
- Produce the sound by letting air flow out through your nose.
- Your vocal cords should vibrate.

2. Practice the Sound

A. Practice the sound /n/, first normally, then with exaggeration, then normally. Listen and repeat.

/n/   /n . . . /   /n/

B. Now practice the sound in words. Notice the phonetic spelling. Listen and re-peat each word twice.

1. <u>n</u>o   /now/   <u>n</u>o
2. <u>n</u>ot   /nɑt/   <u>n</u>ot
3. **di<u>nn</u>**er   /dɪnər/   **di<u>nn</u>**er
4. **fu<u>nn</u>**y   /fəniy/   **fu<u>nn</u>**y
5. brai<u>n</u>   /breyn/   brai<u>n</u>
6. lear<u>n</u>   /lərn/   lear<u>n</u>   •

3. Check Your Listening

A. In the following pairs of words, one word ends with the sound /n/. You will hear one word from each pair. Circle the word that you hear.

1. gay   gai<u>n</u>   5. sue   soo<u>n</u>
2. bee   bea<u>n</u>   6. low   loa<u>n</u>
3. lie   li<u>n</u>e   7. sigh   sig<u>n</u>
4. bow   bo<u>n</u>e   8. pay   pai<u>n</u>

B. In the following pairs of words, one word has a final /n/. The other word has a final /l/. You will hear one word from each pair. Circle the word that you hear.

1. di<u>n</u>e   **di**a<u>l</u>   5. sa<u>n</u>e   sa<u>l</u>e
2. mai<u>n</u>   mai<u>l</u>   6. see<u>n</u>   sea<u>l</u>
3. mea<u>n</u>   mea<u>l</u>   7. sto<u>n</u>e   sto<u>l</u>e
4. mi<u>n</u>e   mi<u>l</u>e   8. te<u>n</u>   te<u>l</u>l

C. In the following pairs of words, one word has a final /n/. The other word has a final /m/. You will hear one word from each pair. Circle the word that you hear.

1. bu<u>n</u>   bu<u>m</u>   5. ra<u>n</u>   ra<u>m</u>
2. co<u>n</u>e   co<u>m</u>b[1]   6. sa<u>n</u>e   sa<u>m</u>e
3. di<u>n</u>e   di<u>m</u>e   7. see<u>n</u>   see<u>m</u>
4. gai<u>n</u>   ga<u>m</u>e   8. war<u>n</u>   war<u>m</u>

---

[1] Note that the "b" in "comb" is silent.

> Reminder: Vowel sounds are held longer before *voiced* consonants than before *voiceless* consonants. (See Unit 4.)

4. Practice the Contrast: Words with final /n/ as in "soo<u>n</u>" and words without final /n/

Some students leave out the sound /n/ when it occurs at the end of a word.

A. Listen and repeat each word pair.

1. me	mea<u>n</u>	4. Joe	Joa<u>n</u>
2. play	pla<u>n</u>e	5. ray	rai<u>n</u>
3. law	law<u>n</u>	6. war	wor<u>n</u>

B. The second sentence of each pair has the final /n/ sound. Listen and repeat.

1a. me	Is it me?
b. mea<u>n</u>	Is it mea<u>n</u>?

2a. play	Did you like the play?
b. pla<u>n</u>e	Did you like the pla<u>n</u>e?

3a. law	It's the law that's bad.
b. law<u>n</u>	It's the law<u>n</u> that's bad.

4a. Joe	Was that Joe at the door?
b. Joa<u>n</u>	Was that Joa<u>n</u> at the door?

5a. ray	I could feel the ray on my face.
b. rai<u>n</u>	I could feel the rai<u>n</u> on my face.

6a. war	They said it was war, **did**n't they?
b. wor<u>n</u>	They said it was wor<u>n</u>, **did**n't they?

5. Practice the Contrast: Final /n/ as in "soo<u>n</u>" with final /l/ as in "we<u>ll</u>"

Some students may confuse the final /n/ sound with the final /l/ sound.

A. Listen and repeat each word pair.

1. bo<u>n</u>e	bow<u>l</u>	4. i<u>n</u>	i<u>ll</u>
2. do<u>n</u>e	du<u>ll</u>	5. pai<u>n</u>	pai<u>l</u>
3. fi<u>n</u>e	fi<u>l</u>e	6. spi<u>n</u>	spi<u>ll</u>

B. The first sentence of each pair has a final /**n**/. The second sentence has a final /**l**/. Listen and repeat.

1a. bo<u>n</u>e	Where's the dog's bo<u>n</u>e?
b. bow<u>l</u>	Where's the dog's bow<u>l</u>?

2a. do<u>n</u>e	Is it **rea**lly do<u>n</u>e?
b. du<u>ll</u>	Is it **rea**lly du<u>ll</u>?

3a. fi<u>n</u>e	That's a fi<u>n</u>e **cab**inet.

b. fi<u>l</u>e	That's a fi<u>l</u>e **cab**inet.

4a. i<u>n</u>   Is the cat i<u>n</u>?

  b. i<u>ll</u>   Is the cat i<u>ll</u>?

5a. pai<u>n</u>   He got the pai<u>n</u> to**day,**
                         didn't he?

  b. pai<u>l</u>   He got the pai<u>l</u> to**day,**
                         didn't he?

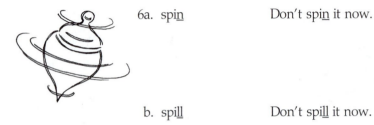

6a. spi<u>n</u>   Don't spi<u>n</u> it now.

  b. spi<u>ll</u>   Don't spi<u>ll</u> it now.

6. Practice the Contrast: Final /n/ as in "soo<u>n</u>" with final /m/ as in "co<u>me</u>"

Some students may confuse the final /n/ sound with the final /m/ sound. When you pronounce /m/, press your lips firmly together.

A. Listen and repeat each word pair.

/n/	/m/		/n/	/m/
1. a<u>n</u>	a<u>m</u>	5.	pho<u>n</u>e	foa<u>m</u>
2. ca<u>n</u>e	ca<u>m</u>e	6.	pa<u>n</u>	Pa<u>m</u>
3. gu<u>n</u>	gu<u>m</u>	7.	ru<u>n</u>	ru<u>m</u>
4. tur<u>n</u>	ter<u>m</u>	8.	ti<u>n</u>	Ti<u>m</u>

B. Each of these sentences has words with a final /**m**/ and a final /**n**/. Listen and repeat.

1. I'<u>m</u> **eat**ing a<u>n</u> **app**le.

2. She ca<u>me</u> with her ca<u>ne</u>.

3. The gu<u>m</u> is on the gu<u>n</u>.

4. Foa<u>m</u> is on the pho<u>ne</u>.

5. Pa<u>m</u> fried eggs in the pa<u>n</u>.

6. Do you drink ru<u>m</u> after you ru<u>n</u>?

7. This ter<u>m</u> it will be our tur<u>n</u>.

8. Ti<u>m</u> wrapped the meat in ti<u>n</u> foil.[2]

7. Syllabic /n/

A. When /n/ is in an unstressed syllable following /t/ or /d/, no vowel sound is produced. This occurs even when a vowel letter appears between /t/ and /n/ or /d/ and /n/. For example,

1. **rott**en   /rɑtn̩/   The food was **rott**en when we bought it.

2. **sudd**en   /sədn̩/   All of a **sudd**en he ran out of the house.

3. **would**n't   /wudn̩t/   I **would**n't see him if I were you.

This syllabic /n/ is similar to the syllabic /l/ (practiced in Unit 24). It is indicated by the symbol /n̩/.

> Reminder: /t/, /d/, /l/, and /n/ are all made with the tongue tip touching the upper gum ridge.
> - To produce /t/ or /d/, press your tongue tip lightly against the upper gum ridge. This action stops the flow of air.
> - Instead of releasing the tongue tip, keep it in place and produce the /n/ sound by letting air escape through your nose.

B. Listen and repeat these words and sentences.

1. **eat**en   /iytn̩/   I've al**ready eat**en.

2. **writt**en   /rɪtn̩/   Have you **writt**en to your friend?

---

[2] _tin foil:_ a thin sheet of aluminum used as a covering, especially for food

3. **kitt**ens	/kɪtn̩z/	The cat had six **kitt**ens.
4. **bitt**en	/bɪtn̩/	He was **bitt**en by a mad dog.
5. **fatt**en	/fætn̩/	The **far**mer will **fatt**en up his **tur**keys be**fore sell**ing them.
6. **gott**en	/gɑtn̩/	I **would**'ve **gott**en it for you.
7. **straight**en	/streytn̩/	Let's **straight**en up the house be**fore** my **moth**er comes home.
8. **cott**on	/kɑtn̩/	I bought a **cott**on blouse, not a silk one.
9. **butt**on	/bətn̩/	I lost the **butt**on from my coat.
10. **hidd**en	/hɪdn̩/	The toys were **hidd**en in the **clos**et.
11. **gar**den	/gɑrdn̩/	She grows **veg**etables in her **gar**den.
12. **wid**en	/waydn̩/	The **cit**y wants to **wid**en the street.
13. **par**don	/pɑrdn̩/	Be po**lite;** say "**Par**don me."
14. **dead**en	/dɛdn̩/	Can you give me **some**thing to **dead**en the pain?
15. **did**n't [3]	/dɪdn̩t/	**Did**n't you want to see the play?
16. **could**n't [3]	/kʊdn̩t/	He **could**n't go home a**gain.**
17. **had**n't [3]	/hædn̩t/	We **had**n't thought of it.
18. **would**n't [3]	/wʊdn̩t/	Why **would**n't he tell us the truth?

8. Stress and Intonation

1. Read the following sentences before you listen to and repeat them. Use a dictionary to help you with the pronunciation and meaning of new words.

2. Mark the stressed words you hear with a stress mark (✔).

3. Pay attention to the underlined letter(s) representing the sound /n/, pausing, and the intonation patterns that are already marked.

---

[3] Be sure to place your tongue tip on your upper gum ridge when you say /d/ before /n/. Do not release your tongue tip; keep it in place and then produce /n/ and /t/, releasing the air on /t/.

The first sentence is marked for you.

1. <u>N</u>ew York State is <u>in</u> the north**eas**ter<u>n</u> part of the U**nit**ed States.

2. The popu**la**tio<u>n</u> of <u>N</u>ew York State is **o**ver seve**nteen million peo**ple.

3. The popu**la**tio<u>n</u> of <u>N</u>ew York **Cit**y is **o**ver **seve**<u>n</u> **million peo**ple.

4. The **cap**ital of <u>N</u>ew York State is called **Al**ba<u>n</u>y.

5. <u>N</u>ew York **Cit**y is the **larg**est **cit**y <u>in</u> <u>N</u>ew York State.

6. There are five **bor**oughs <u>in</u> <u>N</u>ew York **Cit**y: The Bronx,[4] **Brook**ly<u>n</u>, Ma<u>n</u>**hatt**a<u>n</u>, Quee<u>n</u>s, a<u>n</u>d **Rich**mo<u>n</u>d (or **Stat**e<u>n</u> **Is**la<u>n</u>d).

7. <u>N</u>ew York **Cit**y has two **air**ports, Joh<u>n</u> F. **Kenn**edy a<u>n</u>d La **Guar**dia; both are <u>in</u> Quee<u>n</u>s.

8. Gra<u>n</u>d **Cen**tral a<u>n</u>d Pe<u>n</u><u>n</u>syl**van**ia are the two mai<u>n</u> trai<u>n</u> **sta**tio<u>n</u>s <u>in</u> Ma<u>n</u>**hatt**a<u>n</u>.

9. **Pass**enger ships leave from the piers a**long**[4] the **Hud**so<u>n</u> **Riv**er.

10. The <u>N</u>ew York **Pub**lic **Lib**rary is at Fifth **Av**e<u>n</u>ue a<u>n</u>d **For**ty-**sec**o<u>n</u>d Street.

9. Further Practice

Write a short paragraph describing the town or city you come from. You may want to include the following information:

where the city or town is in your country

how large it is

what the available transportation is

where the vacation areas are, etc.

Be prepared to share your story with the class.

---

[4] The "n" in "Bronx" and the "n" in "along" are pronounced /ŋ/: /brɑŋks/, /əlɔŋ/. See Unit 36.

Unit 36

/ŋ/ as in ki**ng**

1. Producing /ŋ/

EXAMPLES: **an**ger, **sin**gle, i**nk**, **ban**ker, **sing**ing, si**ng**, ri**ng**

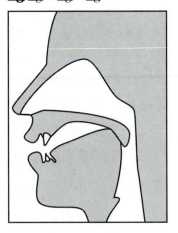

- Note that in English, this sound does not occur at the beginning of words.
- Raise the back of your tongue so that it touches and presses against the roof of your mouth (soft palate). This stops the air from flowing out of the mouth.
- Produce the sound by letting air flow out through your nose.
- Your vocal cords should vibrate.

2. Practice the Sound

A. Practice the sound /ŋ/, first normally, then with exaggeration, then normally. Listen and repeat.

/ŋ/   /ŋ. . . /   /ŋ/

B. Now practice the sound in words. Notice the phonetic spelling. Listen and repeat each word twice.

1. i<u>n</u>k   /ɪŋk/   i<u>n</u>k
2. tha<u>n</u>k   /θæŋk/   tha<u>n</u>k
3. **si<u>n</u>**gle   /sɪŋl̩/   **si<u>n</u>**gle
4. **si<u>ng</u>**er   /sɪŋər/   **si<u>ng</u>**er
5. si<u>ng</u>   /sɪŋ/   si<u>ng</u>
6. ki<u>ng</u>   /kɪŋ/   ki<u>ng</u>

3. Check Your Listening

A. In the following pairs of words, one word has the sound /m/ and the other word has the sound /ŋ/. You will hear one word from each pair. Circle the word that you hear.

1. ham   ha<u>ng</u>   6. swim   swi<u>ng</u>
2. ram   ra<u>ng</u>   7. Sam   sa<u>ng</u>
3. rum   ru<u>ng</u>   8. slim   sli<u>ng</u>
4. rim   ri<u>ng</u>   9. clam   cla<u>ng</u>
5. hum   hu<u>ng</u>   10. bombed   bo<u>ng</u>ed

B. In the following pairs of words, one has a final /n/ and the other word has a final /ŋ/. You will hear one word from each pair. Circle the word that you hear.

1. si<u>n</u>   si<u>ng</u>   6. thi<u>n</u>   thi<u>ng</u>
2. ta<u>n</u>   ta<u>ng</u>   7. ba<u>n</u>   ba<u>ng</u>
3. wi<u>n</u>   wi<u>ng</u>   8. law<u>n</u>   lo<u>ng</u>
4. ra<u>n</u>   ra<u>ng</u>   9. gone   go<u>ng</u>
5. su<u>n</u>   su<u>ng</u>   10. to<u>n</u>   to<u>ng</u>ue

C. In the following pairs of words, one word ends in the sound /ŋk/ and the other word ends in the sound /ŋ/. You will hear one word from each pair. Circle the word that you hear.

1.	cli<u>nk</u>	cli<u>ng</u>	6.	su<u>nk</u>	su<u>ng</u>
2.	thi<u>nk</u>	thi<u>ng</u>	7.	bri<u>nk</u>	bri<u>ng</u>
3.	ba<u>nk</u>	ba<u>ng</u>	8.	ri<u>nk</u>	ri<u>ng</u>
4.	si<u>nk</u>	si<u>ng</u>	9.	wi<u>nk</u>	wi<u>ng</u>
5.	ra<u>nk</u>	ra<u>ng</u>	10.	zi<u>nc</u>	zi<u>ng</u>

> Remember: Vowel sounds are held longer before *voiced* consonants than before *voiceless* consonants. (See Unit 4.)

4. Practice the Contrast : /ŋ/ as in "ki<u>ng</u>," /n/ as in "<u>no</u>," and /ŋk/ as in "ba<u>nk</u>"

Some students may confuse the sounds /n/, /ŋk/, and /ŋ/ when they occur in the final position.

A. Listen and repeat each group of words.

/n/	/ŋk/	/ŋ/
1. ba<u>n</u>	ba<u>nk</u>	ba<u>ng</u>
2. si<u>n</u>	si<u>nk</u>	si<u>ng</u>
3. Mi<u>n</u>	mi<u>nk</u>	Mi<u>ng</u>[1]
4. ta<u>n</u>	ta<u>nk</u>	ta<u>ng</u>[2]
5. wi<u>n</u>	wi<u>nk</u>	wi<u>ng</u>
6. ra<u>n</u>	ra<u>nk</u>	ra<u>ng</u>

---

[1] *Ming:* a Chinese dynasty noted for artistic works
[2] *tang:* a distinct strong taste or odor

B. The first sentence of each group has a final /n/ sound. The second sentence has a final /ŋk/, and the third has a final /ŋ/. Listen and repeat.

1a. ba<u>n</u>   I heard a**bout** the ba<u>n</u>.

b. ba<u>nk</u>   I heard a**bout** the ba<u>nk</u>.

c. ba<u>ng</u>   I heard a**bout** the ba<u>ng</u>.

2a. Mi<u>n</u>   We all thought it was Mi<u>n</u>.

b. mi<u>nk</u>   We all thought it was mi<u>nk</u>.

c. Mi<u>ng</u>   We all thought it was Mi<u>ng</u>.

3a. ta<u>n</u>   He likes that ta<u>n</u>.

b. ta<u>nk</u>   He likes that ta<u>nk</u>.

c. ta<u>ng</u>   He likes that ta<u>ng</u>.

4a.	wi<u>n</u>	She said it's a wi<u>n</u>.
b.	wi<u>nk</u>	She said it's a wi<u>nk</u>.
c.	wi<u>ng</u>	She said it's a wi<u>ng</u>.

5a.	ra<u>n</u>	Did you say we ra<u>n</u>?
b.	ra<u>nk</u>	Did you say we ra<u>nk</u>?
c.	ra<u>ng</u>	Did you say we ra<u>ng</u>?

5. "ng" Rules

There may be some confusion about the sound the letters "ng" represent. The following rules may help to make it clear.

A. Rule No. 1

When a word ends in the spelling "ng" or "ngue," the sound represented is always *one* sound, /ŋ/, as in "ki<u>ng</u>." Listen and repeat.

1.	stro<u>ng</u>	/strɔŋ/
2.	si<u>ng</u>	/sɪŋ/
3.	bri<u>ng</u>	/brɪŋ/
4.	to<u>ngue</u>	/təŋ/

B. Rule No. 2

When a suffix (for example, -s, -er, -ly, -ed, -ing, -ster, -ish) is added to a word ending in the sound /ŋ/ as in "ki<u>ng</u>," the letters "ng" are pronounced /ŋ/, with a few exceptions. Listen and repeat.

1.	si<u>ng</u>s	/sɪŋz/
2.	**sing**ing	/sɪŋɪŋ/
3.	**sing**er	/sɪŋər/
4.	**young**ster	/yəŋstər/
5.	**king**ly	/kɪŋliy/
6.	**young**ish	/yəŋɪʃ/
7.	ba<u>ng</u>ed	/bæŋd/

Exceptions to this rule: In comparative and superlative forms of the following adjectives, "ng" represents two sounds, /ŋ/ + /g/ = /ŋg/.

Adjective		Comparative		Superlative	
long	/lɔŋ/	**long**er	/lɔŋgər/	**long**est	/lɔŋgɪst/
young	/yəŋ/	**young**er	/yəŋgər/	**young**est	/yəŋgɪst/
strong	/strɔŋ/	**strong**er	/strɔŋgər/	**strong**est	/strɔŋgɪst/

C. Rule No. 3

When the spelling "ng" occurs in the middle of the stem or root of a word, it is represented by _two_ sounds, /ŋg/, with a few exceptions. Listen and repeat.

1. **fing**er   /fɪŋgər/

2. **ming**le   /mɪŋgl̩/

3. **sing**le   /sɪŋgl̩/

4. **an**ger   /æŋgər/

Exceptions to this rule:

Proper Names: **Wash**ington   /waʃɪŋtən/
                 Farmingdale   /farmɪŋdeyl/
                 Springfield   /sprɪŋfiyld/

Words: **ging**ham[3]   /gɪŋəm/
          strength   /strɛŋkθ/ or /strɛŋθ/ (alternate pronunciation)
          length   /lɛŋkθ/ or /lɛŋθ/ (alternate pronunciation)

D. Rule No. 4

When "n" is immediately followed by "c," "x," or "k," it is usually pronounced /ŋk/, _two_ sounds. Listen and repeat.

1. **an**chor   /æŋkər/

2. **anx**ious   /æŋkʃəs/

3. li**nk**   /lɪŋk/

4. tha**nk**   /θæŋk/

---

[3] _gingham:_ a cotton material that has a pattern of squares

E.   Rule No. 5

The spelling "nge" in medial or final position usually represents two sounds, /n/ + /d/ = /ndʒ/. Listen and repeat.

1. stra**nge**   /streyndʒ/

2. cha**nge**   /tʃeyndʒ/

3. ar**range**   /əreyndʒ/

4. **or**a**nge**   /ɔrɪndʒ/

6. Stress and Intonation

1. Before you listen to and repeat the following sentences, underline the letter(s) representing the sound /ŋ/.

2. As you listen to the tape, mark the stressed words you hear with a stress mark (ˊ).

3. Pay attention to function words, phrasing, and the intonation that is already marked.

EXAMPLES: a.   He's **com**ing a**long** with his **driv**ing.

b.   Will you **fill** your gas ta**n**k in **En**gland?

1. She was **walk**ing home, **sing**ing a song.

2. Were they **talk**ing a**bout fall**ing in love?

3. Are you **go**ing **surf**ing or **jogg**ing?

4. The girls were **jum**ping rope, and the boys were **play**ing ball.

5. Are you **com**ing up or **stay**ing down?

6. Are you **wrapp**ing gifts and **an**swering the phone at the same time?

7. "**Laugh**ing on the **out**side, **cry**ing on the **in**side" is a line from a song.

8. **Cook**ing and **clean**ing are two things I hate to do.

9. My **neigh**bor's **mov**ing to **Wash**ington, but I'm **mov**ing to Long Island.

10. I'm **find**ing new words and **look**ing them up in the **dic**tionary.

7. Further Practice

A. Work with a partner. In the following words, the underlined letters represent the sounds /m/, /n/, /ŋ/, /ŋg/, /ŋk/, or /ndʒ/. Say the word aloud; then write the correct phonetic symbol or symbols in the blank. Refer to the rules in Section 5. Your instructor may ask you to hand in your work on a separate piece of paper.

	EXAMPLES:	a.	ti<u>m</u>e	/m/
		b.	su<u>n</u>	/n/
		c.	ri<u>ng</u>	/ŋ/
		d.	**a<u>n</u>**gry	/ŋg/
		e.	**a<u>n</u>**kle	/ŋk/
		f.	spo<u>ng</u>e	/ndʒ/

1. **ju<u>n</u>**gle   /_____/
2. **si<u>ng</u>**er   /_____/
3. **i<u>n</u>**sti<u>nct</u>   /_____/
4. **al**bu<u>m</u>   /_____/
5. **dur**i<u>ng</u>   /_____/
6. **Lin**col<u>n</u>   /_____/
7. **sav**i<u>ng</u>   /_____/
8. **lo<u>ng</u>**er   /_____/

9. ra<u>ng</u>e   /_____/
10. you<u>ng</u>   /_____/
11. **E<u>n</u>**gland   /_____/
12. **ha<u>mm</u>**er   /_____/
13. zi<u>nc</u>   /_____/
14. law<u>n</u>   /_____/
15. **wedd**i<u>ng</u>   /_____/

B. Write six sentences with words containing the sounds /m/, /n/, /ŋ/, /ŋg/, /ŋk/, and /ndʒ/. Read your partner's sentences. Check each other for the correct production of the above sounds.

Appendix

Homophones

Homophones are words that sound the same but have different spellings and meanings.

1a.	ate	/eyt/	We *ate* all the food.
b.	eight		Wake up. It's *eight* o'clock.

2a.	be	/biy/	Will you *be* there?
b.	bee		A *bee* is an insect that makes honey.

3a.	bare (adj)	/bɛr/	The sign said, "No *bare* feet allowed in this store."
b.	bear (n)		A *bear* is an animal that lives in the forest.
c.	bear (v)		I dislike him; I can't *bear* to be with him in the same room.

4a.	beat	/biyt/	He *beat* out the rhythm on the drum.
b.	beet		A *beet* is a dark red vegetable.

5a.	brake	/breyk/	Put your foot on the *brake* of the car.
b.	break		The dish will *break* if you drop it.

6a.	blue	/bluw/	*Blue* is a nice color, but I like red.
			Blue is also the way I feel, unhappy.
b.	blew		The wind *blew* the paper away.

7a.	board	/bɔrd/	A *board* is a piece of wood.
b.	bored		To be *bored* is to be uninterested.

8a.	**berr**y	/bɛriy/	A **berr**y is a small fruit.
b.	**bur**y		When people die, we **bur**y them.

9a.	been	/bɪn/	I've *been* to the movies.
b.	bin		A *bin* is a container that holds things.

10a.	by	/bay/	We went *by* the house and looked at the door.
b.	buy		We would like to *buy* the house.
c.	bye		The baby waved *bye-bye* as we left the house.
11a.	cell	/sɛl/	The prisoner is in the jail *cell.*
b.	sell		Does the man in the store *sell* pens?
12a.	**cell**ar	/sɛlər/	A ***cell**ar* is a space underneath a building, like a basement.
b.	**sell**er		A ***sell**er* is someone who sells something.
13a.	cent	/sɛnt/	A *cent* is 1/100 of a dollar, or a penny.
b.	sent		I couldn't go, so I *sent* my sister to get it for me.
c.	scent		The sweet *scent* of the flowers filled the room.
14a.	chord	/kɔrd/	He played a *chord* on the piano.
b.	cord		Before you send the package, tie it with a *cord.*
15a.	**cap**ital	/kæpətl̩/	The ***cap**ital* of the United States is Washington, D.C.
			***Cap**ital* is money you invest in a business.
b.	**cap**itol		The ***cap**itol* is a building in which the Congress of the United States meets.
16a.	**cer**eal	/sɪrɪəl/	***Cer**eal* is a grain used as a food, usually eaten for breakfast.
b.	**ser**ial		A ***ser**ial* is a story that is told in several parts, not all at one time.
17a.	**car**ats	/kærəts/	Diamonds are measured in ***car**ats.*
b.	**carr**ots		***Carr**ots* are long orange-red pointed vegetables.

| 18a. | chews | /ʧuwz/ | He *chews* his food before swallowing it. |
| b. | choose | | Please *choose* the movie you want to see. |

19a.	coarse	/kɔrs/	*Coarse* is not smooth; it is rough, like sandpaper.
b.	course		I took a psychology *course* in college.
			The golf *course* is not too far away.

20a.	cite	/sayt/	To *cite* is to mention something. (The Mayor *cited* the recent crime figures.)
b.	sight		He's blind; he lost his *sight*; he can't see.
c.	site		A *site* can be a place. (The *site* of the new building will be on Main Street.)

| 21a. | chute | /ʃuwt/ | A *chute* is a passage through which various things can slide, such as a mail *chute* or a laundry *chute.* |
| b. | shoot | | The man with the gun will *shoot* you. |

| 22a. | close | /klowz/ | The door is open; please *close* it. |
| b. | clothes | | Pack your *clothes* in a suitcase. |

| 23a. | dear | /dɪr/ | *Dear* is the opposite of cheap. |
| b. | deer | | A *deer* is an animal. |

| 24a. | die | /day/ | He's very sick; we expect him to *die.* |
| b. | dye | | In order to change the color of her hair, she'll *dye* it. |

25a.	do	/duw/	I want to go. *Do* you?
b.	due		My rent is *due* the beginning of the month.
c.	dew		The morning *dew* on the grass wet our feet.

26a.	draws	/drɔz/	A horse *draws* a wagon.
			I like to *draw* pictures.
b.	drawers[1]		The desk *drawers* are hard to open.

---

[1] In many dialects, these are not homophones and "drawers" is pronounced /drɔrz/.

27a.	eye	/ay/	He couldn't read because his *eye* hurt.
b.	I		Do you believe that? *I* do.
c.	aye		When you say *aye*, you're saying "yes."
28a.	fair (adj)	/fɛr/	The movie was only *fair*, not good.
			The "*fair* sex" refers to the female sex.
b.	fair (n)		We went on lots of rides at the *fair*.
c.	fair (adv)		Play *fair*; don't cheat.
d.	fare (n)		We pay a *fare* when we go on the bus.
29a.	flew	/fluw/	The bird *flew* from tree to tree.
b.	flu		I was very sick; I had the *flu*.
c.	flue		Smoke goes up through a chimney *flue*.
30a.	for	/fɔr/	Jim will get it *for* you.
b.	four		The book costs *four* dollars.
31a.	fourth	/fɔrθ/	That was the *fourth* time he called.
b.	forth		She walked back and *forth*, waiting impatiently.
32a.	heal	/hiyl/	To *heal* is to make someone well after being sick.
b.	heel		The *heel* is the back part of the foot, under the ankle.
c.	he'll		*He'll* is a contraction for "he will."
33a.	hear	/hɪr/	If you listen closely, you will *hear* me.
b.	here		You said, "Come *here*," so I came.
34a.	hair	/hɛr/	I cut my *hair*; it was very long.
b.	hare		A *hare* is a rabbit with long ears and a short tail.
35a.	him	/hɪm/	Don't give it to her; give it to *him*.
b.	hymn		We sang a *hymn* in church.
36a.	horse	/hɔrs/	A *horse* is a four-legged animal.
b.	hoarse		When I have a cold, it's hard for me to speak because of my *hoarse* voice.

37a. hole   /howl/   There's a *hole* in my sock.
  b. whole   We ate the *whole* pie; nothing was left.

38a. hour   /awər/   The *hour* is late; we have to go now.
  b. our   That's *our* house, not yours.

39a. I'll   /ayl/   *I'll* is a contraction of "I will."
  b. aisle   In a theater you walk down the *aisle* to
                      get to your seat.
  c. isle   An *isle* is a small island.

40a. in   /ɪn/   You put sugar *in* your coffee.
  b. inn   An *inn* is a small hotel.

41a. knew   /nuw/   *Knew* is the past tense of "to know."
  b. new   I bought a pair of *new* shoes.

42a. know   /now/   I think I *know* you.
  b. no   I said "*no*," not "yes."

43a. knot   /nɑt/   A *knot* was tied at the end of the rope.
  b. not   She said she would *not* go.

44a. led   /lɛd/   *Led* is the past tense of "to lead."
  b. lead   *Lead* is a metal; it is found in a pencil.

45a. leased /liyst/ We *leased* the apartment for one year.
  b. least   The smallest amount is the *least*.

46a. made   /meyd/   *Made* is the past tense of "to make."
  b. maid   The *maid* in a hotel cleans the rooms.

47a. male   /meyl/   He is of the *male* sex.
  b. mail   The letter was sent by express *mail*.

48a. meat (n) /miyt/ We buy *meat* in the butcher shop.
  b. meet (v)   I'll *meet* you for lunch at one o'clock.
  c. meet (n)   Our college had a track *meet* with
                       another college.

49a.	**med**al	/mɛdl̩/	The winner of the race received a **med**al.
	b. **medd**le		Leave us alone; don't **medd**le in our business.
50a.	**min**er	/maynər/	A **min**er is someone who works in a mine.
	b. **min**or (n)		A **min**or is a person below the age of 18.
	c. **min**or (adj)		**Min**or also means something is less important: He played a *minor* role in the school play.
51a.	Mrs.	/mɪsəz/	She's married; her name is *Mrs.* Smith.
	b. **miss**es		He's never on time; he always **miss**es his plane.
52a.	night	/nayt/	We think of him day and *night.*
	b. knight		A *knight* was a noble soldier.
			A *knight* is also a chess piece.
53a.	nose	/nowz/	The *nose* is the organ for smelling.
	b. knows		Who *knows* the answer to the question?
54a.	pail	/peyl/	A *pail* is a container for liquids: Get a *pail* of water and we'll wash the car.
	b. pale		To look *pale* is to have little color in your face.
55a.	pain	/peyn/	After I got hurt, I was in *pain.*
	b. pane		The window *pane* broke; there was glass all over the floor.
56a.	paws	/pɔz/	The feet of four-legged animals are called *paws.*
	b. pause		To *pause* is to stop for a short time.
57a.	peace	/piys/	After the war there was *peace.*
	b. piece		Cut the cake and give me a *piece.*

58a. pear   /pɛr/   A *pear* is a fruit.

  b. pair   A *pair* is two things that are the same or that are joined together: a *pair* of shoes, scissors, pants.

  c. pare   You *pare* an apple by peeling off its skin with a knife.

59a. plain   /pleyn/   When something is *plain,* it's ordinary.

  b. plane   A *plane* can be an airplane or a carpenter's tool that makes wood smooth.

60a. **prin**cipal   /prɪnsəpl̩/   The **prin***cipal* is the head of a school.

  b. **prin**ciple   To act on **prin***ciple* is to act on a rule or standard of behavior.

61a. **proph**et   /prɑfɪt/   A **proph***et* is a person who tells you what the future can bring.

  b. **prof**it   I made a **prof***it* on the sale of my house. (I got more money than I paid for it.)

62a. **pal**ate   /pælɪt/   The **pal***ate* is the roof of your mouth.

  b. **pal**ette   A **pal***ette* is a piece of wood on which an artist mixes paints.

63a. rain   /reyn/   It's very cloudy; it looks like *rain.*

  b. reign   A *reign* refers to the period of time that a king or queen rules.

  c. rein   A *rein* is a long piece of narrow leather used by a rider to control a horse.

64a. rays   /reyz/   The *rays* of the sun are very strong.

  b. raise   *Raise* your head and look at me.

  c. raze   A bomb will *raze* the building to the ground.

65a. red   /rɛd/   *Red* is the name of a color.

  b. read   *Read* is the past tense of "to read."

66a.	real	/riyl/	It's a *real* diamond, not a fake.
b.	reel		A *reel* is a round object on which recording tape, film, wire, or a fishing line is stored.
67a.	right	/rayt/	It's not wrong; it's *right*.
b.	write		Don't call; *write* a letter.
68a.	road	/rowd/	The *road* was crowded with autos.
b.	rode		*Rode* is the past tense of "to ride."
c.	rowed		We *rowed* the boat on a small lake.
69a.	roll	/rowl/	May I have a *roll* with butter?
b.	role		He played the *role* of a thief in a play.
70a.	route	/ruwt/	Look at the map and see which *route* to take.
b.	root		A *root* is part of a plant that grows beneath the soil or ground. The square *root* of 9 is 3.
71a.	sail	/seyl/	The boat was due to *sail* at noon.
b.	sale		We bought the chair for less money because it was on *sale*.
72a.	see	/siy/	We went to *see* the play.
b.	sea		They went sailing on the *sea*.
73a.	seam	/siym/	The tailor sewed the torn *seam* of my jacket.
b.	seem		They *seem* to be enjoying themselves.
74a.	seen	/siyn/	They were *seen* together yesterday.
b.	scene		The play has three acts, and each act has two *scenes*.

75a.	sees	/siyz/	He *sees* me every day.
b.	seas		*Seas* are large bodies of salt water enclosed by land.
c.	seize		To *seize* is to take and hold on to something. (He will *seize* the opportunity when it comes.)

| 76a. | son | /sən/ | His wife gave birth to a *son*. |
| b. | sun | | The *sun* shines in the sky. |

77a.	so	/sow/	I like it, *so* I'll buy it.
b.	sew		I like to *sew* my own clothes.
c.	sow		To *sow* is to plant seeds for growing.

78a.	sole (adj)	/sowl/	He is the *sole* owner of the store. He has no partners.
b.	sole (n)		*Sole* is a kind of fish; a *sole* is also the bottom of a foot.
c.	soul (n)		The *soul* is the part of the person that is believed to live on after death.

| 79a. | **sta**tionary | /steyʃənɛry/ | To be **sta**tionary is not to move. |
| b. | **sta**tionery | | To buy **sta**tionery is to buy writing paper. |

| 80a. | steal | /stiyl/ | The thief tried to *steal* my money. |
| b. | steel | | *Steel* is a metal. Some pipes are made of *steel*. |

| 81a. | sum | /səm/ | Five plus five equals the *sum* of ten. |
| b. | some | | Would you like to have *some* cake? |

| 82a. | tail | /teyl/ | A dog wags his *tail* when he's happy. |
| b. | tale | | A *tale* is the same as a story. |

| 83a. | threw | /θruw/ | He *threw* the ball to me. |
| b. | through | | She walked *through* the door. |

84a. their   /ðɛr/   *Their* books are on the table.

  b. there   I looked, but they weren't *there.*

  c. they're   *They're* is a contraction for "they are."

85a. throne   /θrown/   The king sits on his *throne.*

  b. thrown   *Thrown* is past tense of "to throw."

86a. to   /tuw/   I'm going *to* the store.

  b. too   We spend *too* much money on books.

  c. two   I ate *two* pieces of pie.

87a. toe   /tow/   The ballet dancer stood on one *toe.*

  b. tow   My car broke down; *tow* it to the garage.

88a. waist   /weyst/   You wear a belt around your *waist.*

  b. waste   Save the paper; don't *waste* it.

89a. wait   /weyt/   I'll be right there; *wait* for me.

  b. weight   His *weight* is 165 pounds.

90a. way   /wey/   Show me which *way* to go.

  b. weigh   When I eat more, I *weigh* more.

91a. wore   /wɔr/   *Wore* is the past tense of "to wear."

  b. war   World *War* II, for the United States, began on December 7, 1941.

92a. warn   /wɔrn/   Don't *warn* her that I'm here; I want to surprise her.

  b. worn   My clothes are old and *worn.*

93a. weak   /wiyk/   After my illness I felt very *weak.*

  b. week   There are seven days in one *week.*

94a. **weath**er /wɛðər/   The **weath**er is bad; it rained all week.

  b. **wheth**er   I can't decide **wheth**er to go with John or with you.

95a.	we'll	/wiyl/	*We'll* is a contraction of "we will."
b.	wheel		The *wheel* on my bicycle is broken.
96a.	witch	/wɪtʃ/	A *witch* is a woman who is believed to have powers of magic.
b.	which		*Which* tie did you get, the red or the green?
97a.	who's	/huwz/	*Who's* is a contraction of "who is."
b.	whose		In *whose* house is the party?
98a.	won	/wən/	I *won* the lottery.
b.	one		I bought *one* ticket.
99a.	would	/wʊd/	*Would* you like to come with us?
b.	wood		Furniture is usually made from *wood*.
100a.	your	/yɔr/	*Your* brother is waiting for you.
b.	you're		*You're* is a contraction of "you are."